INTRODUCTION
MODERN ENGLISH LIT
FOR STUDENTS OF

Modern Plays

Alex Martin and Robert Hill

ENGLISH LANGUAGE TEACHING

Prentice Hall

New York London Toronto Sydney Tokyo Singapore

Published 1995 by
Prentice Hall International
Campus 400, Maylands Avenue
Hemel Hempstead, Hertfordshire
HP2 7EZ

Typeset in Syntax, Plantin and Bembo
by Derek Lee

Printed and bound in Great Britain by
Redwood Books, Trowbridge, Wiltshire

British Library Cataloguing in Publication Data

A catalogue record for this book is available from the British Library

ISBN 0-13-017815-2

6 5 4 3 2 1
99 98 97 96 95

Cover illustration: *The Rehearsal* (1987, oil on canvas) by Stephen McKenna, reproduced by kind permission of the artist and Kerlin Gallery, Dublin

For
Jeremy, Jessica and Lucy Howe
in memory of Lizzie
author of *The First English Actresses*

Acknowledgements

The Editors and Publishers would like to thank the following for their kind permission to reproduce the following extracts:

Michael Imison Playrights Ltd, 28 Almeida Street, London N1 1TD for *Our Country's Good* © 1988 by Timberlake Wertenbaker based on the novel *The Playmaker* by Thomas Keneally © 1987 The Serpentine Publishing Company Pty, published by Hodder and Stoughton and Sceptre; The Society of Authors on behalf of the Bernard Shaw Estate for *Pygmalion* by George Bernard Shaw; Penguin Books Ltd for *Roots* from *The Wesker Trilogy* by Arnold Wesker (Penguin Books, 1959) copyright © Arnold Wesker, 1959, 1960; Jonathan Cape, Cadwalader, Wickersham & Taft and the Estate of the Author for *Long Day's Journey Into Night* from *Collected Plays* by Eugene O'Neill copyright 1955 Carlotta Monterey O'Neill, copyright renewed 1983 Yale University; A P Watt Ltd for *My Mother Said I Never Should* by Charlotte Keatley; World Book, Inc. for the article on 'Witchcraft' from *The World Book Encyclopedia* © 1992, 1994 World Book Inc by permission of the publisher; Greene & Heaton Ltd for *The Crucible* by Arthur Miller; Faber and Faber Ltd for *The Birthday Party* by Harold Pinter, *Man Of The Moment* by Alan Ayckbourn, *Act Without Words II* by Samuel Beckett, *Translations* by Brian Friel; Casarotto Ramsay Ltd for *A Streetcar Named Desire* copyright 1947 by Tennessee Williams and *The Glass Menagerie* copyright 1945 by Tennessee Williams and Edwina D Williams (all rights in these plays are strictly reserved and application for performance etc must be made before rehearsal to Casarotto Ramsay Ltd, National House, 60-66 Wardour Street, London W1V 4ND; no performance may be given unless a licence has been obtained); Athol Fugard, John Kani and Winston Ntshona for *Sizwe Bansi Is Dead*; Methuen London for *Shirley Valentine* by Willy Russell; Macmillan London Ltd for *The Plough And The Stars* by Sean O'Casey; B T Batsford Ltd for *Ireland From Easter Uprising To Civil War* by Michael Hodges.

While every endeavour has been made to trace copyright owners, the Publishers would be pleased to hear from any other parties who may feel they hold rights in any of the material that has been included.

The Editors and Publishers are grateful to the following for permission to reproduce photographs and pictures:
The Raymond Mander & Joe Mitchenson Theatre Collection: (stage design and posters) *Venus Observed* (p 18), *Pygmalion* (p 20), *Sizwe Bansi Is Dead / The Island* (p 20); (photographs) *Streetcar Named Desire* (Angus Bean, p 115), *Man Of The Moment* (John Haynes, p 166); Art Books International and Jocelyn Herbert and Cathy Courtney: theatre designs from *Jocelyn Herbert, A Theatre Workbook* (p 19); Hulton Deutsch Collection Ltd (p 33, p 190); Zoe Dominic: *Pygmalion* (p 45), *Roots* (p 53), *Long Day's Journey Into Night* (p 60), *The Birthday Party* (p 106); the Bodleian Library, Douce Collection (p 88); Catherine Ashmore: *The Crucible* (p 101), *Shirley Valentine* (p 162); Camera Press Ltd (p 137); John Haynes: *Sizwe Bansi Is Dead* (p 141), *Translations* (p 215).

Contents

Introduction

1 To The Student

This book is for those who either want to read some plays in English or need to for school, university or exams. You don't need to have studied literature before. The aim of the book is help you understand and enjoy reading plays, and to give you tools and methods for appreciating them in the future.

You can use the book with or without a teacher. If you are studying alone, you will need to check your answers in the Key at the end of the book. The study of literature sometimes requires a purely personal response, however, so not all the exercises have a single correct answer. In these cases it will be useful to discuss your ideas with a teacher or another student.

Like the other books in this series (*Modern Novels, Modern Poetry* and *Modern Short Stories*), this one adopts a double approach: literary and linguistic. Each chapter contains a *Language practice* section divided into *Structures* (ie grammar) and *Vocabulary*, in addition to the literary section on *Close reading*. The Language section is always based on the literature in the chapter and leads back into it. The two approaches feed each other, the language study helping you to appreciate the literature, and the literature helping you to appreciate (and use) the possibilities of the language.

After the *Language practice* section in each chapter there is a section called *Extension*, which gives you the chance to discuss or write about themes raised by the plays, as well as helping you to think practically about the plays as theatre. This is done through creative activities: acting, making posters, stage designs, etc. A final section, *Beyond the text*, offers you an extract from a similar or contrasting play.

You can work on the chapters in any order you like, but we suggest that you begin with Chapter 1, Anatomy of a Play, which takes you round a theatre and introduces some of the basic features of dramatic writing and criticism.

At the back of the book you will find a *Glossary*. In this section are listed the most essential vocabulary items for each play, together with words and phrases which are not usually included in a standard dictionary, such as slang and dialect. These words are listed in the order that they appear in the text, rather than alphabetically.

In order to make the best of this book, you need to have a good monolingual English dictionary, a good bilingual dictionary, and a handbook of English grammar and usage. You may also want to know more about the historical and cultural background to the plays. Here are some suggestions:

Monolingual English dictionaries
Oxford Advanced Learner's Dictionary
Longman Dictionary of Contemporary English

Bilingual dictionaries
This will depend on what is available in your language, but buy a large, modern dictionary if possible. Ask the advice of someone who knows both languages well. A good dictionary is an indispensable intellectual tool which will serve you for many years. It should (a) translate a large number of words, (b) give all possible meanings for these words, and (c) reflect past as well as present usage. Avoid mini-dictionaries, therefore, which have their place in the tourist's suitcase but are useless for the study of literature.

Grammar and usage
Jake Allsop, *Students' English Grammar* (Prentice Hall)
Collins Cobuild English Grammar
Collins Cobuild English Usage
Raymond Murphy, *English Grammar In Use* (Cambridge)
Michael Swan, *Practical English Usage* (Oxford)
A J Thomson & A V Martinet, *A Practical English Grammar* (Oxford)

Historical and cultural background
(a) General
Harry Blamires, *Twentieth Century English Literature* (Macmillan)
Boris Ford (editor), *The New Pelican Guide to English Literature*, Volumes 7, 8 and 9 (Penguin)

(b) History of the theatre
Phyllis Hartnoll, *A Concise History of the Theatre*, (Thames & Hudson)
Richard Southern, *The Seven Ages of the Theatre* (Faber & Faber)
Glynne Wickham, *A History of the Theatre* (Phaidon)
The Revels History of Drama in English, Volumes 7 and 8 (Methuen)

(c) Theory and practice
Eric Bentley (editor), *The Theory of the Modern Stage* (Penguin)
Peter Brook, *The Empty Space* (Penguin)
Martin Esslin, *An Anatomy of Drama* (Abacus)
Malcolm Kelsall, *Studying Drama* (Edward Arnold)
Don Shiach, *From Page to Performance* (Cambridge)

2 To The Teacher

Little needs to be added, except to note that although this book is written with the possibility of private study in mind, practically every exercise will work in the classroom with little or no adaptation. Many of the individual exercises can be transformed by the addition of simple instructions: 'discuss this with a partner', 'report your conclusions', etc.

The use of literature in the language class is now very widely accepted as one of the most effective tools for cultural and linguistic enrichment. Yet in many schools and universities all over the world, literary study is still too often regarded as a form of magic, into which the students are initiated through the ritual repetition of weird and impenetrable spells - otherwise known as critical terminology. This can be the case even at a humble level. How many of us remember being told, at school, to 'analyse the character of Mrs ——' without the faintest idea of (a) what a 'character' is, (b) how to analyse one, or (c) why anyone should want to do this in the first place? And how many of us, who still smart at such memories, continue to set our students such mystifying tasks? There must be a better way of doing things.

One alternative is suggested in this book. The essence of our approach is to apply communicative teaching techniques to the study of literature. To us this means (a) reducing critical jargon to a minimum, (b) defining and thoroughly practising any critical terms that are used, (c) setting practical exercises that are challenging, achievable, and personally engaging, (d) encouraging students to develop and share their ideas with each other. Broadly, it means that the students should talk more and the teacher less. One might add that an ideal class would be like a conversation, or a group of friends out on a walk, rather than the traditional lecture + interrogation format.

Making this approach actually work in the classroom is, of course, up to the teacher - it is ultimately beyond the powers of even the most fanatically thorough textbook writer. Still, we have done what we can. This book is full of classroom activities. You can of course add your own. Time spent on thinking up suitable ways to introduce games, drama improvisations, surveys, quizzes, puzzles, debates, role-plays and projects will almost always pay handsome returns. [For a wealth of further practical ideas on this, see J Collie & S Slater, *Literature Teaching in the Language Classroom*; Françoise Grellet, *Developing Reading Skills*; and Penny Ur, *Discussions that Work*, (all Cambridge University Press).] In setting up any group activity, however (especially a discussion), it is essential to give the student a specific goal - a decision to be reached, in a specific time. The approach of 'discuss Question Four', followed inevitably by 'discuss Question Five' is unlikely to be much of a success in any context.

Unlike the first two books in the series, *Modern Plays* is based on extracts rather than full-length works. This is inevitable in a book of this size, but it also offers certain advantages, allowing students to examine a variety of plays, to go into some depth within that variety, and to sample each dramatist's work as a prelude to further reading. Ideally, they will go on to do that further reading on their own initiative (perhaps with a little encouragement from you).

The *While reading* questions that occur during the main extracts can be done individually, in pairs, groups or as class brainstorming. They are there to:

a) give the students achievable portions of text to be read
b) encourage students to engage in the mechanics of the plot
c) aid, rather than test, comprehension by highlighting the questions that a practised reader would be asking her/himself.

These questions should therefore be dealt with fairly rapidly , and the students should carry on reading the play at the first sign of the class discussion or pair / group work flagging. A more leisurely and deeper analysis of the play is always provided in the *Close reading* section.

The *First reaction* exercise should also be dealt with quickly. The aim of this exercise is to harness that moment when any reader (even the least practised) tends to want to make a subjective response. We hope that this will encourage the less confident students to express their reactions. Detailed discussion of these reactions, however, should be left till after the *Close reading*, when students will have looked at key moments in the extract and should be able to take a more informed critical stance.

Finally, if you find yourself disagreeing violently with the answers in the *Key*, you can of course treat them as further discussion points. It is probably unwise to suggest that all literary questions are debatable, but a good many certainly are, at least to the extent that there is always more to be said.

Alex Martin
Robert Hill

1 Anatomy of a Play

The aim of this chapter is to introduce some of the basic language of drama criticism, as used in this book and elsewhere in the discussion of plays generally. It should enable you to talk and write more confidently about things like plot, theme, character and staging. (More advanced critical terms can be found in the books recommended in the Introduction.)

There are eight sections in this chapter. The first seven can be done sitting at a desk, but in the last section you will be asked to leave your desk behind and stage a scene from a play.

The idea of putting on a play fills some people with excitement and others with horror. 'Great!' cry the extroverts, 'I love acting!' 'Help!' say the shy, 'I can't do this!' (although it's amazing how often they turn out to be excellent actors). In reality, though, this is not a talent contest – but an opportunity to study a play in a practical and creative way.

It's important actually to **do** this, not simply to imagine it. Unlike other forms of literature, which can be enjoyed alone – in an armchair, in the bath, on the beach – drama is active and social. Reading the text is only half the story.

Inside a theatre

I can take any empty space and call it a bare stage. A man walks across this empty space whilst someone else is watching him, and this is all that is needed for an act of theatre to be engaged.
(Peter Brook, *The Empty Space*)

1 Look at the picture and fill in the missing words from the box below.

props scenery spotlights costume make-up auditorium backstage wings stage manager director rehearsal

2 Match the words in the column on the left with the definitions on the right.

a	box-office	*1*	where actors put on costumes and make-up
b	curtain	*2*	another word for 'scenery'
c	set	*3*	sunken area where an orchestra plays
d	dressing-room	*4*	where you buy tickets for the play
e	pit	*5*	the actors' entrance to the theatre
f	stalls	*6*	upper rows of seats in the auditorium
g	flies	*7*	lights in the auditorium
h	curtain call	*8*	the public entrance to the theatre
i	house lights	*9*	where you buy drinks
j	foyer	*10*	the best seats, in front of the stage
k	bar	*11*	where scenery is stored above the stage
l	circle	*12*	when the actors bow at the end of a play
m	stage door	*13*	this comes down at the end of the play

The text

> It was as though the act of speaking a word sent through him vibrations that echoed back meanings far more complex than his rational thinking could find: he would pronounce a word like 'night' and then he would be compelled to pause: listening with all his being to the amazing impulses stirring in some mysterious inner chamber, he would experience the wonder of discovery at the moment when it happened.
>
> (Peter Brook, describing the actor Paul Scofield, in *The Empty Space*)

Plays are usually divided into numbered **scenes** and sometimes into **acts** as well. A scene can last for as little as a few seconds, or up to about half an hour. An act is longer, lasting around an hour and completing one major section of the play.

Scenes are made up of

- **dialogue** (words for the actors to speak, also known as 'speeches' or 'lines') and/or
- **stage directions** (instructions to the actors and director about how the play should be performed)

Styles of dialogue and stage directions vary greatly from author to author. Shakespeare's plays are written in verse, with some scenes in prose. Almost all modern plays are written in prose.

Shakespeare's stage directions are minimal. This is how *Macbeth* begins:

ACT I
SCENE I
A desert Heath
Thunder and lightning. Enter three WITCHES.

FIRST WITCH: When shall we three meet again
In thunder, lightning, or in rain?
SECOND WITCH: When the hurlyburly's done,
When the battle's lost and won.
THIRD WITCH: That will be ere the set of sun.
FIRST WITCH: Where the place?
SECOND WITCH: Upon the heath.
THIRD WITCH: There to meet with Macbeth.
FIRST WITCH: I come, Graymalkin!
SECOND WITCH: Paddock calls.
THIRD WITCH: Anon.
ALL: Fair is foul, and foul is fair:
Hover through the fog and filthy air. [*Exeunt.*

Notice that there are no instructions about how the witches should be dressed, their voices, ages, movements, or actions. All Shakespeare says in his stage directions is that they enter and go out ('*Exeunt*'). The dialogue, though, suggests a taste for dirt, wild places and bad weather, and an atmosphere of evil. Most productions of *Macbeth* take up this suggestion and portray the witches as ugly, ragged, filthy creatures with horrible voices.

Compare this to the opening of *Krapp's Last Tape* by Samuel Beckett:

A late evening in the future.

KRAPP*'s den.*

Front centre a small table, two drawers of which open towards the audience. Sitting at the table, facing front, ie across from the drawers, a wearish old man: KRAPP.

Rusty black narrow trousers too short for him. Rusty black sleeveless waistcoat, four capacious pockets. Heavy silver watch and chain. Grimy white shirt open at neck, no collar. Surprising pair of dirty white boots, size ten at least, very narrow and pointed.

White face. Purple nose. Disordered grey hair. Unshaven.

Very near-sighted (but unspectacled). Hard of hearing.

Cracked voice. Distinctive intonation.

Laborious walk.

On the table a tape-recorder with microphone and a number of cardboard boxes containing reels of recorded tapes.

Table and immediately adjacent area in strong white light. Rest of stage in darkness.

Beckett gives plenty of detail, because he wants to create a precise visual image which is as important to the play as the words that are spoken. Krapp makes us curious. Why does he wear this 'surprising pair of dirty white boots'? Why is his nose purple? He may be a clown, or a drunkard (or both), or there may be another explanation. Nothing in the rest of the play explains these features. They remain as mysterious, as ambiguous at the end as they are at the beginning. They are part of Beckett's dramatic statement.

The characters

> We know characters in plays are not real people. We know actors create the roles. In certain kinds of play, however, we like to watch *as if* the characters were real.
> (Malcolm Kelsall, *Studying Drama*)

The list of characters in the play is usually printed on the first page. The actors in the play are called the **cast** or sometimes the **company**.

We talk about an actor or actress **playing a part** – this means acting a character in the play.

Sometimes people 'play a part' in real life too, when they have to say things they don't want to say or when their work requires them to 'perform' in front of other people: teachers, air hostesses, doctors, lawyers, waiters, schoolchildren, salesmen, soldiers, priests … there is an element of theatre, of acting, in all their lives.

William Shakespeare, in his play *As You Like It*, takes this idea further, when one of the characters, Jaques, declares that **everyone** is an actor:

> All the world's a stage,
> And all the men and women merely players:
> They have their exits and their entrances;
> And one man in his time plays many parts ….
> (*As You Like It*, Act II, Scene vii, lines 139–42)

Can you think of any scenes from your own life which were theatrical in some way, or in which someone was clearly 'playing a part'?

When we read a play we take our ideas about a character from:

- lines spoken by the character
- lines spoken to or about the character
- actions by the character
- reactions by other characters
- stage directions

When we see a play, there are other indications too – the actors, their costumes and make-up, but also subtle hints like the way they enter a room, the unspoken reactions of other actors – what is often called 'body language' – added by the director and actors during rehearsals.

Talking about characters is not as difficult as one might think. We do it every day about real people with great skill – so why not about people in a play?

With real people, we judge character by all sorts of signs: their appearance, facial expression, eyes, clothes, actions, habits, words, manner of speaking – as well as what other people say about them. We then compare all these and decide whether we like that person or not, whether we trust them, whether we want to spend time with them. Judging character is an essential skill in life. It is also extremely useful in reading literature.

Imagine this situation. You are in a crowded train. Opposite you is an unhappy-looking man, poorly dressed, unshaven, smelling strongly of alcohol. He makes you and everybody else in the compartment feel uncomfortable.

What sort of character do you judge him to be? Write down or discuss your answer before going on.

Then the train stops at a station. A young woman comes in with a small child and a heavy suitcase. The man sitting opposite at once stands up and offers to lift her suitcase onto the luggage rack. He also offers her his seat.

What is your opinion of him now?

Later, the child begins to cry. The mother tries to console him with biscuits, drinks and toys, but he takes no notice and cries louder than ever. The other passengers start to get annoyed. Suddenly the man kneels down in front of the child, pulls a handkerchief and some coins from his pocket and performs a series of brilliant magic tricks. At once the child stops crying.

What do you think of the man now?

When we read or see a play, we make similar judgements all the time, revising our opinions whenever a character does something unexpected or shows a new aspect of his or her personality.

Think of a person you know – someone you once liked but now dislike, or vice versa.

1 Write a short dramatic dialogue showing what it was that changed your mind.

2 Find a partner and read each other's dialogues. As you read, try to guess as much as you can about the person, then tell your partner what you have understood. Is your interpretation right?

3 Choose one of the dialogues, improve it if necessary, and perform it to the rest of the class. Then check their understanding of the characters in the dialogue.

Plot, theme and structure

> Plays tell stories, and the enjoyment of a good story is a fundamental human pleasure.
> (Malcolm Kelsall, *Studying Drama*)

As in a short story, novel or film, the **plot** of a play is what happens in it. When describing what happens, it is important to specify certain things. These can be summed up in four simple questions: Who? Where? What? When?

Who are the characters?
Where are they?
What do they do?
When does the action take place?

Summarising a play, or a scene or act in a play, usually means describing these four things. It is very useful to be able to do this quickly and without too many irrelevant details. Like describing character, this is something we all do in ordinary conversation – when telling a joke or a story, or describing an incident that we have seen.

A related idea is **theme**. This is the general moral or philosophical subject of the play. A great play may have many themes. Shakespeare's *Hamlet*, for example, is the story of a prince who is ordered by the ghost of his dead father to kill his uncle. Hamlet finds this very difficult to do, despite evidence that his uncle murdered his father in order to become king. The themes of the play include revenge, conscience, courage, family relationships, politics and morality, the purpose of human existence, Christianity and humanism, love, men and women, idealism, art, heroism, death ... in fact, they seem endless, which is one of the reasons why the play is so fascinating.

Structure can be defined as the way the various parts of the play (characters, plot, themes) are put together. Many plays use contrasting characters and actions as part of their structure. In *Hamlet*, the thoughtful, indecisive hero is contrasted with a series of much more determined, aggressive characters who don't think much but certainly get things done. Similarly, a scene of action may be followed by a scene of contemplation, a scene of tenderness by one of violence, comedy by tragedy, and so on. Parallel characters and scenes are another common structural device, as are verbal repetitions, music and songs. There are examples of many of these devices in the plays in this book.

Stage design

> The objection arising from the impossibility of passing the first hour at Alexandria and the next at Rome, supposes that when the play opens, the spectator really imagines himself at Alexandria and believes that his walk to the theatre has been a voyage to Egypt, and that he lives in the days of Antony and Cleopatra. ... The truth is that spectators are always in their senses and know, from the first act to the last, that the stage is only a stage, and that the players are only players.
>
> (Samuel Johnson, *Preface to Shakespeare*, 1765)

Before a play can be performed, a designer has to make a plan for the stage, showing scenery and furniture, and where the actors will enter and exit. Some dramatists give long and precise instructions about the stage design (see the extracts from *Krapp's Last Tape* above and *Pygmalion* and *The Plough and the Stars* later in this book); others give very little.

When we read a play, we create our own 'theatre of the mind' – an imaginary stage in our thoughts where the characters speak and move about as if on a real stage. It can therefore be very helpful when reading a play if we have a stage design in mind – and the best way to do this is to sketch one out. This should be based on the stage directions at the start of the play, however brief. Your sketch can take any form you like. The important thing is that it should be clear.

Here are some examples of stage designs. Next to each one, write down what you think it represents.

a ____

b ______________________________

c ______________________________

LOVING
14

FIGHTING
15

19
JUSTICE
JUSTICE
JUSTICE
JUSTICE

20
20

Publicity

Whenever a play is put on in a theatre, publicity has to be organised in order to attract audiences. This includes writing a **press release** (usually a summary of the play, with information about the author and the new production, emphasising its topical interest, comedy or some other features thought likely to appeal to the public), taking **photographs** of rehearsals, setting up **interviews** with the director and actors, designing **advertisements** for magazines and newspapers, and making **posters** to put up outside the theatre and around the town.

In order to produce these materials, people in the press office of a theatre need to see the play and choose what aspects will be most attractive to audiences. Is there romance? Murder? Political intrigue? A famous actor in the main part? Great music or dancing? …

Later in this book (in Chapters 2, 5, and 7, 'Extension') you will be asked to make a poster for a play. This is a chance to think about its popular appeal, about what is important to you in the play, and to use your imagination and

Here are some examples of different poster designs.

artistic skills to express your ideas. In discussing your posters with other students you will also, of course, exchange ideas about characters, themes, and plot – in other words, you will be analysing the play, but from a new perspective.

Before you make a poster, have a look at some examples from local cinemas, theatres and other places in your town that interest you. Look carefully at the designs. What images are used? What is appealing about them? What do they suggest to you? Look at the words on the posters also. How are they placed in relation to the images? What information do they convey? What lettering is used? Does it suggest anything? What about the colours? Are they bright or dark? Why?

Staging a play

> In Greek the word *drama* simply means action. Drama is mimetic action, action in imitation or representation of human behaviour.
>
> (Martin Esslin, *An Anatomy of Drama*)

It's important to remember as you read a play that the words on the page are not the play – they are only instructions for the play – just as musical notation is not in itself music but a set of instructions for playing it. Acting out a playscript (or seeing it performed) is an essential part of understanding it.

There isn't always time to work up a fully-rehearsed performance of every play you study, or even the opportunity to see the play performed; but even if you spend a short time in class staging a single scene – perhaps just working out the actors' moves – you'll find that the play suddenly means more to you, you'll remember it more vividly, and you'll have begun to make the exciting transition from printed words to action and speech which is the essence of theatre.

Here are some things to consider when you act out a playscript.

1 Define your stage area. Where do actors come in and go out? Where is the audience?

2 Do you need any furniture, props or scenery? Sometimes a single well-chosen object can make a scene real in a surprising and powerful way.

3 Do you need any costumes? What is the minimum necessary to define a character? A hat? A pair of boots? A raincoat?

4 Do you need any sound effects or music?

5 Who is going to play which part? Make sure that everyone, as far as

possible, plays a part which appeals to them and which they feel comfortable with.

6 When you rehearse a scene, make sure the audience can see all the important actions and hear all the words. Arrange the actors on the stage so that the action is clearly focussed.

7 Try to make everything that happens on the stage as real as possible. Conviction, belief in what you are doing, is infinitely more important than fine costumes or grandiose stage effects.

A rehearsal

Here is a chance for you to try out some of the ideas in this chapter. Read the scene printed below, then stage it following the suggestions given in the previous section. As well as 10 actors (6 male, 4 female), you may also want a director, stage-manager, designer, and someone to make music or sound-effects. With a large group – 20 or more – you could produce two 'rival' versions of the scene.

The scene comes from *Our Country's Good* by Timberlake Wertenbaker. The play is set in Sydney, Australia, 200 years ago, where a group of criminals deported from England are establishing a colony under military guard. One of the army officers, Ralph Clark, has decided to put on a play (*The Recruiting Officer* by George Farquhar, an 18th century comedy) using the prisoners as actors. In this scene Clark holds his first rehearsal.

1 Read the scene as far as line 57, then, using information from the text, write down who is to play which part in *The Recruiting Officer*.

Our Country's Good	*The Recruiting Officer*
Mary Brenham	Silvia
____________	Melinda
____________	Lucy (Melinda's maid)
____________	Rose, a country girl
____________	Captain Plume
____________	Sergeant Kite
____________	Mr Worthy
____________	Justice Balance
____________	Captain Brazen

The play is directed by ____________

2 Look at the diagram below, and decide where you would put 'acting' on the scale. Is it a totally 'natural' process, or does it require some (or a great deal of) artificiality and technique? Can you think of any famous actors or actresses that you would place at different ends of the scale?

0	50	100%
NATURAL		ARTIFICIAL

As you read, decide where you would put the following characters from *Our Country's Good* on the scale as actors.

Sideway Liz Dabby Duckling Mary

0	50	100%
NATURAL		ARTIFICIAL

Our Country's Good (1988) Timberlake Wertenbaker

See the Glossary section at the back of the book for vocabulary.

ACT I

SCENE ELEVEN

THE FIRST REHEARSAL

RALPH CLARK, ROBERT SIDEWAY, JOHN WISEHAMMER, MARY BRENHAM, LIZ MORDEN, DABBY BRYANT, DUCKLING SMITH, KETCH FREEMAN.

RALPH: Good afternoon, ladies and gentlemen –
DABBY: We're ladies now. Wait till I tell my husband I've become a lady.
MARY: Sshht.
RALPH: It is with pleasure that I welcome you –
SIDEWAY: Our pleasure, Mr Clark, our pleasure.
RALPH: We have many days of hard work ahead of us.
LIZ: Work! I'm not working. I thought we was acting.
RALPH: Now, let me introduce the company –
DABBY: We've all met before, Lieutenant, you could say we know

each other, you could say we'd know each other in the dark.

SIDEWAY: It's a theatrical custom, the company is formally introduced to each other, Mrs Bryant.

DABBY: Mrs Bryant? Who's Mrs Bryant?

SIDEWAY: It's the theatrical form of address, Madam. You may call me Mr Sideway.

RALPH: If I may proceed –

KETCH: Shhh! You're interrupting the director.

DABBY: So we are, Mr Hangman.

The women all hiss and spit at KETCH.

RALPH: The ladies first: Mary Brenham who is to play Silvia. Liz Morden who is to play Melinda. Duckling Smith who is to play Lucy, Melinda's maid.

DUCKLING: I'm not playing Liz Morden's maid.

RALPH: Why not?

DUCKLING: I live with an officer. He wouldn't like it.

DABBY: Just because she lives chained up in that old toss pot's garden.

DUCKLING: Don't you dare talk of my Harry –

RALPH: You're not playing Morden's maid, Smith, you're playing Melinda's. And Dabby Bryant, who is to play Rose, a country girl.

DABBY: From Devon.

DUCKLING (*to* DABBY): Screw jaws!

DABBY (*to* DUCKLING): Salt bitch!

RALPH: That's the ladies. Now, Captain Plume will be played by Henry Kable.

He looks around.

Who seems to be late. That's odd. I saw him an hour ago and he said he was going to your hut to learn some lines, Wisehammer?

WISEHAMMER *is silent.*

Sergeant Kite is to be played by John Arscott, who did send a message to say he would be kept at work an extra hour.

DABBY: An hour! You won't see him in an hour!

LIZ (*under her breath*): You're not the only one with new wrinkles in your arse, Dabby Bryant.

RALPH: Mr Worthy will be played by Mr Sideway.

SIDEWAY *takes a vast bow.*

SIDEWAY: I'm here.

RALPH: Justice Balance by James Freeman.

DUCKLING: No way I'm doing a play with a hangman. The words would stick in my throat.

More hisses and spitting. KETCH *shrinks.*

RALPH: You don't have any scenes with him, Smith. Now if I could finish the introductions. Captain Brazen is to be played by John Wisehammer.

The small parts are still to be cast. Now. We can't do the first scene until John Arscott appears.

DABBY: There won't be a first scene.

RALPH: Bryant, will you be quiet please! The second scene. Wisehammer, you could read Plume.

WISEHAMMER *comes forward eagerly.*

No, I'll read Plume myself. So, Act One, Scene Two, Captain Plume and Mr Worthy.

SIDEWAY: That's me. I'm at your command.

RALPH: The rest of you can watch and wait for your scenes. Perhaps we should begin by reading it.

SIDEWAY: No need, Mr Clark, I know it.

RALPH: Ah, I'm afraid I shall have to read Captain Plume.

SIDEWAY: I know that part too. Would you like me to do both?

RALPH: I think it's better if I do it. Shall we begin? Kite, that's John Arscott, has just left –

DABBY: Running.

RALPH: Bryant! I'll read the line before Worthy's entrance: 'None at present. 'Tis indeed the picture of Worthy, but the life's departed.' Sideway? Where's he gone?

SIDEWAY *has scuttled off. He shouts from the wings.*

SIDEWAY: I'm preparing my entrance, Mr Clark, I won't be a minute. Could you read the line again, slowly?

RALPH: ''Tis indeed the picture of Worthy, but the life's departed. What, arms-a-cross, Worthy!'

SIDEWAY *comes on, walking sideways, arms held up in a grandiose eighteenth-century theatrical pose. He suddenly stops.*

SIDEWAY: Ah yes, I forgot. Arms-a-cross. I shall have to start again.

He goes off again and shouts.

Could you read the line again louder please?

RALPH: 'What, arms-a-cross, Worthy!'

SIDEWAY *rushes on.*

SIDEWAY: My wiper! Someone's buzzed my wiper! There's a wipe drawer in this crew, Mr Clark.

RALPH: What's the matter?

SIDEWAY: There's a pickpocket in the company.

DABBY: Talk of the pot calling the kettle black.

SIDEWAY *stalks around the company threateningly.*

SIDEWAY: My handkerchief. Who prigged my handkerchief?

RALPH: I'm sure it will turn up, Sideway, let's go on.

SIDEWAY: I can't do my entrance without my handkerchief. (*Furious.*) I've been practising it all night. If I get my mittens on the rum diver I'll –

He lunges at LIZ, *who fights back viciously. They jump apart, each taking threatening poses and* RALPH *intervenes with speed.*

RALPH: Let's assume Worthy has already entered, Sideway. Now, I say: 'What, arms-a-cross, Worthy! Methinks you should hold 'em open when a friend's so near. I must expel this melancholy spirit.'

SIDEWAY *has dropped to his knees and is sobbing in a pose of total sorrow.*

What are you doing down there, Sideway?

SIDEWAY: I'm being melancholy. I saw Mr Garrick being melancholy once. This is what he did. Hamlet it was.

He stretches his arms to the ground and begins to repeat.

'Oh that this too, too solid flesh would melt. Oh that this too, too solid flesh would melt. Oh that this too, too –'

RALPH: This is a comedy, It is perhaps a little lighter. Try simply to stand normally and look melancholy. I'll say the line again. (SIDEWAY *is still sobbing.*) The audience won't hear Captain Plume's lines if your sobs are so loud, Sideway.

SIDEWAY: I'm still establishing my melancholy.

RALPH: A comedy needs to move quite fast. In fact, I think we'll cut that line and the two verses that follow and go straight to Worthy greeting Plume.

WISEHAMMER: I like the word melancholy.

SIDEWAY: A greeting. Yes. A greeting looks like this.

He extends his arms high and wide.

'Plume!' Now I'll change to say the next words. 'My dear Captain', that's affection isn't it? If I put my hands on my heart, like this. Now, 'Welcome'. I'm not quite sure how to do 'Welcome'.

RALPH: I think if you just say the line.

SIDEWAY: Quite. Now.

He feels RALPH.

RALPH: Sideway! What are you doing?

SIDEWAY: I'm checking that you're safe and sound returned. That's what the line says: 'Safe and sound returned.'

RALPH: You don't need to touch him. You can see that!

SIDEWAY: Yes, yes. I'll check his different parts with my eyes. Now, I'll put it all together, 'Plume! My dear Captain, welcome. Safe and sound returned!'

He does this with appropriate gestures.

RALPH: Sideway – it's a very good attempt. It's very theatrical. But could you try and be a little more – euh – natural.

SIDEWAY: Natural! On the stage! But Mr Clark!

RALPH: People must – euh – believe you. Garrick after all is admired for his naturalness.

SIDEWAY: Of course. I thought I was being Garrick – but never mind. Natural. Quite. You're the director, Mr Clark.

RALPH: Perhaps you could look at me while you're saying the lines.

SIDEWAY: But the audience won't see my face.

RALPH: The lines are said to Captain Plume. Let's move on. Plume says: 'I 'scaped safe from Germany', shall we say – America? It will make it more contemporary –

WISEHAMMER: You can't change the words of the playwright.

RALPH: Mm, well, 'and sound, I hope, from London: you see I have –'

BLACK CAESAR *rushes on.*

RALPH: Caesar, we're rehearsing – would you –

CAESAR: I see that well, Monsieur Lieutenant. I see it is a piece of theatre, I have seen many pieces of theatre in my beautiful island of Madagascar so I have decided to play in your piece of theatre.

RALPH: There's no part for you.

CAESAR: There is always a part for Caesar.

SIDEWAY: All the parts have been taken.

CAESAR: I will play his servant.

He stands next to SIDEWAY.

RALPH: Farquhar hasn't written a servant for Worthy.

DUCKLING: He can have my part. I want to play something else.

CAESAR: There is always a black servant in a play, Monsieur Lieutenant. And Caesar is that servant. So, now I stand here just behind him and I will be his servant.

RALPH: There are no lines for it, Caesar.

CAESAR: I speak in French. That makes him a more high up gentleman if he has a French servant, and that is very good. Now he gets the lady with the black servant. Very chic.

RALPH: I'll think about it. Actually, I would like to rehearse the ladies now. They have been waiting patiently and we don't have much time left. Freeman, would you go and see what's happened to Arscott. Sideway, we'll come back to this scene another time, but that was very good, very good. A little, a little euh, but very good.

SIDEWAY *bows out, followed by* CAESAR.

Now we will rehearse the first scene between Melinda and

Silvia. Morden and Brenham, if you would come and stand here. Now the scene is set in Melinda's apartments. Silvia is already there. So, if you stand here, Morden. Brenham, you stand facing her.

LIZ (*very, very fast*): 'Welcome to town cousin Silvia I envied you your retreat in the country for Shrewsbury methinks and all your heads of shires are the most irregular places for living –'

RALPH: Euh, Morden –

LIZ: Wait, I haven't finished yet. 'Here we have smoke noise scandal affectation and pretension in short everything to give the spleen and nothing to divert it then the air is intolerable –'

RALPH: Morden, you know the lines very well.

LIZ: Thank you, Lieutenant Clark.

RALPH: But you might want to try and act them.

Pause.

Let's look at the scene.

LIZ *looks.*

You're a rich lady. You're at home. Now a rich lady would stand in a certain way. Try to stand like a rich lady. Try to look at Silvia with a certain assurance.

LIZ: Assurance.

WISEHAMMER: Confidence.

RALPH: Like this. You've seen rich ladies, haven't you?

LIZ: I robbed a few.

RALPH: How did they behave?

LIZ: They screamed.

RALPH: I mean before you – euh – robbed them.

LIZ: I don't know. I was watching their purses.

RALPH: Have you ever seen a lady in her own house?

LIZ: I used to climb into the big houses when I was a girl, and just stand there, looking. I didn't take anything. I just stood. Like this.

RALPH: But if it was your own house, you would think it was normal to live like that.

WISEHAMMER: It's not normal. It's not normal when others have nothing.

RALPH: When acting, you have to imagine things. You have to imagine you're someone different. So, now, think of a rich lady and imagine you're her.

LIZ *begins to masticate.*

What are you doing?

LIZ: If I was rich I'd eat myself sick.

DABBY: Me too, potatoes.

The convicts speak quickly and over each other.

SIDEWAY: Roast beef and Yorkshire pudding.

CAESAR: Hearts of palm.

WISEHAMMER: Four fried eggs, six fried eggs, eight fried eggs.

LIZ: Eels, oysters –

RALPH: Could we get on with the scene, please? Brenham, it's your turn to speak.

MARY: 'Oh, Madam, I have heard the town commended for its air.'

LIZ: 'But you don't consider Silvia how long I have lived in't!'

RALPH (*to* LIZ): I believe you would look at her.

LIZ: She didn't look at me.

RALPH: Didn't she? She will now.

LIZ: 'For I can assure you that to a lady the least nice in her constitution no air can be good above half a year change of air I take to be the most agreeable of any variety in life.'

MARY: 'But prithee, my dear Melinda, don't put on such an air to me.'

RALPH: Excellent, Brenham. You could be a little more sharp on the 'don't'.

MARY: 'Don't.' (MARY *now tries a few gestures.*) 'Your education and mine were just the same, and I remember the time when we never troubled our heads about air, but when the sharp air from the Welsh mountains made our noses drop in a cold morning at the boarding-school.'

RALPH: Good! Good! Morden?

LIZ: 'Our education cousin was the same but our temperaments had nothing alike.'

RALPH: That's a little better, Morden, but you needn't be quite so angry with her. Now go on, Brenham.

LIZ: I haven't finished my speech!

RALPH: You're right, Morden, please excuse me.

LIZ (*embarrassed*): No, no, there's no need for that, Lieutenant. I only meant – I don't have to.

RALPH: Please do.

LIZ: 'You have the constitution of a horse.'

RALPH: Much better, Morden. But you must always remember you're a lady. What can we do to help you? Lucy.

DABBY: That's you, Duckling.

RALPH: See that little piece of wood over there? Take it to Melinda. That will be your fan.

DUCKLING: I'm not fetching nothing for Liz.

RALPH: She's not Morden, she's Melinda, your mistress. You're her servant, Lucy. In fact, you should be in this scene. Now take her that fan.

DUCKLING (*gives the wood to* LIZ): Here.

LIZ: Thank you, Lucy, I do much appreciate your effort.

RALPH: No, you would nod your head.

WISEHAMMER: Don't add any words to the play.

RALPH: Now, Lucy, stand behind Morden.

DUCKLING: What do I say?

RALPH: Nothing.

DUCKLING: How will they know I'm here? Why does she get all the lines? Why can't I have some of hers?

RALPH: Brenham, it's your speech.

MARY: 'So far as to be troubled with neither spleen, colic, nor vapours –'

The convicts slink away and sink down, trying to make themselves invisible as MAJOR ROSS, *followed by* CAPTAIN CAMPBELL, *come on.*

'I need no salt for my stomach, no –'

She sees the officers herself and folds in with the rest of the convicts.

RALPH: Major Ross, Captain Campbell, I'm rehearsing.

ROSS: Rehearsing! Rehearsing!

CAMPBELL: Tssaach. Rehearsing.

ROSS: Lieutenant Clark is rehearsing. Lieutenant Clark asked us to give the prisoners two hours so he could rehearse, but what has he done with them? What?

CAMPBELL: Eeeh. Other things, eh.

ROSS: Where are the prisoners Kable and Arscott, Lieutenant?

CAMPBELL: Eh?

RALPH: They seem to be late.

ROSS: While you were rehearsing, Arscott and Kable slipped into the woods with three others, so five men have run away and it's all because of your damned play and your so-called thespists. And not only have your thespists run away, they've stolen food from the stores for their renegade escapade, that's what your play has done.

RALPH: I don't see what the play –

ROSS: I said it from the beginning. The play will bring down calamity on this colony.

RALPH: I don't see –

ROSS: The devil, Lieutenant, always come through the mind, here, worms its way, idleness and words.

RALPH: Major Ross, I can't agree –

ROSS: Listen to me, my lad, you're a Second Lieutenant and you don't agree or disagree with Major Ross.

CAMPBELL: No discipline, tcchhha.

ROSS *looks over the convicts.*

ROSS: Caesar! He started going with them and came back.

RALPH: That's all right, he's not in the play.

CAESAR: Yes I am, please Lieutenant, I am a servant.

ROSS: John Wisehammer!

WISEHAMMER: I had nothing to do with it!

ROSS: You're Jewish, aren't you? You're guilty. Kable was last seen near Wisehammer's hut. Liz Morden! She was observed next to the colony's stores late last night in the company of Kable who was supposed to be repairing the door. (*To* LIZ.) Liz Morden, you will be tried for stealing from the stores. You know the punishment? Death by hanging. (PAUSE.) And now you may continue to rehearse, Lieutenant.

ROSS *goes.* CAMPBELL *lingers, looking at the book.*

CAMPBELL: Ouusstta. *The Recruiting Officer.* A good title. Arara. But a play, tss, a play.

He goes. RALPH *and the convicts are left in the shambles of their rehearsal. A silence.*

Author

Timberlake Wertenbaker is one of England's leading contemporary playwrights. An American, educated in France, now living in London, she is an unashamed intellectual who has declared, 'Theatre is for people who take responsibility. There is no point in trying to attract idiots.' *Our Country's Good*, like many of her earlier plays, was written for the Royal Court Theatre in London, which over the past half-century has been the foremost nursery of new theatre writing in Britain. In her Preface to *Our Country's Good*, she describes how during rehearsals for the play she went with the director and cast to see a play performed by a group of prisoners at Wormwood Scrubs (one of London's prisons): 'It was an unforgettable evening. We huddled in the forecourt as the prison gates closed behind us, and then were led through the courtyard: high walls, barbed wire – upstairs to the barking of guard dogs and finally into a small room. But, once the play began, we were at the theatre: the intensity of the performances, the extremely good acting of some of the prisoners, the understanding they seemed to have of this complex play, made it a riveting evening ... That night was pivotal for the acting and writing of *Our Country's Good*: it confirmed all our feelings about the power and value of theatre.' *Our Country's Good* was performed in London, New York, Bucharest and Australia, winning many awards. It has also been performed in prisons. Wertenbaker's other plays, many of them on feminist themes, include *New Anatomies* (1981), *Abel's Sister* (1984), *The Grace of Mary Traverse* (1985), and *Three Birds Alighting on a Field* (1991).

2 Language, Class and Power

Before you read

1 Look at the picture on the previous page.
  a Imagine what each boy is thinking.
  b What does the picture suggest to you about differences between the social classes in England?
  c Could a similar scene be found in your country – either in the past or today?

2 Imagine you are conducting a survey on social class today, either in your country or in England.
  a Write a list of five interview questions designed to reveal which class a person belongs to.
  b If you could ask just **one** of these questions, which would you choose?

3 Now read these two passages. What do these two writers choose as the most important indication of a person's class?

Very early, at the age of only ten or eleven, I reached the conclusion – no one told me this, but on the other hand I did not simply make it up out of my own head: somehow it was in the air I breathed – that you were no good unless you had £100,000. I had perhaps fixed on this particular sum as a result of reading Thackeray. The interest on £100,000 would be £4,000 a year ... and this seemed to me the minimum income that you must possess if you were to belong to the real top crust, the people in the country houses. But it was clear that I could never find my way into that paradise, to which you did not really belong unless you were born into it. You could only make money, if at all, by a mysterious operation called 'going into the City'*, and when you came out of the City, having won your £100,000, you were fat and old. But the truly enviable thing about the top-notchers was that they were rich while young. For people like me, the ambitious middle class, the examination-passers, only a bleak, laborious kind of success was possible. You clambered upwards on a ladder of scholarships into the Civil Service or the Indian Civil Service, or possibly you became a barrister. And if at any point you 'slacked' or 'went off' and missed one of the rungs in the ladder, you became 'a little office boy at forty pounds a year'. But even if you climbed to the highest niche that was open to you, you could still only be an underling, a hanger-on of the people who really counted. ...

Looking back, it is astonishing how intimately, intelligently snobbish we all were, how knowledgeable about names and addresses, how swift to detect small differences in accents and manners and the cut of clothes. There were some boys who seemed to drip money from their pores even in the bleak misery of the middle of a winter term. ...

(George Orwell, 'Such, Such Were the Joys' from *Collected Essays, Journalism and Letters*, Penguin 1970, pp 407–8)

*ie getting a job in banking, insurance or investments, in London's business district, known as 'the City'.

That there are speech differences associated with social class differences is something well-known to every member of the speech community. In 1972 a survey carried out by National Opinion Polls included the question 'Which two of these [eleven specified factors] would you say are most important in being able to tell which class a person is?' The respondents were a random sample of the British public. The factor which scored highest overall was 'The way they speak'; next in order came 'Where they live'. 'The friends they have', 'Their job, 'The sort of school they went to', 'The way they spend their money', and only then 'The amount of money they have' and various other factors. Hence speech was regarded as more indicative of social class than occupation, education, and income; and the likelihood is that by 'the way they speak' respondents meant, above all, 'accent'.

(J C Wells, *Accents of English*, Cambridge University Press, 1982, Vol I, p 15)

4 Bernard Shaw was very concerned about the way English is spoken and written. His interest in language, accent and class led him to write the play *Pygmalion* (later made into a musical, *My Fair Lady*), in which a poor London girl is taught to speak like a lady. Shaw also wished to reform English spelling so that it would be *phonetic* – that is, written exactly as it is spoken. In his Preface to the play, he wrote:

The English have no respect for their language, and will not teach their children to speak it. They cannot spell it because they have nothing to spell it with but an old foreign alphabet of which only the consonants – and not all of them – have any agreed speech value. Consequently no man can teach himself what it should sound like from reading it, and it is impossible for an Englishman to open his mouth without making some other Englishman despise him. ... The reformer we need most today is an energetic phonetic enthusiast: that is why I have made such a one the hero of a popular play.

One consequence of Shaw's belief in the reform of English can be found in the text from *Pygmalion* that follows. Here are the first two lines of dialogue. What do you notice about the spelling and punctuation?

HIGGINS: Well, I think thats the whole show.
PICKERING: It's really amazing. I havnt taken half of it in, you know.

Pygmalion (1912) Bernard Shaw

See the Glossary section at the back of the book for vocabulary.

ACT 2

Next day at 11 a.m. Higgins's laboratory in Wimpole Street. It is a room on the first floor, looking on the street, and was meant for the drawing room. The double doors are in the middle of the back wall; and persons entering find in the corner to their right two tall file cabinets at right angles to one another against the walls. In this corner stands a flat writing-table, on which are a phonograph, a laryngoscope, a row of tiny organ pipes with a bellows, a set of lamp chimneys for singing flames with burners attached to a gas plug in the wall by an indiarubber tube, several tuning-forks of different sizes, a life-size image of half a human head, shewing in section the vocal organs, and a box containing a supply of wax cylinders for the phonograph.

Further down the room, on the same side, is a fireplace, with a comfortable leather-covered easy-chair at the side of the hearth nearest the door, and a coal-scuttle. There is a clock on the mantelpiece. Between the fireplace and the phonograph table is a stand for newspapers.

On the other side of the central door, to the left of the visitor, is a cabinet of shallow drawers. On it is a telephone and the telephone directory. The corner beyond, and most of the side wall, is occupied by a grand piano, with the keyboard at the end furthest from the door, and a bench for the player extending the full length of the keyboard. On the piano is a dessert dish heaped with fruit and sweets, mostly chocolates.

The middle of the room is clear. Besides the easy-chair, the piano bench, and two chairs at the phonograph table, there is one stray chair. It stands near the fireplace. On the wall, engravings: mostly Piranesis and mezzotint portraits. No paintings.

PICKERING *is seated at the table, putting down some cards and a tuning-fork which he has been using.* HIGGINS *is standing up near him, closing two or three file drawers which are hanging out. He appears in the morning light as a robust, vital, appetizing sort of man of forty or thereabouts, dressed in a professional-looking black frock-coat with a white linen collar and black silk tie. He is of the energetic, scientific type, heartily, even violently interested in everything that can be studied as a scientific subject, and careless about himself and other people, including their feelings. He is, in fact, but for his years and size, rather like a very impetuous baby 'taking notice' eagerly and loudly, and requiring almost as much watching to keep him out of unintended mischief. His manner varies from genial bullying when he is in a good humor to stormy petulance when anything goes wrong; but he is so entirely frank and void of malice that he remains likeable even in his least reasonable moments.*

> *Judging by the furnishings of this room, which social class do you think Higgins belongs to?*

HIGGINS (*as he shuts the last drawer*): Well, I think thats the whole show.

PICKERING: It's really amazing. I havnt taken half of it in, you know.

HIGGINS: Would you like to go over any of it again?

PICKERING (*rising and coming to the fireplace, where he plants himself with his back to the fire*): No, thank you: not now. I'm quite done up for this morning.

HIGGINS (*following him, and standing beside him on his left*): Tired of listening to sounds?

PICKERING: Yes. It's a fearful strain. I rather fancied myself because I can pronounce twenty-four distinct vowel sounds; but your hundred and thirty beat me. I cant hear a bit of difference between most of them.

HIGGINS (*chuckling, and going over to the piano to eat sweets*): Oh, that comes with practice. You hear no difference at first; but you keep on listening, and presently you find theyre all as different as A from B. (MRS PEARCE *looks in: she is* HIGGINS*'s housekeeper*). Whats the matter?

MRS PEARCE (*hesitating, evidently perplexed*): A young woman asks to see you, sir.

HIGGINS: A young woman! What does she want?

MRS PEARCE: Well, sir, she says youll be glad to see her when you know what she's come about. She's quite a common girl, sir. Very common indeed. I should have sent her away, only I thought perhaps you wanted her to talk into your machines. I hope Ive not done wrong; but really you see such queer people sometimes – youll excuse me, I'm sure, sir –

HIGGINS: Oh, thats all right, Mrs Pearce. Has she an interesting accent?

MRS PEARCE: Oh, something dreadful, sir, really. I dont know how you can take an interest in it.

HIGGINS (*to* PICKERING): Lets have her up. Shew her up, Mrs Pearce (*he rushes across to his working table and picks out a cylinder to use on the phonograph*).

MRS PEARCE (*only half resigned to it*): Very well, sir. It's for you to say. (*She goes downstairs*).

HIGGINS: This is rather a bit of luck. I'll shew you how I make records. We'll set her talking; and I'll take it down first in Bell's Visible Speech; then in broad Romic; and then we'll get her on the phonograph so that you can turn her on as often as you like with the written transcript before you.

MRS PEARCE (*returning*): This is the young woman, sir.

THE FLOWER GIRL *enters in state. She has a hat with three ostrich feathers, orange, sky-blue, and red. She has a nearly clean apron, and the shoddy coat has been tidied a little. The pathos of this deplorable figure, with its innocent vanity and consequential air, touches* PICKERING, *who has already straightened himself in the presence of* MRS PEARCE. *But as to* HIGGINS, *the only distinction he makes between men and women is that when he is neither bullying nor exclaiming to the heavens against some feather-weight cross, he coaxes women as a child coaxes its nurse when it wants to get anything out of her.*

HIGGINS (*brusquely, recognising her with unconcealed disappointment, and at once, babylike, making an intolerable grievance of it*): Why, this is the girl I jotted down last night. She's no use: Ive got all the records I want of the Lisson Grove lingo; and I'm not going to waste another cylinder on it. (*To the girl*) Be off with you: I dont want you.

THE FLOWER GIRL: Dont you be so saucy. You aint heard what I come for yet. (*To* MRS PEARCE, *who is waiting at the door for further instructions*) Did you tell him I come in a taxi?

MRS PEARCE: Nonsense, girl! what do you think a gentleman like Mr Higgins cares what you came in?

THE FLOWER GIRL: Oh, we are proud! He aint above giving lessons, not him: I heard him say so. Well, I aint come here to ask for any compliment; and if my money's not good enough I can go elsewhere.

HIGGINS: Good enough for what?

THE FLOWER GIRL: Good enough for yə-oo. Now you know, dont

you? I'm come to have lessons, I am. And to pay for em tə-oo: make no mistake.

HIGGINS (*stupent*): Well!!! (*Recovering his breath with a gasp*) What do you expect me to say to you?

THE FLOWER GIRL: Well, if you was a gentleman, you might ask me to sit down, I think. Dont I tell you I'm bringing you business?

HIGGINS: Pickering: shall we ask this baggage to sit down, or shall we throw her out of the window?

THE FLOWER GIRL (*running away in terror to the piano, where she turns at bay*): Ah-ah-oh-ow-ow-ow-oo! (*Wounded and whimpering*) I wont be called a baggage when Ive offered to pay like any lady. *Motionless, the two men stare at her from the other side of the room, amazed.*

PICKERING (*gently*): But what is it you want?

THE FLOWER GIRL: I want to be a lady in a flower shop stead of sellin at the corner of Tottenham Court Road. But they wont take me unless I can talk more genteel. He said he could teach me. Well, here I am ready to pay him – not asking any favor – and he treats me zif I was dirt.

MRS PEARCE: How can you be such a foolish ignorant girl as to think you could afford to pay Mr Higgins?

THE FLOWER GIRL: Why shouldnt I? I know what lessons cost as well as you do; and I'm ready to pay.

HIGGINS: How much?

Do you think Higgins will accept her offer?

THE FLOWER GIRL (*coming back to him, triumphant*): Now youre talking! I thought youd come off it when you saw a chance of getting back a bit of what you chucked at me last night. (*Confidentially*) Youd had a drop in, hadnt you?

HIGGINS (*peremptorily*): Sit down.

THE FLOWER GIRL: Oh, if youre going to make a compliment of it –

HIGGINS (*thundering at her*): Sit down.

MRS PEARCE (*severely*): Sit down, girl. Do as youre told.

THE FLOWER GIRL: Ah-ah-ah-ow-ow-oo! (*She stands, half rebellious, half bewildered.*)

PICKERING (*very courteous*): Wont you sit down? (*He places the stray chair near the hearthrug between himself and* HIGGINS.)

THE FLOWER GIRL (*coyly*): Dont mind if I do. (*She sits down.* PICKERING *returns to the hearthrug.*)

HIGGINS: Whats your name?

THE FLOWER GIRL: Liza Doolittle.

HIGGINS (*declaiming gravely*):

Eliza, Elizabeth, Betsy and Bess,
They went to the woods to get a bird's nes':

PICKERING: They found a nest with four eggs in it:

HIGGINS: They took one apiece, and left three in it.

They laugh heartily at their own fun.

LIZA: Oh, dont be silly.

MRS PEARCE (*placing herself behind* ELIZA*'s chair*): You mustnt speak to the gentleman like that.

LIZA: Well, why wont he speak sensible to me?

HIGGINS: Come back to business. How much do you propose to pay me for the lessons?

LIZA: Oh, I know whats right. A lady friend of mine gets French lessons for eighteenpence an hour from a real French gentleman. Well, you wouldnt have the face to ask me the same for teaching me my own language as you would for French; so I wont give more than a shilling. Take it or leave it.

HIGGINS (*walking up and down the room, rattling his keys and his cash in his pockets*): You know, Pickering, if you consider a shilling, not as a simple shilling, but as a percentage of this girl's income, it works out as fully equivalent to sixty or seventy guineas from a millionaire.

PICKERING: How so?

HIGGINS: Figure it out. A millionaire has about £150 a day. She earns about half-a-crown.

LIZA (*haughtily*): Who told you I only –

HIGGINS (*continuing*): She offers me two-fifths of her day's income for a lesson. Two fifths of a millionaire's income for a day would be somewhere about £60. It's handsome. By George, it's enormous! it's the biggest offer I ever had.

LIZA (*rising, terrified*): Sixty pounds! What are you talking about? I never offered you sixty pounds. Where would I get –

HIGGINS: Hold your tongue.

LIZA (*weeping*): But I aint got sixty pounds. Oh –

MRS PEARCE: Dont cry, you silly girl. Sit down. Nobody is going to touch your money.

HIGGINS: Somebody is going to touch you, with a broomstick, if you dont stop snivelling. Sit down.

LIZA (*obeying slowly*): Ah-ah-ah-ow-oo-o! One would think you was my father.

HIGGINS: If I decide to teach you, I'll be worse than two fathers to you. Here (*he offers her his silk handkerchief*) !

LIZA: Whats this for?

HIGGINS: To wipe your eyes. To wipe any part of your face that feels moist. Remember: thats your handkerchief; and thats your sleeve. Dont mistake the one for the other if you wish to become a lady in a shop.

LIZA, *utterly bewildered, stares helplessly at him.*

MRS PEARCE: It's no use talking to her like that, Mr Higgins: she doesnt understand you. Besides, youre quite wrong: she doesnt do it that way at all (*she takes the handkerchief*).

LIZA (*snatching it*): Here! You give me that handkerchief. He gev it to me, not to you.

PICKERING (*laughing*): He did. I think it must be regarded as her property, Mrs Pearce.

MRS PEARCE (*resigning herself*): Serve you right, Mr Higgins.

PICKERING: Higgins: I'm interested. What about the ambassador's garden party? I'll say youre the greatest teacher alive if you make that good. I'll bet you all the expenses of the experiment you cant do it. And I'll pay for the lessons.

LIZA: Oh, you are real good. Thank you, Captain.

HIGGINS (*tempted, looking at her*): It's almost irresistible. She's so deliciously low – so horribly dirty –

LIZA (*protesting extremely*): Ah-ah-ah-ah-ow-ow-oo-oo!!! I aint dirty: I washed my face and hands afore I come, I did.

PICKERING: Youre certainly not going to turn her head with flattery, Higgins.

MRS PEARCE (*uneasy*): Oh, dont say that sir: theres more ways than one of turning a girl's head; and nobody can do it better than Mr Higgins, though he may not always mean it. I do hope, sir, you wont encourage him to do anything foolish.

What sort of 'foolish' things might she be thinking of?

HIGGINS (*becoming excited as the idea grows on him*): What is life but a series of inspired follies? The difficulty is to find them to do. Never lose a chance: it doesnt come every day. I shall make a duchess of this draggletailed guttersnipe.

LIZA (*strongly deprecating this view of her*): Ah-ah-ah-ow-ow-oo!

HIGGINS (*carrried away*): Yes: in six months – in three if she has a good ear and a quick tongue – I'll take her anywhere and pass her off as anything. We'll start today: now! this moment! Take her away and clean her, Mrs Pearce. Monkey Brand, if it wont come off any other way. Is there a good fire in the kitchen?

MRS PEARCE (*protesting*): Yes; but –

HIGGINS (*storming on*): Take all her clothes off and burn them. Ring up Whiteley or somebody for new ones. Wrap her up in brown paper til they come.

LIZA: Youre no gentleman, youre not, to talk of such things. I'm a good girl, I am; and I know what the like of you are, I do.

HIGGINS: We want none of your Lisson Grove prudery here, young woman. Youve got to learn to behave like a duchess. Take her away, Mrs Pearce. If she gives you any trouble, wallop her.

LIZA (*springing up and running between* PICKERING *and* MRS PEARCE *for protection*): No! I'll call the police, I will.

MRS PEARCE: But Ive no place to put her.

HIGGINS: Put her in the dustbin.

LIZA: Ah-ah-ah-ow-ow-oo!

PICKERING: Oh come, Higgins! Be reasonable.

MRS PEARCE (*resolutely*): You must be reasonable, Mr Higgins: really you must. You cant walk over everybody like this.

HIGGINS, *thus scolded, subsides. The hurricane is succeeded by a zephyr of amiable surprise.*

HIGGINS (*with professional exquisiteness of modulation*): *I* walk over everybody! My dear Mrs Pearce, my dear Pickering, I never had the slightest intention of walking over anyone. All I propose is that we should be kind to this poor girl. We must help her to prepare and fit herself for her new station in life. If I did not express myself clearly it was because I did not wish to hurt her delicacy, or yours.

LIZA, *reassured, steals back to her chair.*

MRS PEARCE (*to* PICKERING): Well, did you ever hear anything like that, sir?

PICKERING (*laughing heartily*): Never, Mrs Pearce: never.

HIGGINS (*patiently*): Whats the matter?

MRS PEARCE: Well, the matter is, sir, that you cant take a girl up like that as if you were picking up a pebble on the beach.

HIGGINS: Why not?

Can you answer Higgins's question?

MRS PEARCE: Why not! But you dont know anything about her. What about her parents? She may be married.

LIZA: Garn!

HIGGINS: There! As the girl very properly says, Garn! Married indeed! Dont you know that a woman of that class looks a worn out drudge of fifty a year after she's married?

LIZA: Whood marry me?

HIGGINS (*suddenly resorting to the most thrillingly beautiful low tones in *his best elocutionary style*): By George, Eliza, the streets will be strewn with the bodies of men shooting themselves for your sake before Ive done with you.

MRS PEARCE: Nonsense, sir. You mustnt talk like that to her.

LIZA (*rising and squaring herself determinedly*): I'm going away. He's off his chump, he is. I dont want no balmies teaching me.

HIGGINS (*wounded in his tenderest point by her insensibility to his elocution*): Oh, indeed! I'm mad, am I? Very well, Mrs Pearce: you neednt order the new clothes for her. Throw her out.

LIZA (*whimpering*): Nah-ow. You got no right to touch me.

MRS PEARCE: You see now what comes of being saucy. (*Indicating the door*) This way, please.

LIZA (*almost in tears*): I didnt want no clothes. I wouldnt have taken them (*she throws away the handkerchief*). I can buy my own clothes.

HIGGINS (*deftly retrieving the handkerchief and intercepting her on her reluctant way to the door*): Youre an ungrateful wicked girl. This is my return for offering to take you out of the gutter and dress you beautifully and make a lady of you.

MRS PEARCE: Stop, Mr Higgins. I wont allow it. It's you that are wicked. Go home to your parents, girl; and tell them to take better care of you.

LIZA: I aint got no parents. They told me I was big enough to earn my own living and turned me out.

MRS PEARCE: Wheres your mother?

LIZA: I aint got no mother. Her that turned me out was my sixth stepmother. But I done without them. And I'm a good girl, I am.

HIGGINS: Very well, then, what on earth is all the fuss about? The girl doesnt belong to anybody – is no use to anybody but me. (*He goes to* MRS PEARCE *and begins coaxing.*) You can adopt her, Mrs Pearce: I'm sure a daughter would be a great amusement to you. Now dont make any more fuss. Take her downstairs; and –

MRS PEARCE: But whats to become of her? Is she to be paid anything? Do be sensible, sir.

HIGGINS: Oh, pay her whatever is necessary: put it down in the housekeeping book. (*Impatiently*) What on earth will she want with money? She'll have her food and her clothes. She'll only drink if you give her money.

LIZA (*turning on him*): Oh you are a brute. It's a lie: nobody ever saw the sign of liquor on me. (*To* PICKERING) Oh sir: youre a gentleman: dont let him speak to me like that.

PICKERING (*in good-humoured remonstrance*): Does it occur to you, Higgins, that the girl has some feelings?

HIGGINS (*looking critically at her*): Oh no, I dont think so. Not any feelings that we need bother about. (*Cheerily*) Have you, Eliza?

LIZA: I got my feelings same as anyone else.

HIGGINS (*to* PICKERING, *reflectively*): You see the difficulty?

PICKERING: Eh? What difficulty?

HIGGINS: To get her to talk grammar. The mere pronunciation is easy enough.

LIZA: I dont want to talk grammar. I want to talk like a lady in a flower-shop.

MRS PEARCE: Will you please keep to the point, Mr Higgins. I want to know on what terms the girl is to be here. Is she to have any wages? And what is to become of her when youve finished your teaching? You must look ahead a little.

HIGGINS (*impatiently*): Whats to become of her if I leave her in the gutter? Tell me that, Mrs Pearce.

MRS PEARCE: Thats her own business, not yours, Mr Higgins.

HIGGINS: Well, when Ive done with her, we can throw her back into the gutter; and then it will be her own business again; so thats all right.

What do you think of this answer? Is Higgins right?

LIZA: Oh, youve no feeling heart in you: you dont care for nothing but yourself. (*She rises and takes the floor resolutely*). Here! Ive had enough of this. I'm going (*making for the door*). You ought to be ashamed of yourself, you ought.

HIGGINS (*snatching a chocolate cream from the piano, his eyes suddenly beginning to twinkle with mischief*): Have some chocolates, Eliza.

LIZA (*halting, tempted*): How do I know what might be in them? Ive heard of girls being drugged by the like of you.

HIGGINS *whips out his penknife; cuts a chocolate in two; puts one half into his mouth and bolts it; and offers her the other half.*

HIGGINS: Pledge of good faith, Eliza. I eat one half: you eat the other. (LIZA *opens her mouth to retort: he pops the half chocolate into it*). You shall have boxes of them, barrels of them, every day. You shall live on them. Eh?

LIZA (*who has disposed of the chocolate after being nearly choked by it*): I wouldnt have ate it, only I'm too ladylike to take it out of my mouth.

HIGGINS: Listen, Eliza. I think you said you came in a taxi.

LIZA: Well, what if I did? Ive as good a right to take a taxi as anyone else.

HIGGINS: You have, Eliza; and in future you shall have as many

taxis as you want. You shall go up and down and round the town in a taxi every day. Think of that, Eliza.

MRS PEARCE: Mr Higgins: youre tempting the girl. It's not right. She should think of the future.

HIGGINS: At her age! Nonsense! Time enough to think of the future when you havnt any future to think of. No, Eliza: do as this lady does: think of other people's futures; but never think of your own. Think of chocolates, and taxis, and gold, and diamonds.

LIZA: No: I dont want no gold, and no diamonds. I'm a good girl, I am. (*She sits down again, with an attempt at dignity*).

HIGGINS: You shall remain so, Eliza, under the care of Mrs Pearce. And you shall marry an officer in the Guards, with a beautiful moustache: the son of a marquis, who will disinherit him for marrying you, but will relent when he sees your beauty and goodness –

PICKERING: Excuse me, Higgins: but I really must interfere. Mrs Pearce is quite right. If this girl is to put herself in your hands for six months for an experiment in teaching, she must understand thoroughly what she's doing.

HIGGINS: How can she? She's incapable of understanding anything. Besides, do any of us understand what we are doing? If we did, would we ever do it?

PICKERING: Very clever, Higgins; but not to the present point. (*To* ELIZA) Miss Doolittle –

LIZA (*overwhelmed*): Ah-ah-ow-oo!

HIGGINS: There! Thats all youll get out of Eliza. Ah-ah-ow-oo! No use explaining. As a military man you ought to know that. Give her her orders: thats enough for her. Eliza: you are to live here for the next six months, learning how to speak beautifully, like a lady in a florist's shop. If youre good and do whatever youre told, you shall sleep in a proper bedroom, and have lots to eat, and money to buy chocolates and take rides in taxis. If youre naughty and idle you will sleep in the back kitchen among the black beetles, and be walloped by Mrs Pearce with a broomstick. At the end of six months you shall go to Buckingham Palace in a carriage, beautifully dressed. If the King finds out youre not a lady, you will be taken by the police to the Tower of London, where your head will be cut off as a warning to other presumptuous flower girls. If you are not found out, you shall have a present of seven-and-sixpence to start life with as a lady in a shop. If you refuse this offer you will be a most ungrateful wicked girl; and the angels will weep for you. (*To* PICKERING) Now are you satisfied, Pickering? (*To* MRS PEARCE) Can I put it more plainly and fairly, Mrs Pearce?

> *Do you think Higgins is being serious in this speech? What suggests that he is not?*

MRS PEARCE (*patiently*): I think youd better let me speak to the girl properly in private. I dont know that I can take charge of her or consent to the arrangement at all. Of course I know you dont mean her any harm; but when you get what you call interested in people's accents, you never think or care what may happen to them or you. Come with me, Eliza.

HIGGINS: Thats all right. Thank you, Mrs Pearce. Bundle her off to the bath-room.

LIZA (*rising reluctantly and suspiciously*): Youre a great bully, you are. I wont stay here if I dont like. I wont let nobody wallop me. I never asked to go to Bucknam Palace, I didnt. I was never in trouble with the police, not me. I'm a good girl –

MRS PEARCE: Dont answer back, girl. You dont understand the gentleman. Come with me. (*She leads the way to the door, and holds it open for* ELIZA.)

LIZA (*as she goes out*): Well, what I say is right. I wont go near the King, not if I'm going to have my head cut off. If I'd known what I was letting myself in for, I wouldnt have come here. I always been a good girl; and I never offered to say a word to

him; and I dont owe him nothing; and I dont care; and I wont be put upon; and I have my feelings the same as anyone else –
MRS PEARCE *shuts the door; and* ELIZA*'s plaints are no longer audible.*

First reaction

5 Here are three judgements of Higgins. Say which you agree with.
- ***a*** He is 'off his chump' (Liza's opinion).
- ***b*** He is 'wicked' (Mrs Pearce's opinion).
- ***c*** He is 'so entirely frank and void of malice that he remains likeable even in his least reasonable moments' (Shaw's description).

Close reading

Stage design

6 Which of these plans corresponds to Shaw's stage directions at the start of the scene?

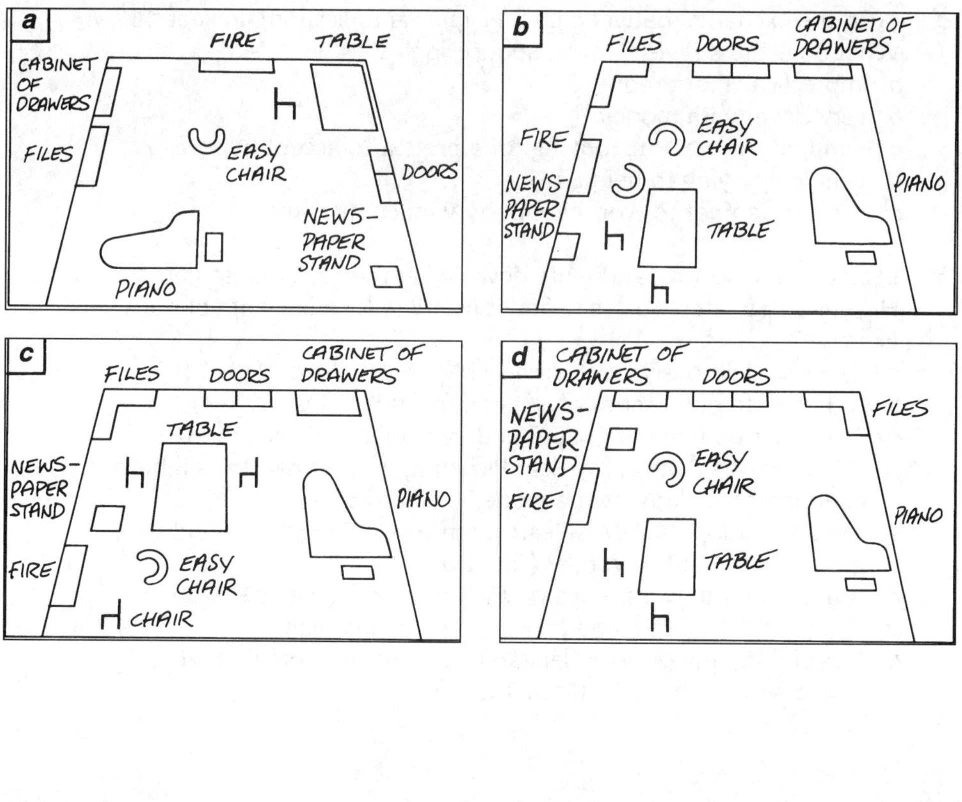

Characters

7 Which of the words below can be used to describe:

a Higgins? ***c*** Mrs Pearce?
b Pickering? ***d*** Liza?

impulsive down-to-earth noisy practical discreet considerate insensitive well-mannered sensible blunt brusque friendly

HIGGINS	PICKERING	MRS PEARCE	LIZA

Add some words of your own.

8 Read the exchange between Liza, Higgins and Pickering in lines 162–84. What does this suggest to you about Higgins? Is he:

a impractical about money?
b very clever with money?
c tempted by Liza, and looking for a pretext to accept her offer?
d genuinely trying to help Liza?
e rich enough not to worry about how much he earns?

9 Look at the following and write down what they suggest to you about Higgins's character. You may find it useful to look back at your answers to Exercise 7.

a 'She's so deliciously low – so horribly dirty.' (lines 213–14)
b 'What is life but a series of inspired follies?' (lines 223–4)
c 'Wrap her up in brown paper til they come.' (lines 235–6)
d 'My dear Mrs Pearce, my dear Pickering, I never had the slightest intention of walking over anyone.' (lines 253–4)
e 'You can adopt her, Mrs Pearce: I'm sure a daughter would be a great amusement to you.' (lines 305–7)
f 'What on earth will she want with money?' (lines 311–12)
g 'Think of chocolates, and taxis, and gold, and diamonds.' (lines 366–7)
h 'Besides, do any of us understand what we are doing? If we did, would we ever do it?' (lines 380–1)

10 Find two similar quotations and two contradictory quotations among those in Exercise 9. Does the fact that Higgins contradicts himself suggest anything else about his character?

11 When Mrs Pearce first enters, she is described as 'hesitating, evidently perplexed' (line 60). Say which of the following explanations seem probable. She hesitates because:

a she does not want to disturb Higgins.
b she is a shy and hesitant person.
c she does not know how to describe the person waiting downstairs.
d she has not worked for Higgins for very long.

She is perplexed because:

e she does not understand Higgins's work.
f she finds life generally bewildering.
g she finds Higgins a puzzling character.
h she cannot understand why a 'common girl' is calling on a gentleman like Higgins.

12 Read the rest of Mrs Pearce's speeches in the scene. Choose one or two which show her to be:

a sympathetic to Liza.
b outspoken and strong-willed.
c practical and down-to-earth.
d psychologically perceptive.

13 At what point do you think Shaw makes Mrs Pearce begin to develop as a character? (If you have difficulty with this question, see Chapter 1, 'The Characters' p 15.)

14 Mrs Pearce's function in the scene is partly *naturalistic* (people like Higgins had housekeepers in 1912), partly *practical* (to bring Liza in and take her out again). Do you think she also plays a *moral* role, contributing to our understanding of what happens? Look at the following interpretations, and for each one decide whether you **agree**, **disagree**, or **partly agree**.

a She is a balancing figure to Higgins. He treats people as objects of scientific interest, but she treats them as human beings.
b She represents reason, prudence, common sense.
c She is an example of working-class snobbery, placed in the scene to show what happens when the working class accept middle-class values.
d She is a narrow-minded figure, intended to contrast with the free-thinking Higgins, and to make his opinions seem more exciting.
e She is a purely comic figure, in the long master-servant tradition of European theatre. She makes no serious contribution to the scene. If Higgins took her advice he would simply return Liza to the streets and there would be no play!

15 Which of the interpretations of Mrs Pearce's character in Exercise 14 could also be applied to Colonel Pickering?

Language practice

Good and bad manners

16 Read this exchange.

HIGGINS (*peremptorily*): Sit down.
THE FLOWER GIRL: Oh, if youre going to make a compliment of it –
HIGGINS (*thundering at her*): Sit down.
MRS PEARCE (*severely*): Sit down, girl. Do as youre told.
THE FLOWER GIRL: Ah-ah-ah-ow-ow-oo! (*She stands, half rebellious, half bewildered.*)
PICKERING (*very courteous*): Wont you sit down?
(*He places the stray chair near the hearthrug between himself and* HIGGINS.)
LIZA (*coyly*): Dont mind if I do. (*She sits down.*)

a Why does Liza not sit down until Colonel Pickering asks her to?
b What is the *grammatical* difference between Colonel Pickering's words and those of Higgins and Mrs Pearce?
c What other differences are there?

17 An **order** is when you tell someone to do something.
Example: 'Leave the room!'
A **polite request** is when you ask someone politely to do something.
Example:'Could you leave the room please? I'd like to be alone.'
An **invitation** is when you ask someone if they would like something or would like to do something. (Note: this may not always take the form of a question.)
Example: 'You must be terribly bored. Would you like to leave the room?' (or: 'Do leave the room if you'd like to.')

Take a careful look at these ways of saying 'sit down', try saying them aloud, then sort them into one of the categories given below. (Note: where the circles overlap you can put phrases which in your opinion may belong to more than one category depending on the way they are spoken.)

a Would you like to sit down?
b Do sit down.
c Will you please sit down?
d Can I offer you a seat?
e Please sit down.
f Would you mind sitting down, please?
g For Heaven's sake, sit down.
h Would you sit down, please?
i Would you like a seat?
j Could you sit down, please?
k Have a seat.
l Won't you sit down?

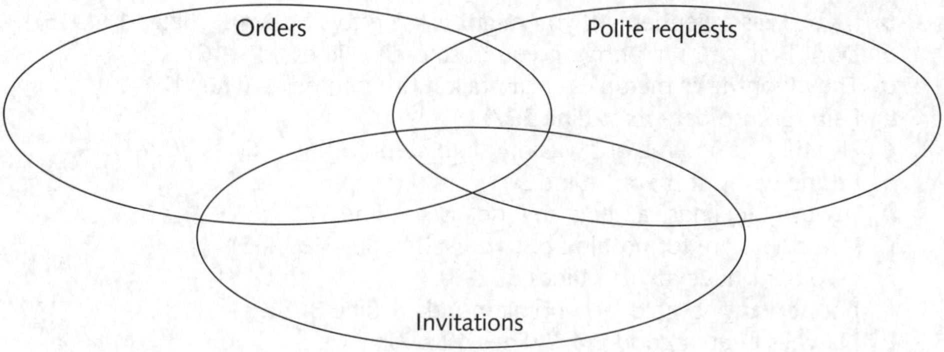

Check your answer in the Key before going on.

18 Make Higgins and Liza sound more polite. Change the following orders to polite requests, using some of the forms given in Exercise 17. Suggest at least **two** possibilities for each one.

a Shew her up, Mrs Pearce. (line 73)
b Here! You give me that handkerchief. (line 203)
c Take her away and clean her, Mrs Pearce. (lines 230–1)

19 **Class activity:** divide into groups of four. One member of the group is Liza, the other three play Pickering, Mrs Pearce, and Higgins. Each practise giving Liza some simple orders, polite requests or invitations (eg 'Sit down') in the style of the character you have chosen. Present your work in the form of a short scene to the rest of the class, who must try to guess who is playing which character.
Some suggestions:

have a cup of tea	*open the door*	*have a bath*
bring the newspaper	*go for walk*	*read a book*

Varieties of English

Liza speaks the working-class London dialect known as Cockney. This differs from Standard English in (a) pronunciation, (b) some grammatical forms, (c) a number of special idioms and slang. During Shaw's lifetime, Cockney and other regional dialects of English were regarded as socially inferior or 'common' – which is why Liza wants to learn to 'talk more genteel'. In the last 40 years, however, fashion has gradually changed and regional dialects are now widely regarded as socially acceptable varieties of English.

20 Here are some examples of Liza's Cockney grammar. Can you convert them to Standard English, and say in each case what her mistakes are?

Example: You aint heard what I come for yet. (lines 99–100)
You haven't heard what I've come for (or *I came for*) *yet.*
'aint' for 'haven't'; present tense form instead of past simple or present perfect.

a I come in a taxi. (line 101)
b If you was a gentleman, you might ask me to sit down. (lines 114–15)
c Dont I tell you I'm bringing you business? (lines 115–16)
d They wont take me unless I can talk more genteel. (lines 126–7)
e I aint got no parents. (line 297)
f Her that turned me out was my sixth stepmother. (lines 300–1)
g I done without them. (line 301)
h I got my feelings same as anyone else. (line 321)
i You dont care for nothing but yourself. (lines 338–9)
j I wouldnt have ate it. (lines 352–3)
k I dont want no gold, and no diamonds. (line 368)
l I always been a good girl. (lines 426–7)

Extension

21 Imagine that you are one of the characters in this scene. Write a letter to a friend describing what has happened.

22 Design a poster (an advertisement for a performance) for *Pygmalion* based on this scene (see Chapter 1, Publicity, p 20).

23 Apart from the change from Cockney to Standard English what else would be necessary to pass Liza off as a duchess at the ambassador's garden party? Make an educational programme for her.

24 **Class project/improvisation**: in groups of 3–5, find out as much as you can about the following stories and work out a short dramatic presentation of them for the rest of the class.
Group 1: the Greek myth of Pygmalion
Group 2: the story of Frankenstein
Group 3: the story of Cinderella

Beyond the text

25 Read this extract from Arnold Wesker's play *Roots*. As you read, make notes on:

a what social class you think the characters belong to, and why.
b what differences in habits, behaviour and attitudes between social classes are revealed in Beatie's description of Ronnie.

Roots (1959) Arnold Wesker

See the Glossary section at the back of the book for vocabulary.

ACT 1

A rather ramshackle house in Norfolk where there is no water laid on, nor electricity, nor gas. Everything rambles and the furniture is cheap and old. If it is untidy it is because there is a child in the house and there are few amenities, so that the mother is too overworked to take much care.

An assortment of clobber lies around: papers and washing, coats and basins, a tin wash-tub with shirts and underwear to be cleaned, Tilley lamps and Primus stoves. Washing hangs on a line in the room. It is September.

JENNY BEALES *is by the sink washing up. She is singing a recent pop song. She is short, fat and friendly, and wears glasses. A child's voice is heard crying 'Sweet, Mamma, sweet.'*

JENNY (*good-naturedly*): Shut you up Daphne and get you to sleep now. (*Moves to get a dishcloth.*)
CHILD'S VOICE: Daphy wan' sweet, sweet, sweet.

JENNY (*going to cupboard to get sweet*): My word child, Father come home and find you awake he'll be after you. (*Disappears to bedroom with sweet.*) There – now sleep, gal, don't wan' you grumpy wi' me in mornin'.

Enter JIMMY BEALES. *Also short, chubby, blond though hardly any hair left, ruddy complexion. He is a garage mechanic. Wears blue dungarees and an army pack slung over his shoulder. He wheels his bike in and lays it by the wall. Seems to be in some sort of pain – around his back.* JENNY *returns.*

Waas matter wi' you then?

JIMMY: I don' know gal. There's a pain in my guts and one a'tween my shoulder blades I can hardly stand up.

JENNY: Sit you down then an' I'll git you your supper on the table.

JIMMY: Blust gal! I can't eat yit.

JIMMY *picks up a pillow from somewhere and lies down on the sofa holding pillow to stomach.* JENNY *watches him a while.*

JENNY: Don't you know what 'tis yit?

JIMMY: Well, how should *I* know what 'tis.

JENNY: I told Mother about the pain and she says it's indigestion.

JIMMY: What the hell's indigestion doin' a'tween my shoulder blades then?

JENNY: She say some people get indigestion so bad it go right through their stomach to the back.

JIMMY: Don't be daft.

JENNY: That's what I say. Blust Mother, I say, you don't git indigestion in the back. Don't you tell me, she say, I hed it!

JIMMY: What hevn't she hed.

JENNY *returns to the washing up while* JIMMY *struggles a while on the sofa.* JENNY *hums. No word. Then –*

JENNY: Who'd you see today?

JIMMY: Only Doctor Gallagher.

JENNY (*wheeling round*): You see who?

JIMMY: Gallagher. His wife driv him up in the ole Armstrong.

JENNY: Well I go t'hell if that ent a rum thing.

JIMMY (*rising and going to table; pain has eased*): What's that then?

JENNY (*moving to get him supper from oven*): We was down at the whist drive in the village and that Judy Maitland say he were dead. 'Cos you know he've hed a cancer this last year and they don't give him no longer'n three weeks don't you?

JIMMY: Ole crows. They don' wan' nothin' less than a death to wake them up.

JENNY: No. No longer'n three weeks.

GIRL'S VOICE (*off*): Yoo-hoo! Yoo-hoo!

JIMMY: There's your sister.

JENNY: That's her.

GIRL'S VOICE (*off*): Yoo-hoo! Anyone home?

JENNY (*calling*): Come you on in gal, don't you worry about yoo-hoo.

Enter BEATIE BRYANT, *an ample, blonde, healthy-faced young woman of twenty-two years. She is carrying a case.*

JIMMY: Here she is.

JENNY (*with reserve, but pleased*): Hello, Beatrice – how are you?

BEATIE (*with reserve, but pleased*): Hello, Jenny – how are you? What's that lovely smell I smell?

JENNY: Onions for supper and bread for the harvest festival.

BEATIE: Watcha Jimmy Beales, how you doin' bor?

JIMMY: Not so bad gal, how's yourself?

BEATIE: All right you know. When you comin' to London again for a football match?

JIMMY: O blust gal, I don' wanna go to any more o' those things. Ole father Bryant was there in the middle of that crowd and he turn around an' he say (*imitating*), Stop you a-pushin' there, he say, stop you a-pushin'.

JENNY: Where's Ronnie?

BEATIE: He's comin' down at the end of two weeks.

JIMMY: Ent you married yit?

BEATIE: No.

JIMMY: You wanna hurry then gal, a long engagement don't do the ole legs any good.

JENNY: Now shut you up Jimmy Beales and get that food down you. Every time you talk, look, you miss a mouthful! That's why you complain of pain in your shoulder blades.

BEATIE: You bin hevin' pains then Jimmy?

JIMMY: Blust yes! Right a'tween my shoulder blades.

JENNY: Mother says it's indigestion.

BEATIE: What the hell's indigestion doin' a'tween his shoulder blades?

JENNY: Mother reckon some people get indigestion so bad it go right though their stomach to the back.

BEATIE: Don't talk daft!

JENNY: That's what I say. Blust Mother, I say, you don't git indigestion in the back. Don't you tell me, she say, I hed it!

BEATIE: What hevn't she hed. How is she?

JENNY: Still the same you know. How long you staying this time?

BEATIE: Two days here – two weeks at home.

JENNY: Hungry gal?

BEATIE: Watcha got?

JENNY: Watcha see.

BEATIE: Liver? I'll hev it!

BEATIE *makes herself at home. Near by is a pile of comics. She picks one up and reads.*

JENNY: We got some ice-cream after.

BEATIE (*absorbed*): Yearp.

JENNY: Look at her. No sooner she's in than she's at them ole comics. You still read them ole things?

JIMMY: She don't change much do she?

BEATIE: Funny that! Soon ever I'm home again I'm like I always was – it don' even seem I bin away. I do the same lazy things an' I talk the same. Funny that!

JENNY: What do Ronnie say to it?

BEATIE: He don't mind. He don't even know though. He ent never bin here. Not in the three years I known him. But I'll tell you (*she jumps up and moves around as she talks*) I used to read the comics he bought for his nephews and he used to get riled –

Now BEATIE *begins to quote Ronnie, and when she does she imitates him so well in both the manner and intonation that in fact as the play progresses we see a picture of him through her.*

'Christ, woman, what can they give you that you can be so absorbed?' So you know what I used to do? I used to get a copy of the *Manchester Guardian* and sit with that wide open – and a comic behind!

JIMMY: *Manchester Guardian*? Blimey Joe – he don' believe in hevin' much fun then?

BEATIE: That's what I used to tell him. 'Fun?' he say, 'fun? Playing an instrument is fun, painting is fun, reading a book is fun, talking with friends is fun – but a comic? A comic? for a young woman of twenty-two?'

JENNY (*handing out meal and sitting down herself*): He sound a queer bor to me. Sit you down and eat gal.

BEATIE (*enthusiastically*): He's alive though.

JIMMY: Alive? Alive you say? What's alive about someone who can't read a comic? What's alive about a person that reads books and looks at paintings and listens to classical music?

There is a silence at this, as though the question answers itself – reluctantly.

JIMMY: Well, it's all right for some I suppose.

BEATIE: And then he'd sneak the comic away from me and read it his-self!

JENNY: Oh, he didn't really mind then?

BEATIE: No – 'cos sometimes I read books as well. 'There's nothing wrong with comics,' he'd cry – he stand up on a chair when he want to preach but don't wanna sound too dramatic.

JENNY: Eh?

BEATIE: Like this, look. (*Stands on a chair.*) 'There's nothing wrong with comics only there's something wrong with comics all the time. There's nothing wrong with football, only there's something wrong with *only* football. There's nothing wrong with rock 'n' rolling, only God preserve me from the girl that can do nothing else!' (*She sits down and then stands up again, remembering something else.*) Oh yes, 'and there's nothing wrong with talking about the weather, only don't talk to me about it!' (*Sits down.*)

JIMMY *and* JENNY *look at each other as though she, and no doubt Ronnie, is a little barmy.* JIMMY *rises and begins to strap on boots and gaiters ready for going out to an allotment.*

JENNY: He never really row with you then?

BEATIE: We used to. There was a time when he handled all official things for me you know. Once I was in between jobs and I didn't think to ask for my unemployment benefit. *He* told me to. But when I asked they told me I was short on stamps and so I wasn't entitled to benefit. *I* didn't know what to say but he did. He went up and argued for me – he's just like his mother, she argues with everyone – and I got it. I didn't know how to talk see, it was all foreign to me. Think of it! An English girl born and bred and I couldn't talk the language – except for to buy food and clothes. And so sometimes when he were in a black mood he'd start on me. 'What can you talk of?' he'd ask. 'Go on, pick a subject. Talk. Use the language. Do you know what language is?' Well, I'd never thought before – hev you? – it's automatic to you isn't it, like walking? 'Well, language is words,' he'd say, as though he were telling me a secret. 'It's bridges, so that you can get safely from one place to another. And the more bridges you know about the more places you can see!' (*To* JIMMY) And do *you* know what happens when you can see a place but you don't know where the bridge is?

JIMMY (*angrily*): Blust gal, what the hell are you on about?

BEATIE: Exactly! You see, you hev a row! Still, rows is all right. I like a row. So then he'd say: 'Bridges! bridges! bridges! Use your bridges woman. It took thousands of years to build them, use them!' And that riled me. 'Blust your bridges,' I'd say. 'Blust you and your bridges – I want a row.' Then he'd grin at me. 'You want a row?' he'd ask. 'No bridges this time?' 'No bridges,' I'd say – and we'd row. Sometimes he'd hurt me but then, slowly, he'd build the bridge up *for* me – and then we'd make love! (*Innocently continues her meal.*)

JENNY: You'd what, did you say?

BEATIE: Make love. Love in the afternoon gal. Ever had it? It's the only time *for* it. Go out or entertain in the evenings; sleep at night, study, work and chores in the mornings; but love – alert and fresh, when you got most energy – love in the afternoon.

JIMMY: I suppose you take time off from work every afternoon to do it?

BEATIE: I'm talking about week-ends and holidays – daft.

JENNY: Oh, Beatie, go on wi' you!

BEATIE: Well, go t'hell Jenny Beales, you're blushin'. Ent you never had love in the afternoon? Ask Jimmy then.

JENNY (*rising to get sweet*): Shut you up gal and get on wi' your ice-cream. It's strawberry flavour. Want some more, James?

26 Professor Higgins wants to teach Liza to talk like a lady for a bet, though Shaw's intentions in writing the play were less frivolous. Ronnie wants Beatie to talk better: 'Talk. Use the language,' he says. What do you think he might mean by this? What reasons are given in this extract for 'using the language' in the way Ronnie suggests? Can you add some reasons of your own?

27 In Exercise 20 you examined Liza's cockney dialect. In this extract the characters speak another dialect: they come from a rural part of the English county of Norfolk. Pick out three or four examples from lines 12 to 41 which show that they speak a regional variety of English rather than standard English.

Authors

George Bernard Shaw (1856–1950) is widely regarded as the greatest British dramatist (although he was Irish) since Shakespeare. He was born in Dublin into a Protestant family which had 'class' but no money, and left school at 16 to work in an office, although he energetically continued his education by reading and visits to art galleries and museums. In 1876 he decided to become a writer and moved to London. He was unsuccessful for ten years, writing five novels (all rejected by publishers) and numerous unpublished articles. From 1885 he found steady work reviewing books, art and music, and edited the highly influential *Fabian Essays in Socialism* (1889). His first plays and dramatic criticism date from the 1890s, when the works of Ibsen were first seen in London, influencing Shaw deeply with their exposure of hypocrisy, corruption and false, outdated ideals, presented in a 'naturalistic' dramatic style that was to revolutionise European theatre. Shaw soon developed his own style, combining the social truth of Ibsen with a brilliant gift for wit and paradox that is reminiscent of Shaw's fellow Irishman, Oscar Wilde. Apart from *Pygmalion*, his best-known plays include *Arms and the Man* (1894), *Caesar and Cleopatra* (1901), *John Bull's Other Island* (1904, a comic and deadly-accurate portrait of Anglo-Irish relations), *Man and Superman* (1905, expressing Shaw's philosophy of an evolutionary life-force), *Major Barbara* (1905), *Heartbreak House* (1920, an exposure of the spiritual bankruptcy of the generation that brought about the First World War), and *Saint Joan* (1923), which led to the award of the Nobel Prize for Literature (which Shaw refused) in 1925. Of his other work it has been written that he was 'the most trenchant pamphleteer since Swift; the most readable music critic in English; the best theatre critic of his generation; a prodigious lecturer and essayist on politics, economics and sociological subjects; and one of the most prolific letter-writers in literature.' Biographies and guides to Shaw's work are abundant, but a good starting-point for serious study is provided by Michael Holroyd's *Bernard Shaw* (3 volumes, 1988–91).

Arnold Wesker was born in London in 1932 and, like Shaw, left school at 16. For the next ten years he worked at a variety of jobs – furniture-maker's apprentice, carpenter's mate, bookseller, airman, plumber, farm labourer, seed sorter, kitchen porter and pastry cook – before his plays *The Kitchen* and *Chicken Soup with Barley* were read by the director Lindsay Anderson and produced at the Royal Court Theatre in London. *Roots* is the second play in a trilogy (with *Chicken Soup with Barley* and *I'm Talking About Jerusalem*) which explores the possibilities and difficulties of living by humanitarian socialist ideals in modern society, set against a series of memorable family scenes. It became one of the classics of British theatre in the 1960s, and has retained its relevance and power to move audiences ever since. Other plays include *Chips with Everything*, *Their Very Own and Golden City*, *The Friends* and *Caritas*.

3 Family Life

Before you read

1 Find a family photograph taken when you were a child or draw a picture of an episode from family life that you remember vividly. (Don't worry about the artistic quality of the drawing, but try to make the essential details clear.)

2 Write a short description of what is happening in your picture. Begin with the words 'I remember ...'.

3 Is this a happy or unhappy memory? Is it typical of the family life you led as a child? Write down your thoughts.

4 Look back over what you have written and pick out two key words that sum up your memories of family life.
a ____________________
b ____________________

5 How did family life change as you grew up? Did it become happier or less happy?

6 **Group work**: find a partner, and show each other your pictures (but not your written work). Take turns to interview your partner about his / her picture and the family life it portrays. Find out as much as you can about the people in the picture. Go through Exercises 3–5 above with your partner.

7 **Group / individual work**: look at the list in the box below. Which is most important for a happy family life? Which is least important? Grade them on a scale 1–10, with 1 as the most important, 10 as the least.

money a sense of humour religious faith cleanliness one parent who doesn't work full time doing things together love good food tolerance discipline

Is there any other quality you think is important for a happy family life?

Long Day's Journey Into Night (1941)
Eugene O'Neill

Characters in the play: James Tyrone is a famous actor. His wife Mary has been addicted to morphine (a drug similar to heroin) for 20 years, but is now supposedly 'cured'. They have two sons – Jamie, aged 33, who is also an actor, although unsuccessful and a drunkard; and Edmund, aged 23, who is ill – possibly with tuberculosis – after spending several years working on sailing ships, travelling the world and living rough. He is now trying to be a writer. The play shows one day in the life of the Tyrone family at their summer home on the north-east coast of the USA in August 1912. At the start of this extract Tyrone and Jamie are discussing Edmund's health. Yesterday Tyrone went to see their doctor about it.

See the Glossary section at the back of the book for vocabulary.

ACT I

JAMIE: You talked to him when you went uptown yesterday, didn't you?

TYRONE: He couldn't say anything for sure yet. He's to phone me today before Edmund goes to him.

JAMIE (*slowly*): He thinks it's consumption, doesn't he, Papa?

TYRONE (*reluctantly*): He said it might be.

JAMIE (*moved, his love for his brother coming out*): Poor kid! God damn it! (*He turns on his father accusingly.*) It might never have happened if you'd sent him to a real doctor when he first got sick.

TYRONE: What's the matter with Hardy? He's always been our doctor up here.

JAMIE: Everything's the matter with him! Even in this hick burg he's rated third class! He's a cheap old quack!

TYRONE: That's right! Run him down! Run down everybody! Everyone is a fake to you!

JAMIE (*contemptuously*): Hardy only charges a dollar. That's what makes you think he's a fine doctor!

TYRONE (*stung*): That's enough! You're not drunk now! There's no excuse – (*He controls himself – a bit defensively.*) If you mean I can't afford one of the fine society doctors who prey on the rich summer people –

JAMIE: Can't afford? You're one of the biggest property owners around here.

TYRONE: That doesn't mean I'm rich. It's all mortgaged –

JAMIE: Because you always buy more instead of paying off mortgages. If Edmund was a lousy acre of land you wanted, the sky would be the limit!

TYRONE: That's a lie! And your sneers against Doctor Hardy are lies! He doesn't put on frills, or have an office in a fashionable location, or drive around in an expensive automobile. That's what you pay for with those other five-dollars-to-look-at-your-tongue fellows, not their skill.

JAMIE (*with a scornful shrug of his shoulders*): Oh, all right. I'm a fool to argue. You can't change the leopard's spots.

TYRONE (*with rising anger*): No, you can't. You've taught me that lesson only too well. I've lost all hope you will ever change yours. You dare tell me what I can afford? You've never known the value of a dollar and never will! You've never saved a dollar in your life! At the end of each season you're penniless! You've thrown your salary away every week on whores and whiskey!

JAMIE: My salary! Christ!

TYRONE: It's more than you're worth, and you couldn't get that if it wasn't for me. If you weren't my son, there isn't a manager in the business who would give you a part, your reputation stinks so. As it is, I have to humble my pride and beg for you, saying you've turned over a new leaf, although I know it's a lie!

JAMIE: I never wanted to be an actor. You forced me on the stage.

TYRONE: That's a lie! You made no effort to find anything else to do. You left it to me to get you a job and I have no influence except in the theatre. Forced you! You never wanted to do anything except loaf in bar-rooms! You'd have been content to sit back like a lazy lunk and sponge on me for the rest of your life! After all the money I'd wasted on your education, and all you did was get fired in disgrace from every college you went to!

JAMIE: Oh, for God's sake, don't drag up that ancient history!

TYRONE: It's not ancient history that you have to come home every summer to live on me.

JAMIE: I earn my board and lodging working on the grounds. It saves you hiring a man.

TYRONE: Bah! You have to be driven to do even that much! (*His anger ebbs into a weary complaint.*) I wouldn't give a damn if you ever displayed the slightest sign of gratitude. The only thanks is to have you sneer at me for a dirty miser, sneer at my profession, sneer at every damned thing in the world – except yourself.

JAMIE (*wryly*): That's not true, Papa. You can't hear me talking to myself, that's all.

TYRONE (*stares at him puzzledly, then quotes mechanically*): 'Ingratitude, the vilest weed that grows'!

JAMIE: I could see that line coming! God, how many thousand times – ! (*He stops, bored with their quarrel, and shrugs his shoulders.*) All right, Papa, I'm a bum. Anything you like, so long as it stops the argument.

Do you think this will stop the argument?

TYRONE (*with indignant appeal now*): If you'd get ambition in your head instead of folly! You're young yet. You could still make your mark. You had the talent to become a fine actor! You have it still. You're my son – !

JAMIE (*boredly*): Let's forget me. I'm not interested in the subject. Neither are you.

TYRONE *gives up.* JAMIE *goes on casually.*
What started us on this? Oh, Doc Hardy. When is he going to call you up about Edmund?

TYRONE: Around lunch time. (*He pauses – then defensively.*) I couldn't have sent Edmund to a better doctor. Hardy's treated him whenever he was sick up here, since he was knee-high. He knows his constitution as no other doctor could. It's not a question of my being miserly, as you'd like to make out. (*Bitterly.*) And what could the finest specialist in America do for Edmund, after he's deliberately ruined his health by the mad life he's led ever since he was fired from college? Even before that, when he was in prep school, he began dissipating and playing the Broadway sport to imitate you, when he's never had your constitution to stand it. You're a healthy hulk like me – or you were at his age – but he's always been a bundle of nerves like his mother. I've warned him for years his body couldn't stand it, but he wouldn't heed me, and now it's too late.

JAMIE (*sharply*): What do you mean, too late? You talk as if you thought –

TYRONE (*guiltily explosive*): Don't be a damned fool! I meant nothing but what's plain to anyone! His health has broken down and he may be an invalid for a long time.

JAMIE (*stares at his father, ignoring his explanation*): I know it's an Irish peasant idea consumption is fatal. It probably is when you live in a hovel on a bog, but over here, with modern treatment –

TYRONE: Don't I know that! What are you gabbing about, anyway? And keep your dirty tongue off Ireland, with your sneers about peasants and bogs and hovels! (*Accusingly.*) The less you say about Edmund's sickness, the better for your conscience! You're more responsible than anyone!

JAMIE (*stung*): That's a lie! I won't stand for that, Papa!

TYRONE: It's the truth! You've been the worst influence for him. He grew up admiring you as a hero! A fine example you set him! If you ever gave him advice except in the ways of rottenness, I've never heard of it! You made him old before his time, pumping him full of what you consider worldly wisdom, when he was too young to see that your mind was so poisoned by your own failure in life, you wanted to believe every man was a knave with his soul for sale, and every woman who wasn't a whore was a fool!

JAMIE (*with a defensive air of weary indifference again*): All right. I did put Edmund wise to things, but not until I saw he'd started to raise hell, and knew he'd laugh at me if I tried the good advice, older brother stuff. All I did was make a pal of him and be absolutely frank so he'd learn from my mistakes that – (*He shrugs his shoulders – cynically.*) Well, that if you can't be good you can at least be careful.

His father snorts contemptuously. Suddenly JAMIE *becomes really moved.*

That's a rotten accusation, Papa. You know how much the Kid means to me, and how close we've always been – not like the usual brothers! I'd do anything for him.

TYRONE (*impressed – mollifyingly*): I know you may have thought it was for the best, Jamie. I didn't say you did it deliberately to harm him.

JAMIE: Besides, it's damned rot! I'd like to see anyone influence Edmund more than he wants to be. His quietness fools people into thinking they can do what they like with him. But he's stubborn as hell inside and what he does is what he wants to do, and to hell with anyone else! What had I to do with all the crazy stunts he's pulled in the last few years – working his way all over the map as a sailor and all that stuff. I thought that was a damned fool idea, and I told him so. You can't imagine me getting fun out of being on the beach in South America or living in filthy dives, drinking rotgut, can you? No, thanks! I'll stick to Broadway, and a room with a bath, and bars that serve bonded Bourbon.

TYRONE: You and Broadway! It's made you what you are! (*With a touch of pride.*) Whatever Edmund's done, he's had the guts to go off on his own, where he couldn't come whining to me the minute he was broke.

JAMIE (*stung into sneering jealousy*): He's always come home broke finally, hasn't he? And what did his going away get him? Look at him now! (*He is suddenly shame-faced.*) Christ! That's a lousy thing to say. I don't mean that.

Why is Jamie suddenly ashamed?

TYRONE (*decides to ignore this*): He's been doing well on the paper. I was hoping he'd found the work he wants to do at last.

JAMIE (*sneering jealously again*): A hick town rag! Whatever bull they hand you, they tell me he's a pretty bum reporter. If he weren't your son – (*Ashamed again.*) No, that's not true! They're glad to have him, but it's the special stuff that gets him by. Some of the poems and parodies he's written are damned good. (*Grudgingly again.*). Not that they'd ever get him anywhere on the big time. (*Hastily.*) But he's certainly made a damned good start.

TYRONE: Yes. He's made a start. You used to talk about wanting to become a newspaper man but you were never willing to start at the bottom. You expected –

JAMIE: Oh, for Christ's sake, Papa! Can't you lay off me!

TYRONE (*stares at him – then looks away – after a pause*): It's damnable luck Edmund should be sick right now. It couldn't have come at a worse time for him. (*He adds, unable to conceal an almost furtive uneasiness.*) Or for your mother. It's damnable she should have this to upset her, just when she needs peace and freedom from worry. She's been so well in the two months since she came home. (*His voice grows husky and trembles a little.*) It's been heaven to me. This home has been a home again. But I needn't tell you, Jamie.

His son looks at him, for the first time with an understanding sympathy. It is as if suddenly a deep bond of common feeling existed between them in which their antagonisms could be forgotten.

JAMIE (*almost gently*): I've felt the same way, Papa.

TYRONE: Yes, this time you can see how strong and sure of herself she is. She's a different woman entirely from the other times. She has control of her nerves – or she had until Edmund got sick. Now you can feel her growing tense and frightened underneath. I wish to God we could keep the truth from her, but we can't if he has to be sent to a sanatorium. What makes it worse is her father died of consumption. She worshipped him and she's never forgotten. Yes, it will be hard for her. But she can do it! She has the will-power now! We must help her, Jamie, in every way we can!

JAMIE (*moved*): Of course, Papa. (*Hesitantly.*) Outside of nerves, she seems perfectly all right this morning.

TYRONE (*with hearty confidence now*): Never better. She's full of fun and mischief. (*Suddenly he frowns at Jamie suspiciously.*) Why do you say, seems? Why shouldn't she be all right? What the hell do you mean?

Why do you think Tyrone is suspicious?

JAMIE: Don't start jumping down my throat! God, Papa, this ought to be one thing we can talk over frankly without a battle.

TYRONE: I'm sorry, Jamie. (*Tensely.*) But go on and tell me –

JAMIE: There's nothing to tell. I was all wrong. It's just that last night – Well, you know how it is, I can't forget the past. I can't help being suspicious. Any more than you can. (*Bitterly.*) That's the hell of it. And it makes it hell for Mama! She watches us watching her –

TYRONE (*sadly*): I know. (*Tensely.*) Well, what was it? Can't you speak out?

JAMIE: Nothing, I tell you. Just my damned foolishness. Around three o'clock this morning, I woke up and heard her moving around in the spare room. Then she went to the bathroom. I pretended to be asleep. She stopped in the hall to listen, as if she wanted to make sure I was.

TYRONE (*with forced scorn*): For God's sake, is that all? She told me herself the foghorn kept her awake all night, and every night since Edmund's been sick she's been up and down, going to his room to see how he was.

JAMIE (*eagerly*): Yes, that's right, she did stop to listen outside his room. (*Hesitantly again.*) It was her being in the spare room that scared me. I couldn't help remembering that when she starts sleeping alone in there, it has always been a sign –

TYRONE: It isn't this time! It's easily explained. Where else could she go last night to get away from my snoring? (*He gives way to a burst of resentful anger.*) By God, how you can live with a mind that sees nothing but the worst motives behind everything is beyond me!

JAMIE (*stung*): Don't pull that! I've just said I was all wrong. Don't you suppose I'm as glad of that as you are!

TYRONE (*mollifyingly*): I'm sure you are, Jamie. (*A pause. His expression becomes sombre. He speaks slowly with a superstitious dread.*) It would be like a curse she can't escape if worry over Edmund – It was in her long sickness after bringing him into the world that she first –

JAMIE: She didn't have anything to do with it!

TYRONE: I'm not blaming her.

JAMIE (*bitingly*): Then who are you blaming? Edmund, for being born?

TYRONE: You damned fool! No one was to blame.

JAMIE: The bastard of a doctor was! From what Mama's said, he was another cheap quack like Hardy! You wouldn't pay for a first-rate –

TYRONE: That's a lie! (*Furiously.*) So I'm to blame! That's what you're driving at, is it? You evil-minded loafer!

JAMIE (*warningly as he hears his mother in the dining-room*): Ssh!

TYRONE *gets hastily to his feet and goes to look out of the windows at right.* JAMIE *speaks with a complete change of tone.*

Well, if we're going to cut the front hedge today, we'd better go to work.

Why does Jamie suddenly change the subject of conversation?

MARY *comes in from the back parlour. She gives a quick, suspicious glance from one to the other, her manner nervously self-conscious.*

TYRONE (*turns from the window – with an actor's heartiness*): Yes, it's too fine a morning to waste indoors arguing. Take a look out the window, Mary. There's no fog in the harbour. I'm sure the spell of it we've had is over now.

MARY (*going to him*): I hope so, dear. (*To* JAMIE, *forcing a smile.*) Did I actually hear you suggesting work on the front hedge, Jamie? Wonders will never cease! You must want pocket money badly.

JAMIE (*kiddingly*): When don't I? (*He winks at her, with a derisive glance at his father.*) I expect a salary of at least one large iron man at the end of the week – to carouse on!

MARY (*does not respond to his humour – her hands fluttering over the front of her dress*): What were you two arguing about ?

JAMIE (*shrugs his shoulders*): The same old stuff.

MARY: I heard you say something about a doctor, and your father accusing you of being evil-minded.

JAMIE (*quickly*): Oh, that. I was saying again Doc Hardy isn't my idea of the world's greatest physician.

MARY (*knows he is lying – vaguely*): Oh. No, I wouldn't say he was, either. (*Changing the subject – forcing a smile.*) That Bridget! I thought I'd never get away. She told me all about her second cousin on the police force in St Louis. (*Then with nervous irritation.*) Well, if you're going to work on the hedge why don't you go? (*Hastily.*) I mean, take advantage of the sunshine before the fog comes back. (*Strangely, as if talking aloud to herself.*) Because I know it will. (*Suddenly she is self-consciously aware that they are both staring fixedly at her – flurriedly, raising her hands.*) Or I should say, the rheumatism in my hands knows. It's a better weather prophet than you are, James. (*She stares at her hands with fascinated repulsion.*) Ugh! How ugly they are! Who'd ever believe they were once beautiful?

They stare at her with a growing dread.

TYRONE (*takes her hands and gently pushes them down*): Now, now, Mary. None of that foolishness. They're the sweetest hands in the world.

She smiles, her face lighting up, and kisses him gratefully. He turns to his son.

Come on, Jamie. Your mother's right to scold us. The way to

start work is to start work. The hot sun will sweat some of that booze fat off your middle.

He opens the screen door and goes out on the porch and disappears down a flight of steps leading to the ground. JAMIE *rises from his chair and, taking off his coat, goes to the door. At the door he turns back but avoids looking at her, and she does not look at him.*

JAMIE (*with an awkward, uneasy tenderness*): We're all so proud of you, Mama, so darned happy.

She stiffens and stares at him with a frightened defiance.

Why does she react like this to Jamie's words?

He flounders on.

But you've still got to be careful. You mustn't worry so much about Edmund. He'll be all right.

MARY (*with a stubborn, bitterly resentful look*): Of course, he'll be all right. And I don't know what you mean, warning me to be careful.

JAMIE (*rebuffed and hurt, shrugs his shoulders*): All right, Mama. I'm sorry I spoke.

He goes out on the porch. She waits rigidly until he disappears down the steps. Then she sinks down in the chair he had occupied, her face betraying a frightened, furtive desperation, her hands roving over the table top, aimlessly moving objects around. She hears Edmund descending the stairs in the front hall. As he nears the bottom he has a fit of coughing. She springs to her feet, as if she wanted to run away from the sound, and goes quickly to windows at right. She is looking out, apparently calm, as he enters from the front parlour, a book in one hand. She turns to him, her lips set in a welcoming, motherly smile.

MARY: Here you are. I was just going upstairs to look for you.

EDMUND: I waited until they went out. I don't want to mix up in any arguments. I feel too rotten.

MARY (*almost resentfully*): Oh, I'm sure you don't feel half as badly as you make out. You're such a baby. You like to get us worried so we'll make a fuss over you. (*Hastily.*) I'm only teasing, dear. I know how miserably uncomfortable you must be. But you feel better today, don't you? (*Worriedly, taking his arm.*) All the same, you've grown much too thin. You need to rest all you can. Sit down and I'll make you comfortable.

He sits down in the rocking-chair and she puts a pillow behind his back.

There. How's that?

EDMUND: Grand. Thanks, Mama.

MARY (*kisses him – tenderly*): All you need is your mother to nurse you. Big as you are, you're still the baby of the family to me, you know.

EDMUND (*takes her hand – with deep seriousness*): Never mind me. You take care of yourself. That's all that counts.

MARY (*evading his eyes*): But I am, dear. (*Forcing a laugh.*) Heavens, don't you see how fat I've grown! I'll have to have all my dresses let out. (*She turns away and goes to the windows at right. She attempts a light, amused tone.*) They've started clipping the hedge.

First reaction

8 Why are the Tyrone family so unhappy? Complete the sentences in any way you like.

a James Tyrone ______________________________

b Mary ______________________________

c Jamie ______________________________

d Edmund ______________________________

e They ______________________________

Close reading

The plot

9 Look at the following sentence.

'In this scene, we see the Tyrone family after breakfast one summer morning.'

How useful do you find this as a summary of what happens? What else would you add? Write two more sentences. (If you don't know what needs to be added, see Chapter 1, 'Plot, theme and structure', p 17.)

10 Here is a more detailed summary of the extract. The descriptions of what happens – in the right-hand column – are not in order. Match the descriptions in the right-hand column with the line numbers in the left-hand column.

Lines	Descriptions
a 1–34	***1*** Jamie blames Mary's addiction on Tyrone's miserliness.
b 35–79	***2*** Edmund and Mary try unsuccessfully to humour each other.
c 80–107	***3*** Jamie accuses Edmund of stubbornness and irresponsibility; Tyrone defends him for his courage and determination.
d 107–34	***4*** Tyrone blames Edmund for destroying his own health; Jamie accuses Tyrone of giving up hope that Edmund will recover.
e 135–67	***5*** As Mary talks, Tyrone and Jamie suspect that she is taking drugs again, but they pretend they have noticed nothing.
f 168–94	***6*** Tyrone and Jamie stop arguing and share a few moments of sympathy for Mary.
g 194–231	7 Jamie blames Edmund's poor health on his father's meanness.
h 232–41	***8*** Left alone, Mary reveals how tense and agitated she is.
i 242–58	***9*** Jamie and his father argue about Mary's behaviour during the night. Jamie suspects her of taking morphine again.
j 259–302	***10*** Tyrone and Jamie try to humour Mary with light-hearted talk.
k 303–12	***11*** Tyrone accuses Jamie of being a loafer and a parasite.
l 313–34	***12*** Tyrone accuses Jamie of corrupting Edmund; Jamie defends himself by claiming he acted out of love for his brother.

Answers: ***a*** ___ ***b*** ___ ***c*** ___ ***d*** ___ ***e*** ___ ***f*** ___
g ___ ***h*** ___ ***i*** ___ ***j*** ___ ***k*** ___ ***l*** ___

The characters

11 In *Long Day's Journey Into Night*, the audience is forced to revise its opinions of the characters very frequently. This is because new information about them is constantly being revealed, and because the characters are complex and full of contradictions. As we learn more about them, our judgements change.

Jamie is an example of a complex character. Look at his speech in lines 157–63.

JAMIE (*sneering jealously again*): A hick town rag! Whatever bull they hand you, they tell me he's a pretty bum reporter. If he weren't your son – (*Ashamed again.*) No, that's not true! They're glad to have him, but it's the special stuff that gets him by. Some of the poems and parodies he's written are damned good. (*Grudgingly again.*) Not that they'd ever get him anywhere on the big time. (*Hastily.*) But he's certainly made a damned good start.

Here we see him being alternately kind and unkind about his brother. Look at his speech again and write down the words he says under these two headings:

kind *unkind*

12 O'Neill's stage directions help the reader (and the actor) to understand why Jamie says such contradictory things. He is *sneering jealously*, then *ashamed*, then *grudging*. Critics describe such characters as 'divided' or 'torn' between jealousy and love.

Now look at these other examples and write down what they suggest to you about the characters in the play. Some words are given in the box on page 73 to help you. Use them or others of your own.

JAMIE

a Let's forget me. I'm not interested in the subject. Neither are you. (lines 77–8)

b You know how much the Kid means to me, and how close we've always been – not like the usual brothers! (lines 129–31)

c (*with an awkward, uneasy tenderness*) We're all so proud of you, Mama, so darned happy. (lines 292–3)

TYRONE

d You had the talent to become a fine actor! You have it still. You're my son – ! (lines 75–6)

e So I'm to blame! That's what you're driving at, is it? You evil-minded loafer! (lines 240–1)

f Now, now, Mary. None of that foolishness. They're the sweetest hands in the world. (lines 280–2)

MARY

g From what Mama's said, he was another cheap quack like Hardy! (lines 237–8, Jamie speaking)

h (*She stares at her hands with fascinated repulsion.*) Ugh! How ugly they are! Who'd ever believe they were once beautiful? (lines 276–8)

i (*with a stubborn, bitterly resentful look.*) Of course, he'll be all right. And I don't know what you mean, warning me to be careful. (lines 298–300)

EDMUND

j What had I to do with all the crazy stunts he's pulled in the last few years – working his way all over the map as a sailor and all that stuff. (lines 139–41, Jamie speaking)

k They're glad to have him, but it's the special stuff that gets him by. Some of the poems and parodies he's written are damned good. (lines 159–61, Jamie speaking)

l I waited until they went out. I don't want to mix up in any arguments. I feel too rotten. (lines 314–15)

talented, but in an unusual way *trying to be optimistic* *bitter* *proud* *cynical* *aggressive* *defensive* *often blames others* *self-obsessed* *weary* *adventurous* *caring*

Explicit and implicit meaning

13 When Jamie says, 'she seems perfectly all right this morning' (lines 191–2), his father at first takes it as an innocent remark. Then suddenly he sees a sinister meaning in it. 'Why do you say, seems? Why shouldn't she be all right? What the hell do you mean?'

The implicit meaning of Jamie's remark is that his mother only 'seems' all right: in fact she is not. The implicit meaning of Tyrone's angry question is that he knows she is not all right but doesn't want to admit it. Such implicit meanings are sometimes called the 'subtext' (from 'sub' meaning *under* in Latin).

Long Day's Journey Into Night is full of implicit meanings.

Here are some more examples. Underneath each one, write down what you think the subtext is. (Note: to do this, you need to look each one up in the extract and think about its possible meanings at that point in the play.)
Example: My salary! Christ! (line 41)
Subtext: You don't pay me enough.

a You can't hear me talking to myself, that's all. (lines 65–6)
Subtext: ____________________

b … or you were at his age. (line 93)
Subtext: ____________________

c I know you may have thought it was for the best. (lines 132–3)
Subtext: ____________________

d You and Broadway! It's made you what you are! (line 147)
Subtext: ____________________

e The hot sun will sweat some of that booze fat off your middle. (lines 286–7)
Subtext: ____________________

f We're all so proud of you, Mama, so darned happy. (lines 292–3)
Subtext: ____________________

g They've started clipping the hedge. (line 335)
Subtext: ____________________

14 Sometimes O'Neill implies meanings through stage directions alone. Here are some examples. Write your own interpretations.
Example: *guiltily explosive* (line 99)
This implies that Jamie has guessed Tyrone's secret (and guilty) thoughts.
a *Hastily* (line 163)
b *His voice grows husky and trembles a little* (line 174)
c *almost gently* (line 180)
d *Hesitantly* (line 191)
e *with forced scorn* (line 212)
f *eagerly* (line 216)
g *her hands fluttering over the front of her dress* (lines 259–60)
h *At the door he turns back but avoids looking at her, and she does not look at him* (lines 290–1)

15 Why do you think there are so many implicit meanings in this play? What do they reveal about the tensions in the Tyrone family?

Language practice – structures

Blaming, accusing, suspecting, defending, claiming, pretending (reported speech)

16 Look back at the summaries in Exercise 10 and write down the verbs that correspond to each of these patterns.
a verb + person + **of** +noun or gerund
b verb + person + **for** + noun or gerund
c verb + noun + **on** + person
d verb (+ **that**) + person + finite clause
e verb + person + **by** + gerund

17 Now put the following into reported speech, using the verbs in brackets in the present tense.
a You've never saved a dollar in your life! (lines 38–9) (Tyrone / accuse / Jamie)
b You've thrown your salary away every week on whores and whiskey! (lines 39–40) (Tyrone / accuse / Jamie)
c I earn my board and lodging working on the grounds. (line 58) (Jamie / defend)
d I couldn't have sent Edmund to a better doctor. (lines 82–3) (Tyrone / claim)
e You're more responsible than anyone! (line 109) (Tyrone / blame / Jamie)
f it's the special stuff that gets him by. (line 160) (Jamie / suspect)

g The bastard of a doctor was! (line 237)
(Jamie / blame)

18 Answer these questions using your knowledge of the text.

a What does Jamie accuse his father of?
b How does Tyrone defend himself?
c What does Tyrone accuse Jamie of?
d How does Jamie defend himself?
e What does Jamie suspect his mother of?

19 Remember a family quarrel you once had and describe it using the reporting verbs in Exercise 17.

Language practice – vocabulary

20 Printed below are some of the phrases describing the characters in the play, taken from O'Neill's stage directions in the opening scene. Can you match the phrases with the characters?

TYRONE	MARY	JAMIE	EDMUND

a high forehead, thick white hair
b broad-shouldered, deep chested
c eyes feverish, cheeks sunken, parched sallow skin
d fifty-four, medium height
e a soldierly quality
f a young, graceful figure
g thin grey hair
h plainly in bad health
i face thin and pale, with the bone structure prominent
j wears a shirt, collar and tie, no jacket
k wears a threadbare grey suit, collarless shirt, white handkerchief knotted around his throat
l there is a lot of stolid, earthy peasant in him
m thin and wiry

n eyes unusually large and beautiful
o face has begun to break down but is still good-looking
p smiles rarely; when he does he has the remnant of a humorous, romantic, irresponsible Irish charm
q hands never still
r sixty-five, but looks ten years younger
s dressed in an old sack suit with a collar and tie
t a habitual expression of cynicism
u a high forehead, with brown hair brushed straight back
v big dark eyes in a long, narrow Irish face
w doesn't give a damn how he looks
x thirty-three, prematurely disintegrating

21 Connect the phrases from Exercise 20 into sentences to make a description of each character. Add some details of your own.

22 Now compare your version with O'Neill's.

Mary is fifty-four, about medium height. She still has a young, graceful figure, a trifle plump, but showing little evidence of middle-aged waist and hips, although she is not tightly corseted. Her face is distinctly Irish in type. It must once have been extremely pretty, and is still striking. It does not match her healthy figure but is thin and pale with the bone structure prominent. Her nose is long and straight, her mouth wide with full, sensitive lips. She uses no rouge or any sort of make-up. Her high forehead is framed by thick, pure white hair. Accentuated by her pallor and white hair, her dark brown eyes appear black. They are unusually large and beautiful, with black brows and long curling lashes.

What strikes one immediately is her extreme nervousness. Her hands are never still. They were once beautiful hands, with long, tapering fingers, but rheumatism has knotted the joints and warped the fingers, so that now they have an ugly crippled look. One avoids looking at them, the more so because one is conscious she is sensitive about their appearance and humiliated by her inability to control the nervousness which draws attention to them.

She is dressed simply but with a sure sense of what becomes her. Her hair is arranged with fastidious care. Her voice is soft and attractive. When she is merry, there is a touch of Irish lilt in it.

Her most appealing quality is the simple, unaffected charm of a shy convent-girl youthfulness she has never lost – an innate unworldly innocence.

James Tyrone is sixty-five but looks ten years younger. About five feet eight, broad-shouldered and deep-chested, he seems taller and slenderer because of his bearing, which has a soldierly quality of head up, chest out, stomach in, shoulders squared. His face has begun to break down but he is still remarkably good-looking – a big, finely shaped head, a handsome profile, deep-set light-brown eyes. His grey hair is thin with a bald spot like a monk's tonsure.

The stamp of his profession is unmistakably on him. Not that he indulges in any of the deliberate temperamental posturings of the stage star. He is by nature and preference a simple, unpretentious man, whose inclinations are still close to his humble beginnings and his Irish farmer forebears. But the actor shows in all his unconscious habits of speech, movement and gesture. These have the quality of belonging to a studied technique. His voice is remarkably fine, resonant and flexible, and he takes great pride in it.

His clothes, assuredly, do not costume any romantic part. He wears a threadbare, ready-made, grey sack suit and shineless black shoes, a collar-less shirt with a thick white handkerchief knotted loosely around his throat. There is nothing picturesquely careless about this get-up. It is commonplace shabby. He believes in wearing his clothes to the limit of usefulness, is dressed now for gardening, and doesn't give a damn how he looks.

He has never been really sick a day in his life. He has no nerves. There is a lot of stolid, earthy peasant in him, mixed with streaks of sentimental melancholy and rare flashes of intuitive sensibility ...

Their sons, James, Jr., and Edmund enter together ...

Jamie, the elder, is thirty-three. He has his father's broad-shouldered, deep-chested physique, is an inch taller and weighs less, but appears shorter and stouter because he lacks Tyrone's bearing and graceful carriage. He also lacks his father's vitality. The signs of premature disintegration are on him. His face is still good-looking, despite marks of dissipation, but it has never been handsome like Tyrone's, although Jamie resembles him rather than his mother. He has fine brown eyes, their colour midway between his father's lighter and his mother's darker ones. His hair is thinning and already there is indication of a bald spot like Tyrone's. His nose is unlike that of any other member of the family, pronouncedly aquiline. Combined with his habitual expression of cynicism it gives his countenance a Mephistophelian cast. But on the rare occasions when he smiles without sneering, his personality possesses the remnant of a humorous, romantic, irresponsible Irish charm – that of the beguiling ne'er-do-well, with a strain of the sentimentally poetic, attractive to women and popular with men.

He is dressed in an old sack suit, not as shabby as Tyrone's, and wears a collar and tie. His fair skin is sunburned a reddish, freckled tan.

Edmund is ten years younger than his brother, a couple of inches taller, thin and wiry. Where Jamie takes after his father, with little resemblance to his mother, Edmund looks like both his parents, but is more like his mother. Her big, dark eyes are the dominant feature in his long, narrow Irish face. His mouth has the same quality of hypersensitiveness hers possesses. His high forehead is hers accentuated, with dark brown hair, sunbleached to red at the ends, brushed straight back from it. But his nose is his father's, and his face in profile recalls Tyrone's. Edmund's hands are noticeably like his mother's, with the same exceptionally long fingers. They even have to a minor degree the same nervousness. It is in the quality of extreme nervous sensibility that the likeness of Edmund to his mother is most marked.

He is plainly in bad health. Much thinner than he should be, his eyes appear feverish and his cheeks are sunken. His skin, in spite of being sunburned a deep brown, has a parched sallowness. He wears a shirt, collar and tie, no coat, old flannel trousers, brown sneakers.

Extension

23 Choose one or more of the following tasks.

a Write a short essay about the extract with the title 'Who is to blame?'

b Choose one of the relationships in the play and write about it. Use one of the following forms, or invent one of your own.

- a doctor's report
- a poem (perhaps in two halves, one for each point of view)
- an analysis from your point of view
- a letter from one character to another

c Write a poem whose lines begin with the first letters of a character's name.

Example: J-A-M-I-E T-Y-R-O-N-E

Juvenile still, but
Ageing,
Muddled, handsome,
I despise my own
Existence.

The theatre has done this to me.
Your profession, father.
Rehearse, perform, get drunk,
On and on,
Not knowing who I am, except your
Enemy.

d **Individual / group work**: write or improvise a short dramatic scene showing family life either at its best or at its worst.

Beyond the text

Read the extract on the next page and answer the questions that follow.

My Mother Said I Never Should (1987)
Charlotte Keatley

See the Glossary section at the back of the book for vocabulary.

ACT I

SCENE 6

A council flat in Mosside, Manchester, early December 1971. JACKIE *is* $19\frac{1}{2}$, ROSIE *is 3 months,* MARGARET *is 40. A worn piece of rusty red carpet with ashtrays and mugs strewn on it, also the red transistor from Scene Four, now worn and battered, blares out over* ROSIE*'s crying. A Moses basket of blankets represents* ROSIE *; the actress playing* ROSIE *can be seen making the sounds of the baby crying. As the lights rise,* JACKIE *is packing baby clothes into a holdall.*

RADIO (*Manchester DJ*): ...Today's highest temperature is expected to be a cold 3°, so wrap up warm. Most roads in the city have been cleared now, but there's still ice and snow on the Pennines, and the forecast is more snow tonight. Police are asking motorists leaving Manchester on Northbound routes to drive slowly because of black ice. Meanwhile, here's something to remind you of summer days ...('*Honky Tonk Woman*'.)

JACKIE *(packing hurriedly)*: I wanted it to look nice and now it won't all go in!

ROSIE *yells.*

JACKIE (*hits transistor, which goes off*): Ssh, Rosie, please –

ROSIE *yells.*

JACKIE: Shut up!

ROSIE *stops crying abruptly.*

JACKIE (*gently*): Ssh, ssh, there now ... Where do you get the energy from, yelling all night? (*Bends over Moses basket, sings haphazard tune.*) My little rabbit, in your little basket ...

ROSIE *coos.*

JACKIE: Sleep, beautiful ... ssh ...

ROSIE *makes a little cry as* JACKIE *moves away to pack again.*

JACKIE (*bends over* ROSIE *again*): Please don't be crying when Mummy and Daddy arrive! – Where's your red sock? (*Picks it up and dangles it over* ROSIE, *who quietens during:*) Look, it fell out! Give me a smile – yes! There. I even washed your red sock. Washed everything, don't want Mummy to think – (*Holding back tears.*) I've got to clear up, Rosie.– All these ashtrays. Sandra and Hugh last night, they never think about you, do they? (*Picks up ashtray.*)

MARGARET (*from off*): Hello?

JACKIE: Oh shit, the mess – Come in!

MARGARET (*entering*): Hello Jackie!

JACKIE (*immediately casual*): Hi Mummy.

MARGARET: It's not locked!

JACKIE: I knew it would be you.

MARGARET: You've been smoking.

JACKIE: Journey from London OK?

MARGARET: Not how I remembered, Mosside. All these tower blocks ...

JACKIE: Is Daddy – he's not –

MARGARET: Waiting in the car.

JACKIE: He didn't mind? – I'm sorry, I couldn't face –

MARGARET: He understands.

Pause.

JACKIE: This is Rosie, Mummy.

MARGARET: I – came up the stairs. (*Pause.*) Lift is out of order. (*Pause.*) Lot of stairs.

JACKIE: ... Please.

MARGARET (*long pause*): Three months.

JACKIE: Say hello.

MARGARET (*goes to the Moses basket. Pause*): Pretty.

JACKIE (*goes also*): You think so?

MARGARET: You had curly eyelashes like that.

JACKIE (*pleased*): Did I?

MARGARET: Hello Rosie ... (*Kisses her.*)

JACKIE: Don't wake her!

MARGARET: Of course not!

JACKIE: I'm sorry, it's just –

MARGARET: You think I don't know?

ROSIE *coos quietly.*

MARGARET (*very tenderly*): Ssh, there now.

ROSIE *murmurs.*

JACKIE (*turns away*): I've packed her things ... here. (*Gives* MARGARET *the holdall.*) And her bottles are in this carrier. There's a bit of powdered milk left –

MARGARET: Oh you really don't need –

JACKIE: Well what would I do with it?

Awkward pause. MARGARET *looks through the clothes in the holdall.*

MARGARET: I've been to Mothercare. Got some of those new

disposable nappies, like you said. Quite different from when you were a baby. (*Sees another carrier, goes to pick it up.*) What about this bag – what a sweet – won't she want this dress with the rabbit on?

JACKIE: Leave those! – things she's grown out of.

MARGARET: Why did you have to try! All by yourself! Didn't you believe me?

JACKIE: I wanted to see if our theories worked … (*Pause.*) But when I came back from the hospital everyone had cleared out. You'd think I had VD, not a new baby.

MARGARET: He should be here with you, your – (*Stuck for word.*) – Rosie's father. – You in these flats …

JACKIE (*calm*): Mummy, I told you. He visits; and sends money. It was my decision.

MARGARET: Yes but you had no idea! I told you, I told you! Nothing, for nearly three months, nothing, since the day she was born, then a phone call, out of the blue, the potatoes boiled dry!

JACKIE: You knew I'd phone, one day. (*Slight pause.*)

MARGARET: Look at you now, a year ago you had everything, you were so excited about the art school, new friends, doing so well –

JACKIE (*angry*): I'll go back! Yes I will, finish the degree, I won't fail both things! Only think about her at night, her cheek against mine, soft and furry, like an apricot …

ROSIE *makes a snuffling noise in her sleep.*

JACKIE: … She'll be happy, won't she? …

MARGARET: After you phoned … after you asked us … Daddy went upstairs and got your old high chair down from the attic. (*Pause.*) Like sisters, he said. A new little sister … (*Bends down to* ROSIE.) Aren't you, precious?

JACKIE (*panics*): Mummy – she's got to know – I can't come and visit, with her not knowing, I can't!

MARGARET: Jackie, darling, we can't go over this again – you know as well as I do it would be impossible –

JACKIE: I don't believe you!

MARGARET: When she's grown up, you can tell her; when she's sixteen.

JACKIE: It'll be too late!

Silence.

Give me back the bags.

MARGARET (*gently*): You've got such opportunities.

JACKIE: Expectations.

MARGARET: Yes!

JACKIE: Yours.

MARGARET: You've got to –

JACKIE: Why? (*Pulls away holdall.*) Why not just Rosie?

MARGARET: You've got to go further than me – and Rosie too. (*Quietly.*) Otherwise … what's it been worth?

JACKIE (*pause*): Here, take them. (*Gives* MARGARET *the bags.*) You haven't told Granny and Grandad?

MARGARET: Not yet. I'll talk to them. (*Tentative.*) – Perhaps you could stay with them, just till Christmas, while you find a new flat? … (*Bends to* ROSIE.) My little lamb … What's this?

JACKIE: She has to have a red sock to go to sleep.

MARGARET: You keep one.

JACKIE (*puts one sock in her pocket*): Love her for me …

MARGARET *picks up the Moses basket.*

JACKIE: I'll help you to the car.

MARGARET: It's all right, Daddy will be there. (MARGARET *picks up the bags. As she goes to the door.*)

JACKIE: I'll come for Christmas. And visit, lots. (*Pause.*) Whenever I can afford the fare to London.

MARGARET *exits.*

JACKIE (*calls after them*): Sing to her at bathtime, especially the rabbit song … (*Silence. Pause. She picks up the bag she told* MARGARET *to leave. As she pulls out the clothes, she is suddenly hysterically happy. She holds up the rabbit dress.*) Wore this the day you first smiled, you wouldn't let go of my hair, – do you remember?! (*Holds up another.*) – And your first bonnet … (*Gentle.*) And the shawl … wrapped you up, like a parcel, the day we left hospital; all the way back in a taxi, bringing you home … (*Pause.*) Our secrets, Rosie. I'll take care of them. (*Pause.*) You'll never call me 'Mummy'. (*Silence. Screams.*) Rosie! Come back! – Mummy, Mummy!

Blackout. For a moment in the darkness, the sound of a baby crying. In a dim light we see MARGARET *rocking a bundle. She comforts the baby with the following words, until the baby quietens and coos:*

MARGARET: There now, there now, hush! Did you have a nasty dream? My precious. Mummy's here now. Mummy's here, Rosie. There now … Did you have a bad dream, Jackie? It's all right. Ssh … ssh …

As the lights come up bright for the next scene, MARGARET turns *and billows out the sheet which was forming the bundle.*

24 What has happened here?

a Margaret is taking Rosie home for the Christmas holiday.
b Margaret is taking Rosie home for a few months.
c Margaret is taking Rosie home to live with her.

25 Look again at lines 108–15. What would you do in this situation? When do you think Rosie should be told the truth?

26 What do you imagine Rosie will think of Jackie when she finds out who her real mother is? (Write down or discuss your ideas before going on.)
Now read the following scene from later in the play and answer the questions that follow.

ACT 3

SCENE 5

The garden of KEN *and* MARGARET*'s suburban semi in Raynes Park, London, late May 1987, early morning …* ROSIE *sits on the swing beneath the cherry tree with the old red tranny wearing one of* KEN*'s jumpers, which is much too big, and jeans.* JACKIE *runs across the garden, hot and grubby, carrying her lacquered briefcase, dressed for work. Both have been up all night.*

LBC RADIO: More congestion on the North Circular, meanwhile the overturned tanker is still blocking the Blackwall Tunnel. And it's coming up to 8 o'clock, a lovely May morning … Looking down the Euston Road, here's to the girl in that blue Mini, a thought from the Beatles … (*Plays 'All You Need Is Love'.*)

JACKIE: Rosie? …

Silence. Hold this for as long as possible while JACKIE *has to cope with it.*

ROSIE: I hope you're a success, Jackie. A big, big success.

JACKIE: Rosie, are you all right? Where's Daddy?

ROSIE: I hope lots of people came to your opening and thought your gallery was brill.

JACKIE: It was only twelve hours – I'd never have gone back to Manchester if I'd thought – after Daddy phoned last night, there were no more planes, I got the first plane I could this morning. If only …

ROSIE: In case you want to know, she died at 6.20 last night. Dad was with her. They said it was quicker at the end. It wasn't just stomach cancer, there were secondaries.

JACKIE (*goes to hug* ROSIE *who won't let her*): If only I'd been here with you …

ROSIE (*turns away*): Did you sell lots of your paintings?

JACKIE: Rosie –

ROSIE: Did you?

JACKIE: I didn't sell any. I cancelled the opening.

ROSIE: I don't believe you. You'd never do that.

Silence.

JACKIE: What do we do … now? … I'll call a taxi to the hospital – do we have to take things – her birth certificate? … I don't know …

ROSIE: Dad's done all that. He's been brilliant, like it was before they split up. He knew where Mum kept the box that's got all the family stuff in it. Look – he said I could have this one – (*Holds out a photo.*) That's Mum holding me by the front door when I'd just arrived … And … (*Lays them on grass.*) – Here's Mum's birth certificate, … and here's mine.

Silence.

JACKIE: No.

ROSIE: So now I know.

JACKIE (*desperate*): I was going to tell you – in five months – when you were sixteen … Mummy said to wait till after your exams, so as not to upset you …

ROSIE (*has a handful of photos, throws them down one by one, except for one which she slips into her pocket*): 1972, my first birthday, 1973, my second birthday, Christmas 1975, 1976; then you were in South America, 1979 with my birthday cake, 1982 when we cleared Gran and Grandad's house, – and our holiday in Venice. (*Pause.*) Have them. Have them all.

JACKIE: Rosie – we've got to help each other now.

ROSIE: Why don't you go and get drunk, or whatever it is you lot do to show you're feeling something.

JACKIE: I wanted you to have opportunities I couldn't ever have given you.

ROSIE: No you didn't. You wanted your own life more than you wanted mine!

JACKIE: Don't!

ROSIE: If you were really my Mum you wouldn't have been able to give me away!

JACKIE: How dare you! (*Goes to hit* ROSIE *but cannot.*) You're at the centre of everything I do! (*Slight pause.*) Mummy treated me as though I'd simply fallen over and cut my knee, – picked me up and said you'll be all right now, it won't show much. She wanted to make it all better. (*Quiet.*) … She was the one who wanted it kept secret ... I WANTED you, Rosie. (*Angry.*) For the first time in my life I took care of myself – refused joints, did exercises, went to the clinic. (*Pause.*) 'It's a girl.' (*Smiles irresistibly.*) – After you'd gone I tried to lose that memory. (*Pause. Effort.*) Graham ... your Father. (*Silence.*) He couldn't be there the day you were born, he had to be in Liverpool. He was married. (*Emphatic.*) He loved me, he loved you, you must believe that! (*Pause.*) He said he'd leave his wife, but I knew he wouldn't; there were two children, the youngest was only four ... we'd agreed, separate lives, I wanted to bring you up. He sent money. (*Pause.*) I took you to Lyme Park one day, I saw them together, across the lake, he was buying them ice creams, his wife was taking a photo. I think they live in Leeds now, I saw his name in the Guardian last year, an article about his photographs ... (*Pause.*) It was a very cold winter after you were born. There were power cuts. I couldn't keep the room warm; there were no lights in the tower blocks; I knew he had an open fire, it was trendy; so we took a bus to Didsbury, big gardens, pine kitchens, made a change from concrete. I rang the bell. (*Stops.*) A Punjabi man answered, said he was sorry ... they'd moved. By the time we got back to Mosside it was dark, the lift wasn't working – (*Stops.*) That was the night I phoned Mummy. (*Difficult.*) Asked her. (*Pause.*) I tried! I couldn't do it, Rosie. (*Pause.*) It doesn't matter how much you succeed afterwards, if you've failed once. (*Pause.*) After you'd gone ... I kept waking in the night to feed you ... A week ... in the flat ... Then I went back to art school. Sandra and Hugh thought I was inhuman. I remember the books that came out that winter – how to succeed as a single working mother – fairytales! (*Pause.*) Sandra and Hugh have a family now. Quite a few of my friends do. (*Pause.*) I could give you everything now. Rosie? ....

ROSIE (*pause*): I used to hate you, only I never knew why. (*Gestures.*) Sit down on the swing. I'm going to Oldham, to live with Gran – Great-Gran. Dad says I can.

JACKIE (*hesitates*): I'm frightened.

ROSIE (*gestures*): Sit down on the swing. Put your head back and look up through the cherry tree. The sky is falling. Mum used to sit here with me in her arms, and I'd pretend I was asleep. (*Gets up.*) I'm never having any children. (*Starts towards the house.*)

JACKIE: You might.

ROSIE *hears, but keeps walking away.*

JACKIE *goes to the swing.*
Lights fade to blackout.

27 ***a*** Who do you think is to blame for this situation?
b What similarities can you see between this extract and the extract from *Long Day's Journey Into Night*?
c What differences can you see between Keatley's and O'Neill's dramatic treatment of their theme?

Authors

Until 1912, the life of **Eugene O'Neill** (1888–1953) closely parallels that of Edmund in *Long Day's Journey Into Night*. His father was a highly successful touring actor, his mother was addicted to morphine. He was educated at private boarding schools, then spent a year at Princeton University (1906–7) until he was expelled for drunkenness. He went to sea and led a reckless life for the next six years, attempted suicide, then returned home (to his parents' house in New London, Connecticut) where he worked on the local newspaper, only to fall dangerously ill with tuberculosis. He spent six months in a sanatorium and in that time decided to make something of his life. He spent a year studying drama at Harvard University, then joined an experimental theatre group in the fishing village of Provincetown, Massachusetts. In 1916 the group produced his first one-act play, *Bound East for Cardiff*, in New York. That and a series of further plays about the sea gradually established his reputation. From 1920 to 1943 he wrote 20 full-length plays, including *Anna Christie*, *The Great God Brown*, *Desire Under the Elms*, *Strange Interlude*, *Mourning Becomes Electra* (an American version of the ancient Greek *Oresteia* trilogy by Aeschylus), *The Iceman Cometh* and *Long Day's Journey Into Night*. His work effectively created a serious American theatre, beginning a tradition that led to the work of playwrights such as Arthur Miller, Tennessee Williams, Edward Albee and David Mamet. He won the Pulitzer Prize four times, and is the only American playwright to have received the Nobel prize for Literature.

Charlotte Keatley was born in 1960. She has worked in community theatre as a writer, actor and director, and as a drama critic for the *Financial Times* newspaper. In her preface to the 1990 edition of this play she wrote the following: 'I wrote the first draft of *My Mother Said I Never Should* in 1985, when I was twenty-five. I wrote it because I didn't know of any plays about mothers and daughters, although we have hundreds of years' worth of plays about fathers and sons, or sons and mothers. The women in Shakespeare's plays have no mothers. Yet it seems to me that a woman's relationship with her mother, that strange bond of love and jealousy, has a lifelong and unavoidable influence. … I wanted to acknowledge the debt that my generation owes to past generations of women; 'feminism' is too often presented as a preoccupation of university educated women in their twenties or thirties. I learned my 'feminism' from the kind of women who invest their energy, often their whole lives, in other people. The behaviour of mothers shapes a nation as much as governments or wars do.'

My Mother Said I Never Should was first produced at the Contact Theatre, Manchester in 1987, then at the Royal Court Theatre, London in 1989, and subsequently in Australia, USA, Japan and several European countries.

4 'We're Right and You're Wrong'

Before you read

1 What do you know about witchcraft? Mark the following sentences **True** or **False** or **Don't Know** (**T**, **F** or **?**).

a Witches have always been women.
b Belief in witchcraft exists only in Christian countries.
c No-one believes in the existence of witches today.
d The word 'witch' comes from an Anglo-Saxon word meaning 'evil'.
e Witches are sometimes associated with good actions as well as bad.
f Witches were often blamed for accidents or misfortunes.
g In some cultures witches are believed to harm people simply by looking at them.
h It is estimated that more than a quarter of a million women were executed for witchcraft between 1484 and 1782.
i Witches were believed to be able to fly.
j Most witches were executed by driving a stake through the heart.
k Persecution of witches never spread from Europe to America.
l Witches were believed to have marks on their bodies where the devil had touched them.
m Witches were sometimes accused of having sexual relations with the devil.
n In European culture, witches were generally thought to have made a bargain with the devil.
o A witch's 'familiar' is an animal believed to be an evil spirit in disguise.

2 Read the following text to check your answers to Exercise 1.

Witchcraft is the use of supposed magic powers, generally to harm people or to damage their property. A witch is a person believed to have received such powers from evil spirits. From earliest times, people in all parts of the world have believed in witches. According to some scholars, more than half the people in the world today think witches can influence their lives.

Through the centuries, witchcraft as practised in countries with a European culture has differed from witchcraft elsewhere. European witchcraft is anti-Christian and involves an association with the Devil. For example, a person wanting to be a witch might sell his or her soul to the devil in exchange for magic powers.

On the other hand, witchcraft in Africa and the West Indies and among the Indians of North America does not involve the Devil. Most of the time, such non-European witchcraft seeks to harm people. But it may also be used to help people. For example, a person in love may ask a witch for a love *potion* (drink) to give the loved one. Drinking the potion will supposedly make the loved one return the giver's love.

The word *witch* comes from the Anglo-Saxon word *wicca*,

meaning *wise one* or *magician*. Originally, a witch was either a man or a woman who supposedly had supernatural powers. Through the years, however, only women came to be considered witches. Men with similar powers were called *sorcerers*, *warlocks*, or *wizards*.

The powers of witches

People who believe in witchcraft think a witch can harm people in various ways. In one form of witchcraft, the witch makes a small wax or wooden image of the victim. The witch may put something from the victim's body into the image, such as finger-nail clippings or hair. The witch then destroys the image by cutting it, burning it, or sticking pins into it. The victim supposedly suffers severe pain or even death.

Sometimes a witch casts a spell by reciting a magic formula. The spell makes the victim suffer. The witch usually mutters the victim's name while casting the spell. In some societies, people use false names so that witches can have no power over them.

People once blamed witches for any unexplained misfortune, such as illness, a sudden death, or a crop failure. Many persons accused witches of marrying demons and bearing monster children. Witches might make cows go dry by stealing their milk or cast a spell on a churn to prevent butter from forming. People also thought witches could raise storms and turn people into beasts. In addition, witches could ride through the air on a broom, and make themselves invisible.

Witchcraft has led to many widely believed superstitions. For example, many people in southern Europe and the Middle East fear a power called the *evil eye*. This power enables witches to cause harm or bring bad luck to others by merely looking at them. According to another superstition, a black cat brings bad luck if it crosses a person's path. This superstition came from the belief that every witch had a personal demon called a *familiar*. Many familiars, which lived with and served their witches, existed in the form of a black cat or some other animal.

History

From 1484 to 1782, according to some historians, the Christian church put to death about 300,000 women for practising witchcraft. Many of these women suffered such terrible torture that they confessed to being witches simply to avoid further torment.

People used many kinds of tests to determine whether a woman was a witch. For example, they looked for moles, scars, or other marks on the woman's body where a pin could be stuck without causing pain. Such 'devil's marks' were said to be places where the devil had touched the accused woman. Devil's marks also included birthmarks. In another test, people tied the suspected woman's arms and legs and threw her into deep water. If she floated she was considered guilty of being a witch. If she sank, she was innocent.

During the 1600s and 1700s, an almost hysterical fear of witchcraft swept most of Europe. Thousands of persons were tried and executed as witches. The courts allowed gossip and rumour to be used as evidence. Many children testified against their own parents.

The American colonists took the belief in witchcraft with them from England. Suspected witches suffered persecution in Connecticut, Massachusetts, and Virginia. The most famous witch hunt in American history occurred in Salem, Massachusetts. In 1692, the Massachusetts colonists executed 19 people as witches and one person was pressed to death for refusing to answer the witchcraft charge. In addition, about 150 others were imprisoned.

The Crucible (1953)
Arthur Miller

Arthur Miller's play *The Crucible* is about the witchcraft trials that took place in Salem, Massachusetts, in 1692. The play begins with the village minister (or priest), Reverend Parris, praying over his daughter Betty, who is lying unconscious on her bed. The doctor says he can find nothing wrong with her, and believes she is the victim of witchcraft. Parris does not want to believe this, but last night he saw Betty together with his niece Abigail, his Negro slave Tituba and some other village girls dancing in the forest and performing sinister rituals. He has now sent for the minister of a nearby village, Reverend Hale, an expert on witchcraft, in the hope that he will cure his daughter's illness.

See the Glossary section at the back of the book for vocabulary.

(*He appears loaded down with half a dozen heavy books.*)

HALE: Pray you, someone take these!

PARRIS (*delighted*): Mr Hale! Oh! it's good to see you again! (*Taking some books.*) My, they're heavy!

HALE (*setting down his books*): They must be; they are weighted with authority.

PARRIS (*a little scared*): Well, you do come prepared!

HALE: We shall need hard study if it comes to tracking down the Old Boy.
(*Noticing* REBECCA.) You cannot be Rebecca Nurse?

REBECCA: I am, sir. Do you know me?

HALE: It's strange how I knew you, but I suppose you look as such a good soul should. We have all heard of your great charities in Beverly.

PARRIS: Do you know this gentleman? Mr Thomas Putnam. And his good wife Ann.

HALE: Putnam! I had not expected such distinguished company, sir.

PUTNAM (*pleased*): It does not seem to help us today, Mr Hale. We look to you to come to our house and save our child.

HALE: Your child ails too?

MRS PUTNAM: Her soul, her soul seems flown away. She sleeps and yet she walks …

PUTNAM: She cannot eat.

HALE: Cannot eat! (*Thinks on it. Then, to* PROCTOR *and* GILES COREY.) Do you men have afflicted children?

PARRIS: No, no, these are farmers. John Proctor –

GILES COREY: He don't believe in witches.

PROCTOR (*to* HALE): I never spoke on witches one way or the other. Will you come, Giles?

GILES: No – no, John, I think not. I have some few queer questions of my own to ask this fellow.

PROCTOR: I've heard you to be a sensible man, Mr Hale. I hope you'll leave some of it in Salem.

(PROCTOR *goes.* HALE *stands embarrassed for an instant.*)

PARRIS (*quickly*): Will you look at my daughter, sir? (*Leads* HALE *to the bed.*) She has tried to leap out the window; we discovered her this morning on the highroad, waving her arms as though she'd fly.

HALE (*narrowing his eyes*): Tries to fly.

PUTNAM: She cannot bear to hear the Lord's name, Mr Hale; that's a sure sign of witchcraft afloat.

HALE (*holding up his hands*): No, no. Now let me instruct you. We cannot look to superstition in this. The Devil is precise; the marks of his presence are definite as stone, and I must tell you all that I shall not proceed unless you are prepared to believe me if I should find no bruise of hell upon her.

PARRIS: It is agreed, sir – it is agreed – we will abide by your judgement.

HALE: Good then. (*He goes to the bed, looks down at* BETTY. *To* PARRIS.) Now, sir, what were your first warning of this strangeness?

PARRIS: Why, sir – I discovered her (*indicating* ABIGAIL) – and my niece and ten or twelve of the other girls, dancing in the forest last night.

HALE (*surprised*): You permit dancing?

PARRIS: No, no, it were secret –

MRS PUTNAM (*unable to wait*): Mr Parris's slave has knowledge of conjurin', sir.

PARRIS (*to* MRS PUTNAM): We cannot be sure of that, Goody Ann –

MRS PUTNAM (*frightened, very softly*): I know it, sir. I sent my child – she should learn from Tituba who murdered her sisters.

REBECCA (*horrified*): Goody Ann! You sent a child to conjure up the dead?

MRS PUTNAM: Let God blame me, not you, not you, Rebecca! I'll not have you judging me any more! (*To* HALE.) Is it a natural work to lose seven children before they live a day?

PARRIS: Sssh!

(REBECCA, *with great pain, turns her face away. There is a pause.*)

HALE: Seven dead in childbirth.

MRS PUTNAM (*softly*): Aye. (*Her voice breaks; she looks up at him. Silence.* HALE *is impressed.* PARRIS *looks to him. He goes to his books, opens one, turns pages, then reads. All wait, avidly.*)

What do you think Hale is looking for in his book?

PARRIS (*hushed*): What book is that?

MRS PUTNAM: What's there, sir?

HALE (*with a tasty love of intellectual pursuit*): Here is all the invisible world, caught, defined, and calculated. In these books the Devil stands stripped of all his brute disguises. Here are all your familiar spirits – your incubi and succubi; your witches that go by land, by air, and by sea; your wizards of the night and of the day. Have no fear now – we shall find him out if he has come among us, and I mean to crush him utterly if he has shown his face! (*He starts for the bed.*)

REBECCA: Will it hurt the child, sir?

HALE: I cannot tell. If she is truly in the Devil's grip we may have to rip and tear to get her free.

REBECCA: I think I'll go, then. I am too old for this. (*She rises.*)

PARRIS (*striving for conviction*): Why, Rebecca, we may open up the boil of all our troubles today!

REBECCA: Let us hope for that. I go to God for you, sir.

PARRIS (*with trepidation – and resentment*): I hope you do not mean we go to Satan here! (*Slight pause.*)

REBECCA: I wish I knew. (*She goes out; they feel resentful of her note of moral superiority.*)

PUTNAM (*abruptly*): Come, Mr Hale, let's get on. Sit you here.

GILES: Mr Hale, I have always wanted to ask a learned man – what signifies the readin' of strange books?

HALE: What books?

GILES: I cannot tell; she hides them.

HALE: Who does this?

GILES: Martha, my wife. I have waked at night many a time and found her in a corner, readin' of a book. Now what do you make of that?

HALE: Why, that's not necessarily –

GILES: It discomforts me! Last night – mark this – I tried and tried and could not say my prayers. And then she close her book and walks out of the house, and suddenly – mark this – I could pray again! ...

How would you explain this?

HALE: Ah! The stoppage of prayer – that is strange. I'll speak further on that with you.

GILES: I'm not sayin' she's touched the Devil, now, but I'd admire to know what books she reads and why she hides them. She'll not answer me, y' see.

HALE: Aye, we'll discuss it. (*To all.*) Now mark me, if the Devil is in her you will witness some frightful wonders in this room, so please to keep your wits about you. Mr Putnam, stand close in case she flies. Now, Betty, dear, will you sit up? (PUTNAM *comes in closer, ready-handed.* HALE *sits* BETTY *up, but she hangs limp in his hands.*) Hmmm. (*He observes her carefully. The others watch breathlessly.*) Can you hear me? I am John Hale, minister of Beverly. I have come to help you, dear. Do you remember my two little girls in Beverly?

(*She does not stir in his hands.*)

PARRIS (*in fright*): How can it be the Devil? Why would he choose my house to strike? We have all manner of licentious people in the village!

HALE: What victory would the Devil have to win a soul already bad? It is the best the Devil wants, and who is better than the minister?

GILES: That's deep, Mr Parris, deep, deep!

PARRIS (*with resolution now*): Betty! Answer Mr Hale! Betty!

HALE: Does someone afflict you, child? It need not be a woman, mind you, or a man. Perhaps some bird invisible to others comes to you – perhaps a pig, a mouse, or any beast at all. Is there some figure bids you fly? (*The child remains limp in his hands. In silence he lays her back on the pillow. Now, holding out his hands toward her, he intones.*) In nomine Domini Sabaoth sui filiique ite ad infernos. (*She does not stir. He turns to* ABIGAIL, *his eyes narrowing.*) Abigail, what sort of dancing were you doing with her in the forest?

ABIGAIL: Why – common dancing is all.

PARRIS: I think I ought to say that I – I saw a kettle in the grass where they were dancing.

ABIGAIL: That were only soup.

HALE: What sort of soup were in this kettle, Abigail?

ABIGAIL: Why, it were beans – and lentils, I think, and –

HALE: Mr Parris, you did not notice, did you, any living thing in the kettle? A mouse, perhaps, a spider, a frog – ?

PARRIS (*fearfully*): I – do believe there were some movement – in the soup.

ABIGAIL: That jumped in, we never put it in!

HALE (*quickly*): What jumped in?

ABIGAIL: Why, a very little frog jumped –

PARRIS: A frog, Abby!

HALE (*grasping* ABIGAIL): Abigail, it may be your cousin is dying. Did you call the Devil last night?

ABIGAIL: I never called him! Tituba, Tituba …

PARRIS (*blanched*): She called the Devil?

HALE: I should like to speak with Tituba.

PARRIS: Goody Ann, will you bring her up?

(MRS PUTNAM *exits.*)

HALE: How did she call him?

ABIGAIL: I know not – she spoke Barbados.

HALE: Did you feel any strangeness when she called him? A sudden cold wind, perhaps? A trembling below the ground?

ABIGAIL: I didn't see no Devil! (*Shaking* BETTY.) Betty, wake up. Betty! Betty!

HALE: You cannot evade me, Abigail. Did your cousin drink any of the brew in that kettle?

ABIGAIL: She never drank it!

HALE: Did you drink it?

ABIGAIL: No, sir!

HALE: Did Tituba ask you to drink it?

ABIGAIL: She tried, but I refused.

HALE: Why are you concealing? Have you sold yourself to Lucifer?

ABIGAIL: I never sold myself! I'm a good girl! I'm a proper girl!

What do you think? Has Abigail been practising witchcraft?

(MRS PUTNAM *enters with* TITUBA, *and instantly* ABIGAIL *points at* TITUBA.)

ABIGAIL: She made me do it! She made Betty do it!

TITUBA (*shocked and angry*): Abby!

ABIGAIL: She makes me drink blood!

PARRIS: Blood!!

MRS PUTNAM: My baby's blood?

TITUBA: No, no, chicken blood. I give she chicken blood!

HALE: Woman, have you enlisted these children for the Devil?

TITUBA: No, no, sir, I don't truck with no Devil!

HALE: Why can she not wake? Are you silencing this child?

TITUBA: I love me Betty!

HALE: You have sent your spirit out upon this child, have you not? Are you gathering souls for the Devil?

ABIGAIL: She sends her spirit on me in church; she makes me laugh at prayer!

PARRIS: She have often laughed at prayer!

ABIGAIL: She comes to me every night to go and drink blood!

TITUBA: You beg *me* to conjure! She beg *me* make charm –

ABIGAIL: Don't lie! (*To* HALE): She comes to me while I sleep; she's always making me dream corruptions!

TITUBA: Why you say that, Abby?

ABIGAIL: Sometimes I wake and find myself standing in the open doorway and not a stitch on my body! I always hear her laughing in my sleep. I hear her singing her Barbados songs and tempting me with –

TITUBA: Mister Reverend, I never –

HALE (*resolved now*): Tituba, I want you to wake this child.

TITUBA: I have no power on this child, sir.

HALE: You most certainly do, and you will free her from it now! When did you compact with the Devil?

TITUBA: I don't compact with no Devil.

PARRIS: You will confess yourself or I will take you out and whip you to your death, Tituba!

PUTNAM: This woman must be hanged! She must be taken and hanged!

TITUBA (*terrified, falls to her knees*): No, no, don't hang Tituba! I tell him I don't desire to work for him, sir.

PARRIS: The Devil?

HALE: Then you saw him! (TITUBA *weeps.*) Now Tituba, I know that when we bind ourselves to Hell it is very hard to break with it. We are going to help you tear yourself free –

TITUBA (*frightened by the coming process*): Mister Reverend, I do believe somebody else be witchin' these children.

> *Do you think Tituba is telling the truth here? Or is she trying to protect herself by telling Hale what he wants to hear?*

HALE: Who?

TITUBA: I don't know, sir, but the Devil got him numerous witches.

HALE: Does he! (*It is a clue.*) Tituba, look into my eyes. Come, look into me.

(*She raises her eyes to his fearfully.*)

You would be a good Christian woman, would you not, Tituba?

TITUBA: Aye, sir, a good Christian woman.

HALE: And you love these little children?

TITUBA: Oh, yes, sir, I don't desire to hurt little children.

HALE: And you love God, Tituba?

TITUBA: I love God with all my bein'.

HALE: Now, in God's holy name –

TITUBA: Bless Him. Bless Him. (*She is rocking on her knees, sobbing in terror.*)

HALE: And to His glory –

TITUBA: Eternal glory. Bless Him – bless God …

HALE: Open yourself, Tituba – open yourself and let God's holy light shine on you.

TITUBA: Oh, bless the Lord.

HALE: When the Devil comes to you does he ever come – with another person?

(*She stares up into his face.*)

Perhaps another person in the village? Someone you know.

PARRIS: Who came with him?

PUTNAM: Sarah Good? Did you ever see Sarah Good with him? Or Osburn?

PARRIS: Was it man or woman came with him?

TITUBA: Man or woman. Was – was woman.

PARRIS: What woman? A woman, you said. What woman?

TITUBA: It was black dark, and I –

PARRIS: You could see him, why could you not see her?

TITUBA: Well, they was always talking; they was always runnin' round and carryin' on –

PARRIS: You mean out of Salem? Salem witches?

TITUBA: I believe so, yes, sir.

(*Now* HALE *takes her hand. She is surprised.*)

HALE: Tituba. You must have no fear to tell us who they are, do you understand? We will protect you. The Devil can never overcome a minister. You know that, do you not?

TITUBA (*kisses* HALE*'s hand*): Aye, sir, oh, I do.

HALE: You have confessed yourself to witchcraft, and that speaks a wish to come to Heaven's side. And we will bless you, Tituba.

TITUBA (*deeply relieved*): Oh, God bless you, Mr Hale!

HALE (*with rising exaltation*): You are God's instrument put in our hands to discover the Devil's agents among us. You are selected, Tituba, you are chosen to help us cleanse our village. So speak utterly, Tituba, turn your back on him and face God – face God, Tituba, and God will protect you.

TITUBA (*joining with him*): Oh, God, protect Tituba!

HALE (*kindly*): Who came to you with the Devil? Two? Three? Four? How many?

(TITUBA *pants, and begins rocking back and forth again, staring ahead.*)

Why does she behave like this?

TITUBA: There was four. There was four.

PARRIS (*pressing in on her*): Who? Who? Their names, their names!

TITUBA (*suddenly bursting out*): Oh, how many times he bid me kill you, Mr Parris!

PARRIS: Kill me!

TITUBA (*in a fury*): He say Mr Parris must be kill! Mr Parris no goodly man, Mr Parris mean man and no gentle man, and he bid me rise out of my bed and cut your throat! (*They gasp.*) But I tell him 'No! I don't hate that man. I don't want kill that man.' But he say, 'You work for me, Tituba, and I make you free! I give you pretty dress to wear, and put you way high up in the air, and you gone fly back to Barbados!' And I say, 'You lie, Devil, you lie!' And then he come one stormy night to me, and he say, 'Look! I have *white* people belong to me.' And I look – and there was Goody Good.

PARRIS: Sarah Good!

TITUBA (*rocking and weeping*): Aye, sir, and Goody Osburn.

MRS PUTNAM: I knew it! Goody Osburn were midwife to me three times. I begged you, Thomas, did I not? I begged him not to call Osburn because I feared her. My babies always shrivelled in her hands!

HALE: Take courage, you must give us all their names. How can you bear to see this child suffering? Look at her, Tituba. (*He is indicating* BETTY *on the bed.*) Look at her God-given innocence; her soul is so tender; we must protect her, Tituba; the Devil is out and preying on her like a beast upon the flesh of the pure lamb. God will bless you for your help.

(ABIGAIL *rises, staring as though inspired, and cries out.*)

ABIGAIL: I want to open myself!

(*They turn to her, startled. She is enraptured, as though in a pearly light.*)

I want the light of God, I want the sweet love of Jesus! I danced for the Devil; I saw him; I wrote in his book; I go back to Jesus; I kiss His hand. I saw Sarah Good with the Devil! I saw Goody Osburn with the Devil! I saw Bridget Bishop with the Devil!

(*As she is speaking,* BETTY *is rising from the bed, a fever in her eyes, and picks up the chant.*)

BETTY (*staring too*): I saw George Jacobs with the Devil! I saw Goody Howe with the Devil!

PARRIS: She speaks! (*He rushes to embrace* BETTY.) She speaks!

HALE: Glory to God! It is broken, they are free!

BETTY (*calling out hysterically and with great relief*): I saw Martha Bellows with the Devil!

ABIGAIL: I saw Goody Sibber with the Devil! (*It is rising to a great glee.*)

PUTNAM: The marshal, I'll call the marshal!

(PARRIS *is shouting a prayer of thanksgiving.*)

BETTY: I saw Alice Barrow with the Devil!

(*The curtain begins to fall.*)

HALE (*as* PUTNAM *goes out*): Let the marshal bring irons!

ABIGAIL: I saw Goody Hawkins with the Devil!

BETTY: I saw Goody Bibber with the Devil!

ABIGAIL: I saw Goody Booth with the Devil!

On their ecstatic cries

THE CURTAIN FALLS

First reaction

3 Why do Tituba, Abigail and Betty say they saw these people with the devil? Choose one explanation, and give your reasons.

a They really did see them with the devil.

b They were suffering from hysterical illusions in the forest last night.

c They are suffering from hysterical illusions now.
d They are lying to protect themselves.

4 **Pair/group work**: find someone in the class who disagrees with your answer to Exercise 3. Listen to their reasons, then explain yours. Do you still disagree?

Close reading

The characters

5 Read this extract. What is Hale trying to say here? Choose one explanation from the ones given below.

PUTNAM: She cannot bear to hear the Lord's name, Mr Hale; that's a sure sign of witchcraft afloat.
HALE (*holding up his hands*): No, no. Now let me instruct you. We cannot look to superstition in this. The Devil is precise; the marks of his presence are definite as stone, and I must tell you that I shall not proceed unless you are prepared to believe me if I should find no bruise of hell upon her. (lines 40–46)

a She is not a witch. The proof is that there is no mark on her.
b She is a witch. The proof is that she has definite marks on her.
c She may be a witch. I don't know yet. But even if her 'devil's mark' is invisible, I must ask you to believe me if I find it.
d She may or may not be a witch. We can only be sure by looking for the devil's mark.

6 In a stage direction, Miller describes Hale in the following words:

'... nearing forty, a tight-skinned, eager-eyed intellectual. This is a beloved errand for him; on being called here to ascertain witchcraft he felt the pride of the specialist whose unique knowledge has at last been called for. ... Reverend Hale conceives of himself much as a young doctor on his first call.'

What evidence can you find in the first 100 lines of this scene that
a he is an eager-eyed intellectual?
b this is a beloved errand for him?

7 In plays (as in life) people do not always mean exactly what they say, or say exactly what they mean. In lines 84–94, Rebecca Nurse does not say anything disapproving, yet she makes the other characters 'feel resentful of her note of moral superiority'. When she says, 'I think I'll go, then. I am too old for this' (line 87), what does she really mean? Choose one interpretation.

a I am too weak to help with such violent work.
b I do not like what you are doing.
c I will die of shock if I see violence.

8 Now write your own interpretation of the following.

a Line 90: Let us hope for that.
b Line 90: I go to God for you, sir.
c Line 93: I wish I knew.

9 In lines 179–203, Abigail and Tituba contradict each other over some important details. Complete the sentences and then answer the questions.

Abigail claims that ______________________________

Tituba claims that ______________________________

a Which of them does Reverend Hale believe – Abigail or Tituba?
b Why do you think he believes one rather than the other?
c Which one do you believe?
d If you were the Reverend Hale, what other evidence would you ask for in order to be sure? Would you conduct the investigation differently?

10 Look at Tituba's confession in lines 213–14.

a What persuades her to confess?
b What does this suggest about her confession?

Check your answer in the Key before going on.

11 In the final part of the scene (lines 209–330) a number of village women are named as witches by Tituba, Abigail and Betty. Hale, Putnam and Parris seem to believe them without question. What is your opinion of the interrogation that has just taken place? Was it properly carried out? Do you think the truth has been discovered? Give reasons for your opinion.

Language practice – structures

12 In order to create an appropriate historical atmosphere, Miller uses several words and structures that are archaic (no longer in current use) or found only in dialects of modern English. Look at the following examples, and decide how a person might say them in today's Standard English.

a Pray you, someone take these! (line 2)
b Your child ails too? (line 20)
c He don't believe in witches. (line 27)
d I never spoke on witches one way or the other. (lines 28–9)
e ... waving her arms as though she'd fly. (lines 37–8)
f Now, sir, what were your first warning of this strangeness? (lines 50–1)
g Have no fear now. (line 81)
h Sit you here. (line 95)
i What signifies the readin' of strange books? (lines 96–7)
j I have waked at night many a time and found her in a corner, readin' of a book. (lines 101–2)
k It discomforts me! (line 105)
l I know not – she spoke Barbados. (line 163)

13 Tituba has a dialect of her own – for example she uses 'give' for 'gave' and 'she' for 'her' in the sentence 'I give she chicken blood' (line 184). Look at the speech below and underline all the words and phrases that seem to belong to her dialect rather than Standard English.

He say Mr Parris must be kill! Mr Parris no goodly man, Mr Parris mean man and no gentle man, and he bid me rise out of my bed and cut your throat! ... But I tell him 'No! I don't hate that man. I don't want kill that man.' But he say, 'You work for me, Tituba, and I make you free! I give you pretty dress to wear, and put you way high up in the air, and you gone fly back to Barbados!' And I say, 'You lie, Devil, you lie!' And then he come one stormy night to me, and he say, 'Look, I have *white* people belong to me.' And I look – and there was Goody Good. (lines 281–90)

14 Now rewrite the passage in Standard English. Check your answer in the Key before going on.

15 Compare Tituba's speech with those of Mrs Putnam, Hale and Abigail that follow (lines 293–310). What differences can you see between Tituba's dialect and that of the other characters in

a the use of tenses?

b any other aspect of grammar?

16 How do you think this difference in speech affects the way the other characters treat Tituba?

Language practice – vocabulary

17 All the following words are connected by the theme of religion. Write them in your notebook and next to each word write a simple definition. Use a dictionary if necessary.

belief	Christian	church
convert	defile	discipline
heathen	homage	light
mystery	parish	parishioner
persecute	sect	

18 Here is part of Miller's introductory remarks about the people of Salem. A number of words are missing. Fill in the gaps using the words you defined in Exercise 17, or words derived from them. You will need to use some words more than once.

The edge of the wilderness was close by. The American continent stretched endlessly west, and it was full of _________ (a) for them. It stood, dark and threatening, over their shoulders night and day, for out of it Indian tribes marauded from time to time, and Reverend Parris had _________ (b) who had lost relatives to these _________ (c). The parochial snobbery of these people was partly responsible for their failure to _________ (d) the Indians. Probably they also preferred to take land from _________ (e) rather than from fellow _________ (f). At any rate, very few Indians were converted, and the Salem folk _________ (g) that the virgin forest was the Devil's last preserve, his home base and the citadel of his final stand. To the best of their knowledge the American forest was the last place on earth that was not paying _________ (h) to God.

For these reasons, among others, they carried about an air of innate resistance, even of persecution. Their fathers had, of course, been _________ (i) in England. So now they and their _________ (j) found it necessary to deny any other _________ (k) its freedom, lest their New

Jerusalem be _________ (l) and corrupted by wrong ways and deceitful ideas.

They _________ (m), in short, that they held in their steady hands the candle that would _________ (n) the world. We have inherited this _________ (o), and it has helped and hurt us. It helped them with the _________ (p) it gave them. They were a dedicated folk, by and large, and they had to be to survive the life they had chosen or been born into in this country.

19 Do these introductory remarks help you understand the extract from the play any better?

Extension

20 These are Miller's stage directions for Act 1 of the play.

A small upper bedroom in the home of REVEREND SAMUEL PARRIS, *Salem, Massachusetts, in the spring of the year 1692.*

There is a narrow window at the left. Through its leaded panes the morning sunlight streams. A candle still burns near the bed, which is at the right. A chest, a chair, and a small table are the other furnishings. At the back a door opens on the landing of the stairway to the ground floor. The room gives off an air of clean spareness. The roof rafters are exposed, and the wood colours are raw and unmellowed.

- ***a*** Imagine that you are directing the play. Draw a stage plan on a large sheet of paper, and sketch in the positions of the actors either at the moment when Hale intones over Betty in Latin (line 137), or when the curtain falls.
- ***b*** **Group work (groups of 9)**: each member of the group in turn is the director. Using the other members of the group as actors, the director arranges them in the positions sketched on the stage plan, as if they were in a photograph from a performance of the play.
- ***c*** Decide which version of the two moments is best. Add a few lines of speech to bring your 'photograph' to life. Present your group's work to the rest of the class.

21 Imagine that Tituba and Abigail are left alone at the end of this scene. What do you think Tituba might say to Abigail? How would Abigail reply? Write a short dialogue of not more than 15–20 lines between them.

22 *The Crucible* was written at a time when a similar 'witch-hunt' was going on in the USA against communists and people with left-wing political sympathies. It was led by Senator Joseph McCarthy and the House

Un-American Activities Committee, and it damaged or ended the careers of many actors, film-makers and theatre people, including Charlie Chaplin. Arthur Miller himself was called up before the committee, and his play was intended as an allegorical warning to Americans of the dangers of the 'witch-hunt' mentality.

Can you think of any other witch-hunts that have occurred in this century or previously? What similarities do they have with *The Crucible*? How would you define the witch-hunt mentality?

Beyond the text

23 Look at the following questions. For each one, try to guess (1) who might ask it, (2) to whom, and (3) in what situation. You can use the same answers more than once.

a What were you doing yesterday?
b Why do you behave so badly?
c Where do you keep your suits?
d Why did you leave the organization?
e When did you come to this place?
f When did you last have a bath?
g What can you see without your glasses?
h What have you done with your wife?
i Why did you change your name?
j When did you last pray?
k Why don't you pay the rent?
l What about Ireland?
m Chicken? Egg? Which came first?
n Who are you?
o What makes you think you exist?

24 Now read this extract from Harold Pinter's *The Birthday Party*.

a Which of the characters and situations that you wrote down in Exercise 23 seems the most likely explanation for what happens in this scene?
b At what point (or points) does the questioning become
- more bizarre?
- more sinister?

The Birthday Party (1957)
Harold Pinter

See the Glossary section at the back of the book for vocabulary.

GOLDBERG: A warm night.
STANLEY (*turning*): Don't mess me about!
GOLDBERG: I beg your pardon?
STANLEY (*moving downstage*): I'm afraid there's been a mistake. We're booked out. Your room is taken. Mrs Boles forgot to tell you. You'll have to find somewhere else.
GOLDBERG: Are you the manager here?
STANLEY: That's right.
GOLDBERG: Is it a good game?
STANLEY: I run the house. I'm afraid you and your friend will have to find other accommodation.
GOLDBERG (*rising*): Oh, I forgot, I must congratulate you on your birthday. (*Offering his hand.*) Congratulations.
STANLEY (*ignoring hand*): Perhaps you're deaf.
GOLDBERG: No, what makes you think that? As a matter of fact, every single one of my senses is at its peak. Not bad going, eh? For a man past fifty. But a birthday, I always feel, is a great occasion, taken too much for granted these days. What a thing

to celebrate – birth! Like getting up in the morning. Marvellous! Some people don't like the idea of getting up in the morning. I've heard them. Getting up in the morning, they say, what is it? Your skin's crabby, you need a shave, your eyes are full of muck, your mouth is like a boghouse, the palms of your hands are full of sweat, your nose is clogged up, your feet stink, what are you but a corpse waiting to be washed? Whenever I hear that point of view I feel cheerful. Because I know what it is to wake up with the sun shining, to the sound of the lawnmower, all the little birds, the smell of the grass, church bells, tomato juice –

STANLEY: Get out.

(*Enter* MCCANN, *with bottles.*)

Get that drink out. These are unlicensed premises.

GOLDBERG: You're in a terrible humour today, Mr Webber. And on your birthday too, with the good lady getting her strength up to give you a party.

(MCCANN *puts the bottles on the sideboard.*)

STANLEY: I told you to get those bottles out.

GOLDBERG: Mr Webber, sit down a minute.

STANLEY: Let me – just make this clear. You don't bother me. To me, you're nothing but a dirty joke. But I have a responsibility towards the people in this house. They've been down here too long. They've lost their sense of smell. I haven't. And nobody's going to take advantage of them while I'm here. (*A little less forceful.*) Anyway, this house isn't your cup of tea. There's nothing here for you, from any angle, any angle. So why don't you just go, without any more fuss?

GOLDBERG: Mr Webber, sit down.

STANLEY: It's no good starting any kind of trouble.

GOLDBERG: Sit down.

STANLEY: Why should I?

GOLDBERG: If you want to know the truth, Webber, you're beginning to get on my breasts.

STANLEY: Really? Well, that's –

GOLDBERG: Sit down.

STANLEY: No.

(GOLDBERG *sighs, and sits at the table right.*)

GOLDBERG: McCann.

MCCANN: Nat?

GOLDBERG: Ask him to sit down.

MCCANN: Yes, Nat. (MCCANN *moves to* STANLEY.) Do you mind sitting down?

STANLEY: Yes, I do mind.
MCCANN: Yes now, but – it'd be better if you did.
STANLEY: Why don't you sit down?
MCCANN: No, not me – you.
STANLEY: No thanks.
(*Pause.*)
MCCANN: Nat.
GOLDBERG: What?
MCCANN: He won't sit down.
GOLDBERG: Well, ask him.
MCCANN: I've asked him.
GOLDBERG: Ask him again.
MCCANN (*to* STANLEY): Sit down.
STANLEY: Why?
MCCANN: You'd be more comfortable.
STANLEY: So would you.
(*Pause.*)
MCCANN: All right. If you will I will.
STANLEY. You first.
(MCCANN *slowly sits at the table, left.*)
MCCANN: Well?
STANLEY: Right. Now you've both had a rest you can get out!
MCCANN (*rising*): That's a dirty trick! I'll kick the shite out of him!
GOLDBERG (*rising*): No! I have stood up.
MCCANN: Sit down again!
GOLDBERG: Once I'm up I'm up.
STANLEY: Same here.
MCCANN (*moving to* STANLEY): You've made Mr Goldberg stand up.
STANLEY (*his voice rising*): It'll do him good!
MCCANN: Get in that seat.
GOLDBERG: McCann.
MCCANN: Get down in that seat!
GOLDBERG (*crossing to him*): Webber. (*Quietly.*) SIT DOWN.
(*Silence.* STANLEY *begins to whistle 'The Mountains of Mourne'. He strolls casually to the chair at the table. They watch him. He stops whistling. Silence. He sits.*)
STANLEY: You'd better be careful.
GOLDBERG: Webber, what were you doing yesterday?
STANLEY: Yesterday?
GOLDBERG: And the day before. What did you do the day before that?
STANLEY: What do you mean?
GOLDBERG: Why are you wasting everybody's time, Webber? Why are you getting in everybody's way?

STANLEY: Me? What are you –

GOLDBERG: I'm telling you, Webber. You're a washout. Why are you getting on everybody's wick? Why are you driving that old lady off her conk?

MCCANN: He likes to do it!

GOLDBERG: Why do you behave so badly, Webber? Why do you force that old man out to play chess?

STANLEY: Me?

GOLDBERG: Why do you treat that young lady like a leper? She's not the leper, Webber!

STANLEY: What the –

GOLDBERG: What did you wear last week, Webber? Where do you keep your suits?

MCCANN: Why did you leave the organization?

GOLDBERG: What would your old mum say, Webber?

MCCANN: Why did you betray us?

GOLDBERG: You hurt me, Webber. You're playing a dirty game.

MCCANN: That's a Black and Tan fact.

GOLDBERG: Who does he think he is?

MCCANN: Who do you think you are?

STANLEY: You're on the wrong horse.

GOLDBERG: When did you come to this place?

STANLEY: Last year.

GOLDBERG: Where did you come from?

STANLEY: Somewhere else.

GOLDBERG: Why did you come here?

STANLEY: My feet hurt!

GOLDBERG: Why did you stay?

STANLEY: I had a headache!

GOLDBERG: Did you take anything for it?

STANLEY: Yes.

GOLDBERG: What?

STANLEY: Fruit salts!

GOLDBERG: Enos or Andrews?

STANLEY: En– An–

GOLDBERG: Did you stir properly? Did they fizz?

STANLEY: Now, now, wait, you –

GOLDBERG: Did they fizz? Did they fizz or didn't they fizz?

MCCANN: He doesn't know!

GOLDBERG: You don't know. When did you last have a bath?

STANLEY: I have one every –

GOLDBERG: Don't lie.

MCCANN: You betrayed the organization. I know him!

STANLEY: You don't!

GOLDBERG: What can you see without your glasses?

STANLEY: Anything.

GOLDBERG: Take off his glasses.

(MCCANN *snatches his glasses and as* STANLEY *rises, reaching for them, takes his chair downstage centre, below the table,* STANLEY *stumbling as he follows.* STANLEY *clutches the chair and stays bent over it.*)

Webber, you're a fake. (*They stand on each side of the chair.*) When did you last wash up a cup?

STANLEY: The Christmas before last.

GOLDBERG: Where?

STANLEY: Lyons Corner House.

GOLDBERG: Which one?

STANLEY: Marble Arch.

GOLDBERG: Where was your wife?

STANLEY: In –

GOLDBERG: Answer.

STANLEY (*turning, crouched*): What wife?

GOLDBERG: What have you done with your wife?

MCCANN: He's killed his wife!

GOLDBERG: Why did you kill your wife?

STANLEY (*sitting, his back to the audience*): What wife?

MCCANN: How did he kill her?

GOLDBERG: How did you kill her?

MCCANN: You throttled her.

GOLDBERG: With arsenic.

MCCANN: There's your man!

GOLDBERG: Where's your old mum?

STANLEY: In the sanatorium.

MCCANN: Yes!

GOLDBERG: Why did you never get married?

MCCANN: She was waiting at the porch.

GOLDBERG: You skeddadled from the wedding.

MCCANN: He left her in the lurch.

GOLDBERG: You left her in the pudding club.

MCCANN: She was waiting at the church.

GOLDBERG: Webber! Why did you change your name?

STANLEY: I forgot the other one.

GOLDBERG: What's your name now?

STANLEY: Joe Soap.

GOLDBERG: You stink of sin.

MCCANN: I can smell it.

GOLDBERG: Do you recognise an external force?

STANLEY: What?
GOLDBERG: Do you recognise an external force?
MCCANN: That's the question!
GOLDBERG: Do you recognise an external force, responsible for you, suffering for you?
STANLEY: It's late.
GOLDBERG: Late! Late enough! When did you last pray?
MCCANN: He's sweating!
GOLDBERG: When did you last pray?
MCCANN: He's sweating!
GOLDBERG: Is the number 846 possible or necessary?
STANLEY: Neither.
GOLDBERG: Wrong! Is the number 846 possible or necessary?
STANLEY: Both.
GOLDBERG: Wrong! It's necessary but not possible.
STANLEY: Both.
GOLDBERG: Wrong! Why do you think the number 846 is necessarily possible?
STANLEY: Must be.
GOLDBERG: Wrong! It's only necessarily necessary! We admit possibility only after we grant necessity. It is possible because necessary but by no means necessary through possibility. The possibility can only be assumed after the proof of necessity.
MCCANN: Right!
GOLDBERG: Right? Of course right! We're right and you're wrong, Webber, all along the line.
MCCANN: All along the line!
GOLDBERG: Where is your lechery leading you?
MCCANN: You'll pay for this.
GOLDBERG: You stuff yourself with dry toast.
MCCANN: You contaminate womankind.
GOLDBERG: Why don't you pay the rent?
MCCANN: Mother defiler!
GOLDBERG: Why do you pick your nose?
MCCANN: I demand justice!
GOLDBERG: What's your trade?
MCCANN: What about Ireland?
GOLDBERG: What's your trade?
STANLEY: I play the piano.
GOLDBERG: How many fingers do you use?
STANLEY: No hands!
GOLDBERG: No society would touch you. Not even a building society.

MCCANN: You're a traitor to the cloth.

GOLDBERG: What do you use for pyjamas?

STANLEY: Nothing.

GOLDBERG: You verminate the sheet of your birth.

MCCANN: What about the Albigensenist heresy?

GOLDBERG: Who watered the wicket in Melbourne?

MCCANN: What about the blessed Oliver Plunkett?

GOLDBERG: Speak up, Webber. Why did the chicken cross the road?

STANLEY: He wanted to – he wanted to – he wanted to. …

MCCANN: He doesn't know!

GOLDBERG: Why did the chicken cross the road?

STANLEY: He wanted to – he wanted to. …

GOLDBERG: Why did the chicken cross the road?

STANLEY: He wanted. …

MCCANN: He doesn't know. He doesn't know which came first!

GOLDBERG: Which came first?

MCCANN: Chicken? Egg? Which came first?

GOLDBERG and MCCANN: Which came first? Which came first? Which came first?

(STANLEY *screams.*)

GOLDBERG: He doesn't know. Do you know your own face?

MCCANN: Wake him up. Stick a needle in his eye.

GOLDBERG: You're a plague, Webber. You're an overthrow.

MCCANN: You're what's left!

GOLDBERG: But we've got the answer to you. We can sterilise you.

MCCANN: What about Drogheda?

GOLDBERG: Your bite is dead. Only your pong is left.

MCCANN: You betrayed our land.

GOLDBERG: You betray our breed.

MCCANN: Who are you, Webber?

GOLDBERG: What makes you think you exist?

MCCANN: You're dead.

GOLDBERG: You're dead. You can't live, you can't think, you can't love. You're dead. You're a plague gone bad. There's no juice in you. You're nothing but an odour!

(*Silence. They stand over him. He is crouched in the chair. He looks up slowly and kicks* GOLDBERG *in the stomach.* GOLDBERG *falls.* STANLEY *stands.* MCCANN *seizes a chair and lifts it above his head.* STANLEY *seizes a chair and covers his head with it.* MCCANN *and* STANLEY *circle.*)

GOLDBERG: Steady, McCann.

STANLEY (*circling*): Uuuuuhhhhh!

MCCANN: Right, Judas.
GOLDBERG (*rising*): Steady, McCann.
MCCANN: Come on!
STANLEY: Uuuuuuuhhhhh!
MCCANN: He's sweating.
STANLEY: Uuuuuhhhhh!
GOLDBERG: Easy, McCann.
MCCANN: The bastard sweatpig is sweating.
(*A loud drumbeat off left, descending the stairs.* GOLDBERG *takes the chair from* STANLEY. *They put the chairs down. They stop still. Enter* MEG, *in evening dress, holding sticks and drum.*)
MEG: I brought the drum down. I'm dressed for the party.
GOLDBERG: Wonderful.
MEG: You like my dress?
GOLDBERG: Wonderful. Out of this world.

Authors

Arthur Miller was born in New York in 1915, the son of a prosperous businessman. He was denied the chance to go to university by the collapse of his father's business during the Depression, and took a job instead in an automobile spare parts warehouse. After two years he had saved enough to pay his way through the University of Michigan, where he began writing plays. He later became a radio scriptwriter, then worked in documentary films in World War II. His first stage success was *All My Sons* (1947), in which an aircraft engine manufacturer allows faulty parts to be used in warplanes and then finds that his own son has died in a crash as a result. In 1949 came his greatest success, *Death of a Salesman*, a suburban drama of self-deception and failure, which has been widely acclaimed as an authentic 'tragedy of the common man'. In 1952, the official 'witch-hunt' of former communists and socialists by Senator Joseph McCarthy and the House Un-American Activities Committee prompted Miller to write *The Crucible* as a reminder of the evils of mass paranoia.

Miller's later plays include *A View from the Bridge* (1955), *After the Fall* (1964, concerning his marriage to the film star Marilyn Monroe), *The Price* (1968, a study of success, envy and forgiveness between two brothers) and *The Last Yankee* (1992). His autobiography, *Timebends* (1987) provides many insights into his mind and work.

Harold Pinter was born in London in 1930. He went to drama school and worked as an actor for several years before his first success, *The Caretaker*, in 1960. This was followed by *The Homecoming* (1965), *Landscape* (1969), *Silence* (1969), *Old Times* (1971), *No Man's Land* (1975), *Betrayal* (1978) and others. He has also written several critically acclaimed filmscripts, including

Joseph Losey's *The Servant* (1962) and *The Go-Between* (1971) as well as *The Last Tycoon* (1974) and *The French Lieutenant's Woman* (1981). He continues to work as both an actor and director in the London theatre.

The *Birthday Party* (1957) was his first full-length play. It was a commercial failure (the first production in London ran for only a week), but following his later success came to be regarded, like many of his other plays, as a classic of post-war drama.

At first sight, Pinter's work is puzzling. It mixes elements of Theatre of the Absurd (characters behaving in surreal and unexplained ways) with scenes reminiscent of gangster and spy films. His characters are often comic, but they take part in tragic or sinister events; they are bizarre, yet curiously like ourselves; and, despite their unmistakably British settings and dialogue, the plays seem universal – and are performed and studied all over the world.

5 Lost in New Orleans

Before you read

1 Look at the photograph on the previous page. Imagine you are this woman, arriving alone in a strange city for the first time. What thoughts go through your head? What worries? What hopes? Write down some ideas and discuss them with a partner.

A Streetcar Named Desire (1947)
Tennessee Williams

See the Glossary section at the back of the book for vocabulary.

SCENE ONE

The exterior of a two-storey corner building on a street in New Orleans which is named Elysian Fields and runs between the L & N tracks and the river. The section is poor but, unlike corresponding sections in other American cities, it has a raffish charm. The houses are mostly white frame, weathered grey, with rickety outside stairs and galleries and quaintly ornamented gables to the entrances of both. It is first dark of an evening early in May. The sky that shows around the dim white building is a peculiarly tender blue, almost turquoise, which invests the scene with a kind of lyricism and gracefully attenuates the atmosphere of decay. You can almost feel the warm breath of the brown river beyond the river warehouses with their faint redolences of bananas and coffee. A corresponding air is evoked by the music of Negro entertainers at a bar-room around the corner. In this part of New Orleans you are practically always just around the corner, or a few doors down the street, from a tinny piano being played with the infatuated fluency of brown fingers. This 'Blue Piano' expresses the spirit of the life which goes on here.

(Two women, one white and one coloured, are taking the air on the steps of the building. The white woman is EUNICE, *who occupies the upstairs flat; the coloured woman a neighbour, for New Orleans is a cosmopolitan city where there is a relatively warm and easy intermingling of races in the old part of town.*

Above the music of the 'Blue Piano' the voices of people on the street can be heard overlapping.)

NEGRO WOMAN (*to* EUNICE): ... she says St Barnabas would send out his dog to lick her and when he did she'd feel an icy cold wave all up an' down her. Well, that night when –

A MAN (*to a* SAILOR): You keep right on going and you'll find it. You'll hear them tapping on the shutters.

SAILOR (*to* NEGRO WOMAN *and* EUNICE): Where's the Four Deuces?

VENDOR: Red hot! Red hots!

NEGRO WOMAN: Don't waste your money in that clip joint!

SAILOR: I've got a date there.

VENDOR: Re-e-ed h-o-o-t!

NEGRO WOMAN: Don't let them sell you a Blue Moon cocktail or you won't go out on your own feet!

(*Two men come round the corner,* STANLEY KOWALSKI *and* MITCH. *They are about twenty-eight or thirty years old, roughly dressed in blue denim work clothes.* STANLEY *carries his bowling jacket and a red-stained package from a butcher's.*)

STANLEY (*to* MITCH): Well, what did he say?

MITCH: He said he'd give us even money.

STANLEY: Naw! We gotta have odds!

(*They stop at the foot of the steps.*)

STANLEY (*bellowing*): Hey, there! Stella, Baby!

(STELLA *comes out on the first-floor landing, a gentle young woman, about twenty-five, and of a background obviously quite different from her husband's.*)

STELLA (*mildly*): Don't holler at me like that. Hi, Mitch.

STANLEY: Catch!

STELLA: What?

STANLEY: Meat!

(*He heaves the package at her. She cries out in protest but manages to catch it: then she laughs breathlessly. Her husband and his companion have already started back around the corner.*)

STELLA (*calling after him*): Stanley! Where are you going?

STANLEY: Bowling!

STELLA: Can I come watch?

STANLEY: Come on. (*He goes out.*)

STELLA: Be over soon. (*To the white woman.*) Hello, Eunice. How are you?

EUNICE: I'm all right. Tell Steve to get him a poor boy's sandwich 'cause nothing's left here.

(*They all laugh; the* COLOURED WOMAN *does not stop.* STELLA *goes out.*)

COLOURED WOMAN: What was that package he th'ew at 'er? (*She rises from steps, laughing louder.*)

EUNICE: You hush, now!

NEGRO WOMAN: Catch *what*!

(*She continues to laugh.* BLANCHE *comes around the corner, carrying a valise. She looks at a slip of paper, then at the building, then again at *the slip and again at the building. Her expression is one of shocked disbelief. Her appearance is incongruous to this setting. She is daintily dressed in a white suit with a fluffy bodice, necklace and earrings of pearl, white gloves and hat, looking as if she were arriving at a summer tea or cocktail party in the garden district. She is about five years older than* STELLA. *Her delicate beauty must avoid a strong light. There is something about her uncertain manner, as well as her white clothes, that suggests a moth.*)

> *What might Blanche be doing here? What is written on the slip of paper?*

EUNICE (*finally*): What's the matter, honey? Are you lost?

BLANCHE (*with faintly hysterical humour*): They told me to take a streetcar named Desire, and then transfer to one called Cemeteries and ride six blocks and get off at – Elysian Fields!

EUNICE: That's where you are now.

BLANCHE: At Elysian Fields?

EUNICE: This here is Elysian Fields.

BLANCHE: They mustn't have – understood – what number I wanted …

EUNICE: What number you lookin' for?

(BLANCHE *wearily refers to the slip of paper.*)

BLANCHE: Six thirty-two.

EUNICE: You don't have to look no further.

BLANCHE (*uncomprehendingly*): I'm looking for my sister, Stella DuBois. I mean – Mrs Stanley Kowalski.

EUNICE: That's the party. – You just did miss her, though.

BLANCHE: This – can this be – her home?

EUNICE: She's got the downstairs here and I got the up.

BLANCHE: Oh. She's – out?

EUNICE: You noticed that bowling alley around the corner?

BLANCHE: I'm – not sure I did.

EUNICE: Well, that's where she's at, watchin' her husband bowl. (*There is a pause.*) You want to leave your suitcase here an' go find her?

BLANCHE: No.

NEGRO WOMAN: I'll go tell her you come.

BLANCHE: Thanks.

NEGRO WOMAN: You welcome. (*She goes out.*)

EUNICE: She wasn't expecting you?

BLANCHE: No. No, not tonight.

EUNICE: Well, why don't you just go in and make yourself at home till they get back.

BLANCHE: How could I – do that?

EUNICE: We own this place so I can let you in.

(*She gets up and opens the downstairs door. A light goes on behind the blind, turning it light blue.* BLANCHE *slowly follows her into the downstairs flat. The surrounding areas dim out as the interior is lighted. Two rooms can be seen, not too clearly defined. The one first entered is primarily a kitchen but contains a folding bed to be used by* BLANCHE. *The room beyond this is a bedroom. Off this room is a narrow door to a bathroom.*)

EUNICE (*defensively, noticing* BLANCHE*'s look*): It's sort of messed up right now but when it's clean it's real sweet.

BLANCHE: Is it?

EUNICE: Uh-huh, I think so. So you're Stella's sister?

BLANCHE: Yes. (*Wanting to get rid of her.*) Thanks for letting me in.

EUNICE: *Por nada*, as the Mexicans say, *por nada*! Stella spoke of you.

BLANCHE: Yes?

EUNICE: I think she said you taught school.

BLANCHE: Yes.

EUNICE: And you're from Mississippi, huh?

BLANCHE: Yes.

EUNICE: She showed me a picture of your home-place, the plantation.

BLANCHE: Belle Reve?

EUNICE: A great big place with white columns.

BLANCHE: Yes …

EUNICE: A place like that must be awful hard to keep up.

BLANCHE: If you will excuse me, I'm just about to drop.

EUNICE: Sure, honey. Why don't you set down?

BLANCHE: What I meant was I'd like to be left alone.

EUNICE (*offended*): Aw. I'll make myself scarce, in that case.

BLANCHE: I didn't mean to be rude, but –

EUNICE: I'll drop by the bowling alley an' hustle her up. (*She goes out of the door.*)

What do you think Blanche will do now that she is alone?

(BLANCHE *sits in a chair very stiffly with her shoulders slightly hunched and her legs pressed close together and her hands tightly clutching her purse as if she were quite cold. After a while the blind look goes out of her eyes and she begins to look slowly around. A cat screeches. She catches her breath with a startled gesture. Suddenly she notices something in a half-opened closet. She springs up and crosses to it, and removes a whisky bottle. She pours a half tumbler of whisky and tosses it down. She carefully replaces the bottle and washes out the tumbler at the sink. Then she resumes her seat in front of the table.)*

BLANCHE (*faintly to herself*): I've got to keep hold of myself!

(STELLA *comes quickly around the corner of the building and runs to the door of the downstairs flat.*)

STELLA (*calling out joyfully*): Blanche!

(*For a moment they stare at each other. Then* BLANCHE *springs up and runs to her with a wild cry.*)

BLANCHE: Stella, oh, Stella, Stella! Stella for Star!

(*She begins to speak with feverish vivacity as if she feared for either of them to stop and think. They catch each other in a spasmodic embrace.*)

BLANCHE: Now, then, let me look at you. But don't you look at me, Stella, no, no, no, not till later, not till I've bathed and rested! And turn that over-light off! Turn that off! I won't be looked at in this merciless glare! (STELLA *laughs and complies.*) Come back here now! Oh, my baby! Stella! Stella for Star! (*She embraces her again.*) I thought you would never come back to this horrible place! What am I saying! I didn't mean to say that. I meant to be nice about it and say – Oh, what a convenient location and such – Ha-a-ha! Precious lamb! You haven't said a *word* to me.

STELLA: You haven't given me a chance to, honey! (*She laughs but her glance at* BLANCHE *is a little anxious.*)

BLANCHE: Well, now you talk. Open your pretty mouth and talk while I look around for some liquor! I know you must have some liquor on the place! Where could it be, I wonder? Oh, I spy, I spy!

(*She rushes to the closet and removes the bottle; she is shaking all over and panting for breath as she tries to laugh. The bottle nearly slips from her grasp.*)

> *What does the way she takes the whisky-bottle suggest to you about Blanche?*

STELLA (*noticing*): Blanche, you sit down and let me pour the drinks. I don't know what we've got to mix with. Maybe a coke's in the icebox. Look'n see, honey, while I'm –

BLANCHE: No coke, honey, not with my nerves tonight! Where – where – where is – ?

STELLA: Stanley? Bowling! He loves it. They're having a – found some soda! – tournament …

BLANCHE: Just water, baby, to chase it! Now don't get worried, your sister hasn't turned into a drunkard, she's just all shaken up and hot and tired and dirty! You sit down, now, and explain this place to me! What are you doing in a place like this?

STELLA: Now, Blanche –

BLANCHE: Oh, I'm not going to be hypocritical, I'm going to be honestly critical about it! Never, never, never in my worst dreams could I picture – Only Poe! Only Mr Edgar Allan Poe! – could do it justice! Out there I suppose is the ghoul-haunted woodland of Weir! (*She laughs.*)

STELLA: No, honey, those are the L & N tracks.

BLANCHE: No, now seriously, putting joking aside. Why didn't you tell me, why didn't you write to me, honey, why didn't you let me know?

STELLA (*carefully, pouring herself a drink*): Tell you what, Blanche?

BLANCHE: Why, that you had to live in these conditions!

STELLA: Aren't you being a little intense about it? It's not that bad at all! New Orleans isn't like other cities.

BLANCHE: This has got nothing to do with New Orleans. You might as well say – forgive me, blessed baby! (*She suddenly stops short.*) The subject is closed!

STELLA (*a little drily*): Thanks.

(*During the pause,* BLANCHE *stares at her. She smiles at* BLANCHE.)

What is your impression of Blanche so far?

BLANCHE (*looking down at her glass, which shakes in her hand*): You're all I've got in the world, and you're not glad to see me!

STELLA (*sincerely*): Why, Blanche, you know that's not true.

BLANCHE: No? – I'd forgotten how quiet you were.

STELLA: You never did give me a chance to say much, Blanche. So I just got in the habit of being quiet around you.

BLANCHE (*vaguely*): A good habit to get into … (*then abruptly*) You haven't asked me how I happened to get away from the school before the spring term ended.

STELLA: Well, I thought you'd volunteer that information – if you wanted to tell me.

BLANCHE: You thought I'd been fired?

STELLA: No, I – thought you might have – resigned. …

BLANCHE: I was so exhausted by all I'd been through my – nerves broke. (*Nervously tamping cigarette.*) I was on the verge of – lunacy, almost! So Mr Graves – Mr Graves is the high school superintendent – he suggested I take a leave of absence. I couldn't put all of those details into the wire. … (*She drinks quickly.*) Oh, this buzzes right through me and feels so *good*!

STELLA: Won't you have another?

BLANCHE: No, one's my limit.

STELLA: Sure?

BLANCHE: You haven't said a word about my appearance.

STELLA: You look just fine.

BLANCHE: God love you for a liar! Daylight never exposed so total a ruin! But you – you've put on some weight, yes, you're just as plump as a little partridge! And it's so becoming to you!

STELLA: Now, Blanche –

BLANCHE: Yes, it is, it is or I wouldn't say it! You just have to watch around the hips a little. Stand up.

STELLA: Not now.

BLANCHE: You hear me? I said stand up! (STELLA *complies reluctantly.*) You messy child, you, you've spilt something on that pretty white lace collar! About your hair – you ought to have it cut in a feather bob with your dainty features. Stella, you have a maid, don't you?

STELLA: No. With only two rooms it's –

BLANCHE: What? *Two* rooms, did you say?

STELLA: This one and – (*She is embarrassed.*)

BLANCHE: The other one? (*She laughs sharply. There is an embarrassed silence.*) How quiet you are, you're so peaceful. Look how you sit there with your little hands folded like a cherub in choir!

STELLA (*uncomfortably*): I never had anything like your energy, Blanche.

BLANCHE: Well, I never had your beautiful self-control. I am going to take just one little tiny nip more, sort of to put the stopper on, so to speak. … Then put the bottle away so I won't be tempted. (*She rises.*) I want you to look at *my* figure! (*She turns around.*) You know I haven't put on one ounce in ten years, Stella? I weigh what I weighed the sum – you left Belle Reve. The summer Dad died and you left us …

STELLA (*a little wearily*): It's just incredible, Blanche, how well you're looking.

BLANCHE: You see I still have that awful vanity about my looks even now that my looks are slipping! (*She laughs nervously and glances at* STELLA *for reassurance.*)

STELLA (*dutifully*): They haven't slipped one particle.

BLANCHE: After all I've been through? You think I believe that story? Blessed child! (*She touches her forehead shakily.*) Stella, there's – only two rooms?

STELLA: And a bathroom.

BLANCHE: Oh, you do have a bathroom! First door to the right at the top of the stairs? (*They both laugh uncomfortably.*) But, Stella, I don't see where you're going to put me!

STELLA: We're going to put you in here.

BLANCHE: What kind of bed's this – one of those collapsible things? (*She sits on it.*)

STELLA: Does it feel all right?

BLANCHE (*dubiously*): Wonderful, honey. I don't like a bed that gives much. But there's no door between the two rooms, and Stanley – will it be decent?

STELLA: Stanley is Polish, you know.

BLANCHE: Oh, yes. They're something like Irish, aren't they?

STELLA: Well –

BLANCHE: Only not so – highbrow? (*They both laugh again in the same way.*) I brought some nice clothes to meet all your lovely friends in.

STELLA: I'm afraid you won't think they are lovely.

BLANCHE: What are they like?

STELLA: They're Stanley's friends.

BLANCHE: Polacks?

STELLA: They're a mixed lot, Blanche.

BLANCHE: Heterogeneous – types?

STELLA: Oh, yes. Yes, types is right!

BLANCHE: Well – anyhow – I brought nice clothes and I'll wear them. I guess you're hoping I'll say I'll put up at a hotel, but I'm not going to put up at a hotel. I want to be *near* you, got to be *with* somebody, I *can't* be *alone*! Because – as you must have noticed – I'm *not* very *well*. … (*Her voice drops and her look is frightened.*)

STELLA: You seem a little bit nervous or overwrought or something.

BLANCHE: Will Stanley like me, or will I be just a visiting in-law, Stella? I couldn't stand that.

STELLA: You'll get along fine together, if you'll just try not to – well – compare him with men that we went out with at home.

What is your impression of Stella so far?

BLANCHE: Is he so – different?

STELLA: Yes. A different species.

BLANCHE: In what way; what's he like?

STELLA: Oh, you can't describe someone you're in love with! Here's a picture of him! (*She hands a photograph to* BLANCHE.)

BLANCHE: An officer?

STELLA: A Master Sergeant in the Engineers' Corps. Those are decorations!

BLANCHE: He had those on when you met him?

STELLA: I assure you I wasn't just blinded by all the brass.

BLANCHE: That's not what I –

STELLA: But of course there were things to adjust myself to later on.

BLANCHE: Such as his civilian background! (STELLA *laughs uncertainly.*) How did he take it when you said I was coming?

STELLA: Oh, Stanley doesn't know yet.

BLANCHE (*frightened*): You – haven't told him?

STELLA: He's on the road a good deal.

BLANCHE: Oh. Travels?

STELLA: Yes.

BLANCHE: Good. I mean – isn't it?

STELLA (*half to herself*): I can hardly stand it when he is away for a night. ...

BLANCHE: Why, Stella?

STELLA: When he's away for a week I nearly go wild!

BLANCHE: Gracious!

STELLA: And when he comes back I cry on his lap like a baby. ... (*She smiles to herself.*)

BLANCHE: I guess that is what I meant by being in love. ... (STELLA *looks up with a radiant smile.*) Stella –

STELLA: What?

BLANCHE (*in an uneasy rush*): I haven't asked you the things you probably thought I was going to ask. And so I'll expect you to be understanding about what *I* have to tell *you*.

STELLA: What, Blanche? (*Her face turns anxious.*)

Do you think this is going to be good news or bad news? Why?

BLANCHE: Well, Stella – you're going to reproach me, I know that you're bound to reproach me – but before you do – take into consideration – you left! I stayed and struggled! You came to New Orleans and looked out for yourself! *I* stayed at Belle Reve and tried to hold it together! I'm not meaning this in any reproachful way, but *all* the burden descended on *my* shoulders.

STELLA: The best I could do was make my own living, Blanche. (BLANCHE *begins to shake again with intensity.*)

BLANCHE: I know, I know. But you are the one that abandoned Belle Reve, not I! I stayed and fought for it, bled for it, almost died for it!

STELLA: Stop this hysterical outburst and tell me what's happened? What do you mean fought and bled? What kind of –

BLANCHE: I knew you would, Stella. I knew you would take this attitude about it!

STELLA: About – what? – please!

BLANCHE (*slowly*): The loss – the loss …

STELLA: Belle Reve? Lost, is it? No!

BLANCHE: Yes, Stella.

(*They stare at each other across the yellow-checked linoleum of the table.* BLANCHE *slowly nods her head and* STELLA *looks slowly down at her hands folded on the table. The music of the 'blue piano' grows louder.* BLANCHE *touches her handkerchief to her forehead.*)

STELLA: But how did it go? What happened?

BLANCHE (*springing up*): You're a fine one to ask me how it went!

STELLA: Blanche!

BLANCHE: You're a fine one to sit there *accusing me* of it!

STELLA: *Blanche*!

BLANCHE: I, I, *I* took the blows in my face and my body! All of those deaths! The long parade to the graveyard! Father, mother! Margaret, that dreadful way! So big with it, it couldn't be put in a coffin! But had to be burned like rubbish! You just came home in time for the funeral, Stella. And funerals are pretty compared to deaths. Funerals are quiet, but deaths – not always. Sometimes their breathing is hoarse, and sometimes it rattles, and sometimes they even cry out to you, 'Don't let me go!' Even the old, sometimes, say, 'Don't let me go.' As if you were able to stop them! But funerals are quiet, with pretty flowers. And, oh, what gorgeous boxes they pack them away in! Unless you were there at the bed when they cried out, 'Hold me!' you'd never suspect there was the struggle for breath and bleeding. You didn't dream, but I saw! *Saw! Saw!* And now you sit there telling me with your eyes that I let the place go! How in hell do you think all that sickness and dying was paid for! Death is expensive, Miss Stella! And old Cousin Jessie's right after Margaret's, hers! Why, the Grim Reaper had put up his tent on our doorstep! … Stella. Belle Reve was his headquarters! Honey – that's how it slipped through my fingers! Which of them left us a fortune? Which of them left a cent of insurance even? Only poor Jessie – one hundred to pay for her coffin. That was all, Stella! And I with my pitiful salary at the school. Yes, accuse me! Sit there and stare at me, thinking I let the place go! *I* let the place go! Where were *you*? In bed with your – Polack!

STELLA (*springing*): Blanche! You be still! That's enough! (*She starts out.*)

BLANCHE: Where are you going?

STELLA: I'm going into the bathroom to wash my face.

BLANCHE: Oh, Stella, Stella, you're crying!

STELLA: Does that surprise you?

(STELLA *goes into the bathroom. Outside is the sound of men's voices.* STANLEY, STEVE, *and* MITCH *cross to the foot of the steps.*)

How do you imagine Stanley will react to Blanche?

STEVE: And the old lady is on her way to Mass and she's late and there's a cop standin' in front of th' church an' she comes runnin' up an' says, 'Officer – is Mass out yet?' He looks her over and says, 'No, Lady, but y'r hat's on crooked!' (*They give a hoarse bellow of laughter.*)

STEVE: Playing poker tomorrow night?

STANLEY: Yeah – at Mitch's.

MITCH: Not at my place. My mother's still sick. (*He starts off.*)

STANLEY (*calling after him*): All right, we'll play at my place … but you bring the beer.

EUNICE (*hollering down from above*): Break it up down there! I made the spaghetti dish and ate it myself.

STEVE (*going upstairs*): I told you and phoned you we was playing. (*To the men.*) Jax beer!

EUNICE: You never phoned me once.

STEVE: I told you at breakfast – and phoned you at lunch …

EUNICE: Well, never mind about that. You just get yourself home here once in a while.

STEVE: You want it in the papers?

(*More laughter and shouts of parting come from the men.* STANLEY *throws the screen door of the kitchen open and comes in. He is of medium height, about five feet eight or nine, and strongly, compactly built. Animal joy in his being is implicit in all his movements and attitudes. Since earliest manhood the centre of his life has been pleasure with women, the giving and taking of it, not with weak indulgence, dependently, but with the power and pride of a richly feathered male bird among hens. Branching out from this complete and satisfying centre are all the auxiliary channels of his life, such as his heartiness with men, his appreciation of rough humour, his love of good drink and food and games, his car, his radio, everything that is his, that bears his emblem of the gaudy seed-bearer. He sizes women up at a glance, with sexual classifications, crude images flashing into his mind and determining the way he smiles at them.*)

BLANCHE (*drawing involuntarily back from his stare*): You must be Stanley. I'm Blanche.

STANLEY: Stella's sister?

BLANCHE: Yes.

STANLEY: H'lo. Where's the little woman?

BLANCHE: In the bathroom.

STANLEY: Oh. Didn't know you were coming in town.

BLANCHE: I – uh –

STANLEY: Where you from, Blanche?

BLANCHE: Why, I – live in Laurel.

(*He has crossed to the closet and removed the whisky bottle.*)

STANLEY: In Laurel, huh? Oh, yeah. Yeah, In Laurel, that's right. Not in my territory. Liquor goes fast in hot weather. (*He holds the bottle to the light to observe its depletion.*) Have a shot?

BLANCHE: No, I – rarely touch it.

STANLEY: Some people rarely touch it, but it touches them often.

BLANCHE (*faintly*): Ha-ha.

STANLEY: My clothes're stickin' to me. Do you mind if I make myself comfortable? (*He starts to remove his shirt.*)

BLANCHE: Please, please do.

STANLEY: Be comfortable is my motto.

BLANCHE: It's mine, too. It's hard to stay looking fresh. I haven't washed or even powdered my face and – here you are!

STANLEY: You know you can catch cold sitting around in damp things, especially when you been exercising hard like bowling is. You're a teacher, aren't you?

BLANCHE: Yes.

STANLEY: What do you teach, Blanche?

BLANCHE: English.

STANLEY: I never was a very good English student. How long you here for, Blanche?

BLANCHE: I – don't know yet.

STANLEY: You going to shack up here?

BLANCHE: I thought I would if it's not inconvenient for you all.

STANLEY: Good.

BLANCHE: Travelling wears me out.

STANLEY: Well, take it easy.

(*A cat screeches near the window.* BLANCHE *springs up.*)

BLANCHE: What's that?

STANLEY: Cats. … Hey, Stella!

STELLA (*faintly, from the bathroom*): Yes, Stanley.

STANLEY: Haven't fallen in, have you? (*He grins at* BLANCHE. *She tries unsuccessfully to smile back. There is a silence.*) I'm afraid I'll strike you as being the unrefined type. Stella's spoke of you a good deal. You were married once, weren't you?

(*The music of the polka rises up, faint in the distance.*)

BLANCHE: Yes. When I was quite young.

STANLEY: What happened?

BLANCHE: The boy – the boy died. (*She sinks back down.*) I'm afraid I'm – going to be sick!

(*Her head falls on her arms.*)

First reaction

2 How do you think Blanche's stay will go? Will she 'be comfortable' with Stanley? Will Stanley be comfortable with her?

Close reading

The Characters

3 Look at this exchange.

BLANCHE: Is he so – different?
STELLA: Yes. A different species. (lines 307–8)

a What do you think Stella means by this?

- a different nationality?
- a different culture?
- a different psychological type?
- a different social class?
- a different economic class?

b Why does Stella warn Blanche not to compare him with men they went out with at home?

4 As in *Pygmalion*, much of the effect of this scene depends on differences in the way people speak English. Look at the way Stanley speaks (lines 40–58, 410–84) and compare it to the way Stella and Blanche speak (lines 156–401). What are the main differences? (Look at syntax, vocabulary, topics of conversation.)

5 What do the following suggest to you about the characters in this scene?

BLANCHE

- ***a*** But don't you look at me, Stella, no, no, no, not till later, not till I've bathed and rested! And turn that over-light off! Turn that off! I won't be looked at in this merciless glare! (lines 162–5)
- ***b*** You sit down, now, and explain this place to me! What are you doing in a place like this? (lines 190–1)
- ***c*** No, one's my limit. (line 231)
- ***d*** You came to New Orleans and looked out for yourself! *I* stayed at Belle Reve and tried to hold it together! I'm not meaning this in any reproachful way, but *all* the burden descended on *my* shoulders. (lines 344–7)

STELLA

- ***e*** (*dutifully*) They haven't slipped one particle. (line 267)
- ***f*** I'm afraid you won't think they are lovely. (line 288)
- ***g*** I can hardly stand it when he is away for a night .... (lines 328–9)
- ***h*** Stop this hysterical outburst and tell me what's happened? (line 353)

STANLEY

- ***i*** Hey, there! Stella, Baby! ... Catch! ... Meat! (lines 44–51)
- ***j*** Some people rarely touch it, but it touches them often. (line 452)
- ***k*** My clothes're stickin' to me. Do you mind if I make myself comfortable? (*He starts to remove his shirt.*) (lines 454–5)

Symbolism

6 Tennessee Wiliams uses a number of interesting symbols in this scene. The 'blue piano' in the opening stage directions, for example, 'expresses the spirit of the life which goes on here', and grows louder, or changes its tune, at significant moments in the action. Similarly, the 'red-stained package from a butcher's' that Stanley carries is a symbol of his vigorous, crude, 'red-blooded' nature.

Symbols often have conventional meanings: they symbolise or stand for a well-known idea (a heart = love, an olive branch = peace). They can also have private meanings, or special meanings suggested by a particular context.

What symbolic meanings are suggested to you by the following?

- ***a*** Red hot! Red hots! (line 30)
- ***b*** There is something about her ... that suggests a moth. (lines 75–7)
- ***c*** They told me to take a streetcar named Desire, and then transfer to one called Cemeteries and ... get off at – Elysian Fields! (lines 79–81)
- ***d*** The name 'Belle Reve'. (line 133)
- ***e*** A cat screeches. She catches her breath with a startled gesture. (lines 147–8)
- ***f*** The music of the 'blue piano' grows louder. (line 363)
- ***g*** The music of the polka rises up, faint in the distance. (line 482)

Language practice – structures

Exploring differences and similarities

7 Much of the tension in this scene comes from the differences in background, temperament and attitudes between the characters. Williams also emphasises the special quality of life in New Orleans, for example when Stella says 'New Orleans isn't like other cities' (line 205).

If Stella were asked to explain why or how it isn't like other cities, she might say, as Williams does in his opening stage directions about this section of the city: *The section is poor but, unlike corresponding sections in other American cities, it has a raffish charm.* (lines 3–4)

This is a useful (and grammatically simple) way of describing the differences between two things. It can also be used for describing similarities: *like Blanche, Stella was brought up at Belle Reve*.

Below is a list of people and things in the scene which show important differences.

a Write sentences explaining these differences, using the patterns given above. (Some prompts are given in brackets to help you.)

Stella's home	Belle Reve	(large, elegant)
Stella	Stanley	(poor background)
Stella	Blanche	(stayed at Belle Reve)
men they once went out with	Stanley	(crude, unsophisticated)
Stella	Blanche	(lacks self-control)
Stella	Blanche	(nervous, energetic)

b Now rewrite the sentences you wrote in ***a*** above, using the patterns in the following example.
Example: It differs from poor sections in other cities in that it has a raffish charm.
or: It is unlike poor sections in other cities in that it has a raffish charm.

8 Can you think of any other differences (or similarities) between the characters? Write some sentences using the structures given above.

Language practice – vocabulary

Commonly used verbs with multiple meanings

9 In each of the following sentences, which you can find in the extract, one of these verbs is missing: *let, go, get, take, make, do, put*. Fill in the gaps.

a You'll _________ along fine together.
b How did he _________ it when you said I was coming?
c They told me to _________ a streetcar named Desire.
d I'll _________ myself scarce.
e I was so exhausted by all I'd _________ through.
f We own this place so I can _________ you in.
g I am going to _________ just one tiny nip more.
h Do you mind if I _________ myself comfortable?
i What are you _________ in a place like this?
j _________ the bottle away so I won't be tempted.
k Liquor _________ fast in hot weather.
l Only Mr Edgar Allen Poe could _________ it justice.
m Why don't you just _________ in and _________ yourself at home till they _________ back.
n I knew you would _________ this attitude about it!
o A good habit to _________ into.
p Why didn't you _________ me know?
q This has got nothing to _________ with New Orleans.
r You keep right on _________ and you'll find it.
s The best I could _________ was make my own living.
t Ride six blocks and _________ off at Elysian Fields.
u Now, then, _________ me look at you.
v You've _________ on some weight.
w No, now seriously, _________ joking aside …
x Two women are _________ the air on the steps of the building.
y I _________ the spaghetti dish and ate it myself.
z Wanting to _________ rid of her …

10 Look at the verbs in Exercise 9 again.

a Would you say that they are used very frequently, fairly frequently or rarely in everyday conversation in English?
b What does the frequent use of these verbs by Tennessee Williams tell you about his style?

Extension

11 Imagine that you are making a radio production of *A Streetcar Named Desire.* How would you establish for the listeners that the play is set in New Orleans – and in *this particular part* of New Orleans?

12 Make your own publicity for the play (see Chapter 1, Publicity, p 20). Follow this procedure.

a Using photographs cut out of magazines, make a collage showing a scene from the play. Include pictures of what you imagine Blanche, Stella and Stanley to look like and add any architectural details, furniture, props, etc that you feel are appropriate.

b Work with a partner and use the collage to make either a poster for *A Streetcar Named Desire* or a still photograph from an imaginary film of the play. Put the collage up on the classroom wall and prepare your ideas for the next activity (**c**, below).

c **Class/group activity**: you are the executives of a film company. Some teams of artists have come to present their designs to you (the collages from **b**, above). Interview them about their work. Choose one team as designers for your film and one team as poster artists.

13 **Group work**: stage a part of this scene for other members of your class.

14 Write a poem or very short story with the title 'The Truth About Blanche DuBois'.

Beyond the text

15 Read this extract from another play by one of the American writers in this book. When you have read it, try to decide whether it is by O'Neill, Miller or Williams. Consider (a) where the play is set, (b) the characters, (c) the style, (d) the subject matter. Write down the reasons for your choice, and compare your answer with others in the class.

Guess the Author

See the Glossary section at the back of the book for vocabulary.

AMANDA *and* LAURA *are seated at a drop-leaf table. Eating is indicated by gestures without food or utensils.* AMANDA *faces the audience.* TOM *and* LAURA *are seated in profile.*

The interior has lit up softly and through the scrim we see AMANDA *and* LAURA *seated at the table in the upstage area.*

AMANDA (*calling*): Tom?

TOM: Yes, Mother.

AMANDA: We can't say grace until you come to the table!

TOM: Coming, Mother. (*He bows slightly and withdraws, re-appearing a few moments later in his place at the table.*)

AMANDA (*to her son*): Honey, don't *push* with your *fingers*. If you have to push with something, the thing to push with is a crust of bread. And chew – chew! Animals have sections in their stomachs which enable them to digest food without mastication, but human beings are supposed to chew their food before they swallow it down. Eat food leisurely, son, and really enjoy it. A well-cooked meal has lots of delicate flavours that have to be held in the mouth for appreciation. So chew your food and give your salivary glands a chance to function! (TOM *deliberately lays his imaginary fork down and pushes his chair back from the table.*)

TOM: I haven't enjoyed one bite of this dinner because of your constant directions on how to eat it. It's you that makes me rush through meals with your hawk-like attention to every bite I take. Sickening – spoils my appetite – all this discussion of – animals' secretion – salivary glands – mastication!

AMANDA (*lightly*): Temperament like a Metropolitan star! (*He rises and crosses downstage.*) You're not excused from the table.

TOM: I'm getting a cigarette.

AMANDA: You smoke too much.

(LAURA *rises.*)

LAURA: I'll bring in the blancmange.

(*He remains standing with his cigarette by the portières during the following.*)

AMANDA (*rising*): No, sister, no, sister – you be the lady this time and I'll be the darkey.

LAURA: I'm already up.

AMANDA: Resume your seat, little sister – I want you to stay fresh and pretty – for gentleman callers!

LAURA: I'm not expecting any gentleman callers.

AMANDA (*crossing out to kitchenette. Airily*): Sometimes they come when they are least expected! Why, I remember one Sunday afternoon in Blue Mountain – (*Enters kitchenette.*)

TOM: I know what's coming!

LAURA: Yes. But let her tell it.

TOM: Again?

LAURA: She loves to tell it.

(AMANDA *returns with bowl of dessert.*)

AMANDA: One Sunday afternoon in Blue Mountain – your mother received – *seventeen!* – gentlemen callers! Why, sometimes there weren't chairs enough to accommodate them all. We had to send the nigger over to bring in folding chairs from the parish house.

TOM (*remaining at portières*): How did you entertain those gentleman callers?

AMANDA: I understood the art of conversation!

TOM: I bet you could talk.

AMANDA: Girls in those days *knew* how to talk, I can tell you.

TOM: Yes?

(IMAGE: AMANDA AS A GIRL ON A PORCH, GREETING CALLERS.)

AMANDA: They knew how to entertain their gentlemen callers. It wasn't enough for a girl to be possessed of a pretty face and a graceful figure – although I wasn't slighted in either respect. She also needed to have a nimble wit and a tongue to meet all occasions.

TOM: What did you talk about?

AMANDA: Things of importance going on in the world! Never anything coarse or common or vulgar. (*She addresses* TOM *as though he were seated in the vacant chair at the table though he remains by portières. He plays this scene as though he held the book.*) My callers were gentlemen – all! Among my callers were some of the most prominent young planters of the Mississippi Delta – planters and sons of planters!

(TOM *motions for music and a spot of light on* AMANDA. *Her eyes lift, her face glows, her voice becomes rich and elegiac.*

SCREEN LEGEND: ' OÙ SONT LES NEIGES'.)

There was young Champ Laughlin who later became vice-president of the Delta Planters Bank.

Hadley Stevenson who was drowned in Moon Lake and left his widow one hundred and fifty thousand in Government bonds. There were the Cutrere brothers, Wesley and Bates. Bates was one of my bright particular beaux! He got in a quarrel with that wild Wainwright boy. They shot it out on the floor of Moon Lake Casino. Bates was shot through the stomach. Died in the ambulance on his way to Memphis. His widow was also well provided for, came into eight or ten thousand acres, that's all. She married him on the rebound – never loved her – carried my picture on him the night he died!

And there was that boy that every girl in the Delta had set her cap for! That brilliant, brilliant young Fitzhugh boy from Greene County!

TOM: What did he leave his widow?

AMANDA: He never married! Gracious, you talk as though all of my old admirers had turned up their toes to the daisies!

TOM: Isn't this the first you've mentioned that still survives?

AMANDA: That Fitzhugh boy went North and made a fortune – came to be known as the Wolf of Wall Street! He had the Midas touch, whatever he touched turned to gold! And I could have been Mrs Duncan J. Fitzhugh, mind you! But – I picked your *father*!

LAURA (*rising*): Mother, let me clear the table.

AMANDA: No, dear, you go in front and study your typewriter chart. Or practise your shorthand a little. Stay fresh and pretty! – It's almost time for our gentlemen callers to start arriving. (*She flounces girlishly toward the kitchenette.*) How many do you suppose we're going to entertain this afternoon?

(TOM *throws down the paper and jumps up with a groan.*)

LAURA (*alone in the dining-room*): I don't believe we're going to receive any, Mother.

AMANDA (*reappearing, airily*): What? No one – not one? You must be joking! (LAURA *nervously echoes her laugh. She slips in a fugitive manner through the half-open portières and draws them in gently behind her. A shaft of very clear light is thrown on her face against the faded tapestry of the curtains.*)

(MUSIC UNDER FAINTLY.
Lightly:)

Not one gentleman caller? It can't be true! There must be a flood, there must have been a tornado!

LAURA: It isn't a flood, it's not a tornado, Mother. I'm just not popular like you were in Blue Mountain. … (TOM *utters another groan.* LAURA *glances at him with a faint, apologetic smile. Her voice catching a little.*) Mother's afraid I'm going to be an old maid.

THE SCENE DIMS OUT WITH MUSIC

Author

Tennessee Williams (1911–83) came from an old Southern family in the United States. He had a happy early childhood at his grandparents' home in Columbus, Mississippi, despite a year-long illness which he later believed changed his nature from 'robust, aggressive almost bullying' to one of 'secretive and vulnerable individualism'. 'At the age of fourteen,' he wrote, 'I discovered writing as an escape from a world of reality in which I felt acutely uncomfortable'. His university studies were interrupted in 1931 by the Depression, when his father forced him to take a job in the International Shoe Company, an experience which he hated, although he later admitted that it gave him valuable insights into the lives of ordinary people. In 1934 he left the job and spent the next ten years doing odd bits of work, completing his studies and travelling around the USA and Mexico. His early plays were performed by small theatre groups. His first success was *The Glass Menagerie* (1944), which depicted the frustrations of modern suburban life through the figure of a disabled girl and her discontented brother. The play won the New York Drama Critics Circle Award in 1945 and was filmed in 1950. *A Streetcar Named Desire* was even more successful two years later, running for 855 performances in New York and winning a Pulitzer Prize. It was filmed in 1951, starring Marlon Brando and Vivien Leigh. Further critical and commercial successes followed, both on stage and screen, with *The Rose Tattoo* (1951), *Cat on a Hot Tin Roof* (1955), *Suddenly Last Summer* (1958), *Sweet Bird of Youth* (1959) and *The Night of the Iguana* (1961).

In his *Memoirs* (1975), Tennessee Williams wrote, 'I write of "little people". But are there "little people"? I sometimes think there are only little conceptions of people. Whatever is living and feeling with intensity is not little, and, examined in depth, it would seem to me that most "little people" are living with that intensity that I can use as a writer.

'Was Blanche a "little person"? Certainly not. She was a demonic creature, the size of her feeling was too great for her to contain without the escape of madness.'

Arthur Miller paid a special tribute to Williams in his own autobiography, *Timebends*:

'*Streetcar* – especially when it was still so fresh and the actors almost as amazed as the audience at the vitality of this theatrical experience – opened one specific door for me. Not the story or characters or the direction, but the words and their liberation, the joy of the writer in writing them, the radiant eloquence of the composition, moved me more than all its pathos. ... With *Streetcar*, Tennessee had printed a license to speak at full throat.'

6 Freedom and Laughter

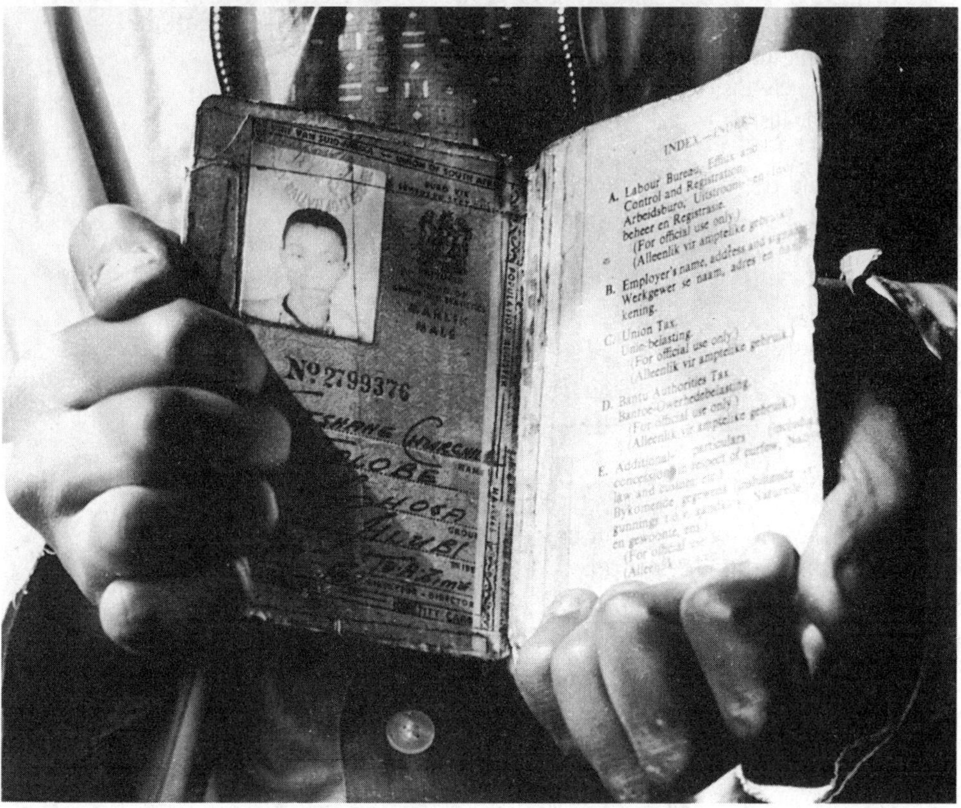

Before you read

Sizwe Bansi Is Dead is a comedy with a serious purpose. It is set in South Africa at a time of increasing social unrest in the early 1970s, and some knowledge of South African history (particularly the last 40 years) is necessary if you want to understand and enjoy the play.

Try to answer the questions below, then read the article which follows to check your answers.

1 Which column correctly shows the racial composition of South Africa – ***a***, ***b***, **c** or ***d***?

	a	***b***	**c**	***d***
Asians	3%	13%	2%	5%
Black Africans	74%	27%	15%	40%
Coloured (mixed race)	9%	18%	13%	4%
Whites	14%	42%	70%	51%

2 Who were the earliest inhabitants of Southern Africa?

a British settlers
b Portuguese colonists
c Black Africans
d Dutch farmers

3 What is the name of the South African policy of racial segregation?

a Lebensraum
b Ethnic cleansing
c Syndicalism
d Apartheid
e Divide and rule
f The Five Year Plan

4 When did the policy of racial segregation begin?

a 1652
b 1848
c 1918
d 1948
e 1963

5 When did racial segregation end?

a 1971
b 1976
c 1981
d 1986
e 1991
f It is still in force.

6 Under the racial laws, which of the following were permitted?

a Blacks and whites swimming at the same beach
b Blacks voting in elections
c Blacks and whites going to the cinema together
d Blacks running shops and small businesses
e Mixed marriages between blacks and whites
f Blacks living, working and travelling wherever they chose

7 When did compulsory free education for black South Africans begin?

a 1940	*d* 1970
b 1950	*e* 1980
c 1960	*f* 1990

Now read this article and check your answers.

Ten thousand years ago, in the late Stone Age, Southern Africa was inhabited by Bushmen (or San) and Khoikhoin, who lived by hunting and gathering. They were the ancestors of today's black South Africans. By the time Europeans first came to the area in the late 15th century, the native inhabitants had developed copper and gold mines, were trading with east Africa, and living in settled, complex communities.

The first European known to have landed in Southern Africa was the Portuguese navigator Bartolemeu Dias in the year 1488. In 1652 a Dutchman, Jan van Riebeeck, established a colony at the Cape of Good Hope as a port of call for Dutch East India Company ships on their way to and from the Orient. The Dutch colonists were eventually known as Boers or Afrikaners. They spoke Afrikaans – derived from their native Dutch language. As the Afrikaner settlers began to spread northwards from the Cape, they interbred with the native San and Khoikhoin, producing an ethnic group known as Cape Coloureds. From the late 18th century they also came into conflict with farmers of the Xhosa people in the region of the Fish River, and the resulting frontier wars lasted almost 100 years. Meanwhile, the Khoikhoin were driven from their land and forced to work on Afrikaner farms, and many thousands of Bushmen were killed or exiled to inhospitable parts of the country.

In 1795 the British captured the Cape, but held on to it for only seven years. In 1806 they returned and took definitive control. In the 1830s the Afrikaners began what is known as the Great Trek, moving northwards with their slaves to resettle north of the Vaal and Orange Rivers, where they established the independent South African Republic (the Transvaal) in 1838, and the Orange Free State in 1854.

The economy of the country grew rapidly in the late 19th century thanks to the discovery of gold and diamonds. British attempts to include the Afrikaner republics in a single confederation led to the Boer War (1899–1902), which ended with defeat for the Boers and the annexation of the republics by Britain.

The Union of South Africa was established in 1910. After the 1914–18 war, in which South African forces fought on the British side, the German colony of South West Africa was mandated to the Union by the League of Nations.

In 1948, the Nationalist Party introduced 'apartheid': a policy of racial segregation designed to create and maintain a hierarchy of economic and political power in which the white minority (less than one in five of the population) were at the top and the black Africans – nearly three-quarters of the population – at the bottom, with the Asians and Cape Coloureds somewhere in between.

One of the principal mechanisms of apartheid was the 'homelands' or Bantustans policy, restricting blacks to ten 'tribal homelands' – poor, undeveloped rural areas – of which every black was made a 'citizen' whether he had any connection with the area or not.

An essential part of this system were the 'pass laws', requiring blacks to carry a 'pass' or document stating which area of the country they had official permission to live and work in. The purpose of this policy was to maintain the supply of black labour to the South African economy while denying the blacks the benefits of South African citizenship (such as the right to vote) and preventing the development of black communities in white-dominated towns and cities.

The apartheid laws established segregated places of public education, recreation and entertainment (schools, theatres, cinemas, beaches) and made it an offence for people of different races to marry or even become lovers.

One result of apartheid was to create enormous social and economic disparities between the different races. The whites generally enjoyed far greater prosperity, higher life expectancy, lower infant mortality and a literacy rate of over 90%, while the blacks had lower life expectancy, higher infant mortality, a significantly higher incidence of malnutrition and infectious diseases, and a literacy rate of less than 50%. Compulsory free education for blacks was not introduced until 1980.

The injustices of apartheid led rapidly to social unrest within South Africa and, more gradually, to ostracism by much of the outside world. By the 1980s it was clear that white supremacy could only be maintained at the cost of unacceptable levels of violence, and apartheid was finally abandoned under President de Klerk in 1991. The country's first black President, Nelson Mandela, was elected in 1994.

Sizwe Bansi Is Dead (1972)
Athol Fugard, John Kani, Winston Ntshona

See the Glossary section at the back of the book for vocabulary.

Styles's Photographic Studio in the African township of New Brighton, Port Elizabeth. Positioned prominently, the name-board.

Styles Photographic Studio. Reference Books;
Passports; Weddings; Engagements; Birthday Parties
and Parties.

Prop. – Styles.

Underneath this a display of photographs of various sizes. Centre stage, a table and chair. This is obviously used for photographs because a camera on a tripod stands ready a short distance away.

There is also another table, or desk, with odds and ends of photographic equipment and an assortment of 'props' for photographs. The setting for this and subsequent scenes should be as simple as possible so that the action can be continuous.

STYLES *walks on with a newspaper. A dapper, alert young man wearing a white dustcoat and bowtie. He sits down at the table and starts to read the paper.*

STYLES (*reading the headlines*): 'Storm buffets Natal. Damage in many areas … trees snapped like … what? … matchsticks. …'

(*He laughs.*)

They're having it, boy! And I'm watching it … in the paper.

(*Turning the page, another headline.*)

'China: A question-mark on South West Africa.' What's China want there? *Yo!* They better be careful. China gets in there …! (*Laugh.*) I'll tell you what happens. …

(*Stops abruptly. Looks around as if someone might be eavesdropping on his intimacy with the audience.*)

No comment.

(*Back to his paper.*)

What's this? … *Ag!* American politics. Nixon and all his votes. Means buggerall to us.

(*Another page, another headline.*)

'Car plant expansion. 1.5 million rand plan.' *Ja.* I'll tell you what *that* means … more machines, bigger buildings … never any expansion to the pay-packet. Makes me fed-up. I know what I'm talking about. I worked at Ford one time. We used to read in the newspaper … big headlines! … 'So and so from America or London made a big speech: "… going to see to it that the conditions of their non-white workers in Southern Africa were substantially improved."' The talk ended in the bloody newspaper. Never in the pay-packet.

Another time we read; Mr Henry Ford Junior Number Two or whatever the hell he is … is visiting the Ford Factories in South Africa!

(*Shakes his head ruefully at the memory.*)

Big news for us, man! When a big man like that visited the plant there was usually a few cents more in the pay-packet at the end of the week.

Ja, a Thursday morning. I walked into the plant … 'Hey! What's this?' … Everything was quiet! Those big bloody machines that used to make so much noise made my head go around …? Silent! Went to the notice-board and read: Mr Ford's visit today!

The one in charge of us … (*laugh*) hey! I remember him. General Foreman Mr 'Baas' Bradley. Good man that one, if you knew how to handle him … he called us all together:

(STYLES *mimics Mr 'Baas' Bradley. A heavy Afrikaans accent.*)

'Listen, boys, don't go to work on the line. There is going to be a General Cleaning first.'

I used to like General Cleaning. Nothing specific, you know, little bit here, little bit there. But that day! Yessus … in came the big machines with hot water and brushes – sort of electric mop – and God alone knows what else. We started on the floors. The oil and dirt under the machines was thick, man. All the time the bosses were walking around watching us:

(*Slapping his hands together as he urges on the 'boys'.*)

'Come on, boys! It's got to be spotless! Big day for the plant!' Even the *big* boss, the one we only used to see lunch-times, walking to the canteen with a big cigar in his mouth and his hands in his pocket … that day? Sleeves rolled up, running around us:

'Come on! Spotless, my boys! Over there, John. …' I thought: What the hell is happening? It was beginning to feel like hard work, man. I'm telling you we cleaned that place – spot-checked after fifteen minutes! … like you would have thought it had just been built.

> *What other preparations do you think will be made for Mr Ford's visit?*

First stage of General Cleaning finished. We started on the second. Mr 'Baas' Bradley came in with paint and brushes. I watched.

W – h – i – t – e   l – i – n – e –

(*Mr 'Baas' Bradley paints a long white line on the floor.*)

What's this? Been here five years and I never seen a white line before. Then:

(*Mr 'Baas' Bradley at work with the paint-brush.*)

CAREFUL THIS SIDE. TOW MOTOR IN MOTION.

(STYLES *laughs.*)

It was nice, man. Safety-precautions after six years. Then another gallon of paint.

Y – e – l – l – o – w   l – i – n – e –

NO SMOKING IN THIS AREA. DANGER!

Then another gallon:

G – r – e – e – n   l – i – n – e –

I noticed that that line cut off the roughcasting section, where we worked with the rough engine blocks as we got them from Iscor. Dangerous world that. Big machines! One mistake there and you're in trouble. I watched them and thought: What's going to happen here? When the green line was finished, down they went on the floor – Mr 'Baas' Bradley, the lot! – with a big green board, a little brush, and a tin of white paint. EYE

PROTECTION AREA. Then my big moment:

'Styles!'

'Yes, sir!'

(*Mr 'Baas Bradley's heavy Afrikaans accent*) 'What do you say in your language for this? Eye Protection Area.'

It was easy, man!

'Gqokra Izi Khuselo Zamehlo Kule Ndawo.'

Nobody wrote it!

'Don't bloody fool me, Styles!'

'No, sir!'

'Then spell it … slowly.'

(STYLES *has a big laugh.*)

Hey! That was my moment, man. Kneeling there on the floor … foreman, general foreman, plant supervisor, plant manager … and Styles? Standing!

(*Folds his arms as he acts out his part to the imaginary figures crouched on the floor.*)

'G – q – o – k – r – a' … and on I went, with Mr 'Baas' Bradley painting and saying as he wiped away the sweat:

'You're not fooling me, hey!'

After that the green board went up. We all stood and admired it. Plant was looking nice, man! Colourful!

Into the third phase of General Cleaning.

'Styles!'

'Yes, sir!'

'Tell all the boys they must now go to the bathroom and wash themselves clean.'

We needed it! Into the bathroom, under the showers … hot water, soap … on a Thursday! Before ten? *Yo!* What's happening in the plant? The other chaps asked me: What's going on, Styles? I told them: 'Big-shot cunt from America coming to visit you.' When we finished washing they gave us towels … (*laugh*).

Three hundred of us, man! We were so clean we felt shy! Stand there like little ladies in front of the mirror. From there to the General Store.

Handed in my dirty overall.

'Throw it on the floor.'

'Yes, sir!'

New overall comes, wrapped in plastic. Brand new, man! I normally take a thirty-eight but this one was a forty-two. Then next door to the tool room … brand new tool bag, set of spanners, shifting spanner, torque wrench – all of them brand new – and because I worked in the dangerous hot test section I was also given a new asbestos apron and fire-proof gloves to replace the ones I had lost about a year ago. I'm telling you I walked back heavy to my spot. Armstrong on the moon! Inside the plant it was general meeting again. General Foreman Mr 'Baas' Bradley called me.

'Styles!'

'Yes, sir.'

'Come translate.'

'Yes, sir!'

Mr 'Baas' Bradley is about to make a speech. What sort of things is he likely to say?

(STYLES *pulls out a chair. Mr 'Baas' Bradley speaks on one side,* STYLES *translates on the other.*)

'Tell the boys in your language, that this is a very big day in their lives.'

'Gentlemen, this old fool says this is a hell of a big day in our lives.'

The men laughed.

'They are very happy to hear that, sir.'

'Tell the boys that Mr Henry Ford the Second, the owner of this place, is going to visit us. Tell them Mr Ford is the big Baas. He owns the plant and everything in it.'

'Gentlemen, old Bradley says this Ford is a big bastard. He owns everything in this building, which means you as well.'

A voice came out of the crowd:

'Is he a bigger fool than Bradley?'

'They're asking, sir, is he bigger than you?'

'Certainly … (*blustering*) … certainly. He is a very big baas. He's a … (*groping for words*) … he's a Makulu Baas.'

I loved that one!

'Mr 'Baas' Bradley says most certainly Mr Ford is bigger than him. In fact Mr Ford is the grandmother baas of them all … that's what he said to me.'

'Styles, tell the boys that when Mr Henry Ford comes into the plant I want them all to look happy. We will slow down the speed of the line so that they can sing and smile while they are working.'

'Gentlemen, he says that when the door opens and his grandmother walks in you must see to it that you are wearing a mask of smiles. Hide your true feelings, brothers. You must sing. The joyous songs of the days of old before we had fools like this one next to me to worry about.' (*To Bradley.*) 'Yes, sir!' 'Say to them, Styles, that they must try to impress Mr Henry Ford that they are better than those monkeys in his own country, those niggers in Harlem who know nothing but strike, strike.'

Yo! I liked that one too.

'Gentlemen, he says we must remember, when Mr Ford walks in, that we are South African monkeys, not American monkeys. South African monkeys are much better trained. …'

Before I could even finish, a voice was shouting out of the crowd:

'He's talking shit!' I had to be careful!

(*Servile and full of smiles as he turns back to Bradley.*)

'No, sir! The men say they are much too happy to behave like those American monkeys.'

Right! Line was switched on nice and slow – and we started working.

(*At work on the Assembly Line; singing.*)

'*Tshotsholoza … Tshotsholoza … kulezondawa. …*'

We had all the time in the world, man! … torque wrench out … tighten the cylinder-head nut … wait for the next one …. (*Singing*) '*Vyabaleka … vyabaleka … kulezondawa. …*' I kept my eye on the front office. I could see them – Mr 'Baas' Bradley, the line supervisor – through the big glass window, brushing their hair, straightening the tie. There was some General Cleaning going on there too.

(*He laughs.*)

We were watching them. Nobody was watching us. Even the old Security Guard. The one who every time he saw a black man walk past with his hands in his pockets he saw another spark-plug walk out of the plant. Today? To hell and gone there on the other side polishing his black shoes.

Then, through the window, I saw three long black Galaxies zoom up. I passed the word down the line: He's come!

What do you think Mr Ford will do during his visit?

Let me tell you what happened. The big doors opened; next thing the General Superintendent, Line Supervisor, General Foreman, Manager, Senior Manager, Managing Director … the bloody lot were there … like a pack of puppies!

(*Mimics a lot of fawning men retreating before an important person.*)

I looked and laughed! 'Yessus, Styles, they're all playing your part today!' They ran, man! In came a tall man, six foot six, hefty, full of respect and dignity … I marvelled at him! Let me show you what he did.

(*Three enormous strides*) *One … two … three. …* (*Cursory look around as he turns and takes the same three strides back.*)

One … two … three … OUT! Into the Galaxie and gone! That's all. Didn't talk to me, Mr 'Baas' Bradley, Line Supervisor, or anybody. He didn't even look at the plant! And what did I see when those three Galaxies disappeared? The white staff at the main switchboard.

'Double speed on the line! Make up for production lost!'

It ended up with us working harder that bloody day than ever before. Just because that big. … (*shakes his head.*)

Six years there. Six years a bloody fool.

(*Back to his newspaper. A few more headlines with appropriate comment, then. …*)

(*Reading*) 'The Mass Murderer! Doom!'

(*Smile of recognition.*)

'For fleas … Doom. Flies … Doom. Bedbugs … Doom. For cockroaches and other household pests. The household insecticide … Doom.' Useful stuff. Remember, Styles? *Ja.*

(*To the audience.*) After all that time at Ford I sat down one day. I said to myself:

'Styles, you're a bloody monkey, boy!'

'What do you mean?'

'You're a monkey, man.'

'Go to hell!'

'Come on, Styles, you're a monkey, man, and you know it. Run up and down the whole bloody day! Your life doesn't belong to you. You've sold it. For what, Styles? Gold wrist-watch in twenty-five years time when they sign you off because you're too old for anything any more?'

I was right. I took a good look at my life. What did I see? A bloody circus monkey! Selling most of his time on this earth to another man. Out of every twenty-four hours I could only properly call mine the six when I was sleeping. What the hell is the use of that?

Think about it, friend. Wake up in the morning, half-past six, out of the pyjamas and into the bath-tub, put on your shirt with one hand, socks with the other, realize you got your shoes on the wrong bloody feet, and all the time the seconds are passing and if you don't hurry up you'll miss the bus. … 'Get the lunch, dear. I'm late. My lunch, please, darling!' … then the children come in … 'Daddy, can I have this? Daddy, I want money for that.' 'Go to your mother. I haven't got time. Look after the children, please, sweetheart!!' … grab your lunch … 'Bye Bye!!' and then run like I-don't-know-what for the bus stop. You call that living? I went back to myself for another chat:

'Suppose you're right. What then?'

'Try something else.'

'Like what?'

Silly question to ask. I knew what I was going to say. Photographer!

What difficulties do you expect Styles to face in becoming a photographer?

It was my hobby in those days. I used to pick up a few cents on the side taking cards at parties, weddings, big occasions. But when it came to telling my wife and parents that I wanted to turn professional … !!

My father was the worst.

'You call that work? Click-click with a camera. Are you mad?'

I tried to explain. 'Daddy, if I could stand on my own two feet and not be somebody else's tool, I'd have some respect for myself. I'd be a man.'

'What do you mean? Aren't you one already? You're circumcised, you've got a wife. …'

Talk about the generation gap!

Anyway I thought: To hell with them. I'm trying it.

It was the Christmas shutdown, so I had lots of time to look around for a studio. My friend Dhlamini at the Funeral Parlour told me about a vacant room next door. He encouraged me. I remember his words. 'Grab your chance, Styles. Grab it before somebody in my line puts you in a box and closes the lid.' I applied for permission to use the room as a studio. After some time the first letter back:

'Your application has been received and is being considered.' A month later: 'The matter is receiving the serious consideration of the Board.' Another month: 'Your application is now on the director's table.' I nearly gave up, friends. But one day, a knock at the door – the postman – I had to sign for a registered letter.

'We are pleased to inform you. …'

(STYLES *has a good laugh.*)

I ran all the way to the Administration Offices, grabbed the key, ran all the way back to Red Location, unlocked the door, and walked in!

What I found sobered me up a little bit. Window panes were all broken; big hole in the roof, cobwebs in the corners. I didn't let that put me off though. Said to myself: 'This is your chance, Styles. Grab it.' Some kids helped me clean it out. The dust! *Yo!* When the broom walked in the Sahara Desert walked out! But at the end of that day it was reasonably clean. I stood here in the middle of the floor, straight! You know what that means? To stand straight in a place of you own? To be your own … General Foreman, Mr 'Baas', Line Supervisor – the lot! I was tall, six foot six and doing my own inspection of the plant.

So I'm standing there – here – feeling big and what do I see on the walls? Cockroaches. *Ja*, cockroaches … in *my* place. I don't mean those little things that run all over the place when you pull out the kitchen drawer. I'm talking about the big bastards, the paratroopers as we call them. I didn't like them. I'm not afraid of them but I just don't like them! All over. On the floors, the walls. I heard the one on the wall say: 'What's going on? Who opened the door?' The one on the floor answered: 'Relax. He won't last. This place is condemned.' That's when I thought: Doom.

Out of here and into the Chinaman's shop. 'Good day, sir, I've got a problem. Cockroaches.'

The Chinaman didn't even think, man, he just said: 'Doom!' I said: 'Certainly.' He said: 'Doom, seventy-five cents a tin.' Paid him for two and went back. *Yo!* You should have seen me! Two-tin Charlie!

(*His two tins at the ready, forefingers on the press-buttons,* STYLES *gives us a graphic re-enactment of what happened. There is a brief respite to 'reload' – shake the tins – and tie a handkerchief around his nose after which he returns to the fight.* STYLES *eventually backs through the imaginary door, still firing, and closes it. Spins the tins and puts them into their holsters.*)

I went home to sleep. *I* went to sleep. Not them (*the cockroaches*). What do you think happened here? General meeting under the floorboards. All the bloody survivors. The old professor addressed them: 'Brothers, we face a problem of serious pollution … contamination! The menace appears to be called Doom. I have recommended a general inoculation of the whole community. Everybody in line, please. (*Inoculation proceeds.*) Next … next … next. …' While poor old Styles is smiling in his sleep! Next morning I walked in. … (*He stops abruptly.*) …

What's this? Cockroach walking on the floor? Another one on the ceiling? Not a damn! Doom did it yesterday. Doom does it today. (*Whips out the two tins and goes in fighting. This time, however, it is not long before they peter out.*) Psssssssss … pssssss … pssss … pss (*a last desperate shake, but he barely manages to get out a squirt*).

Pss.

No bloody good! The old bastard on the floor just waved his feelers in the air as if he was enjoying air-conditioning.

I went next door to Dhlamini and told him about my problem. He laughed. 'Doom? You're wasting your time, Styles. You want to solve your problem, get a cat. What do you think a cat lives on in the township? Milk? If there's any the baby gets it. Meat? When the family sees it only once a week? Mice? The little boys got rid of them years ago. Insects, man, township cats are insect-eaters. Here. …'

He gave me a little cat. I'm … I'm not too fond of cats normally. This one was called Blackie … I wasn't too fond of that name either. But … Kitsy! Kitsy! Kitsy … little Blackie followed me back to the studio.

The next morning when I walked in what do you think I saw? Wings. I smiled. Because one thing I do know is that no cockroach can take his wings off. He's dead!

(*Proud gesture taking in the whole of his studio.*)

So here it is!

(*To his name-board.*)

'Styles Photographic Studio. Reference Books; Passports; Weddings; Engagements; Birthday Parties and Parties. Proprietor: Styles.'

When you look at this, what do you see? Just another photographic studio? Where people come because they've lost their Reference Book and need a photo for the new one? That I sit them down, set up the camera … 'No expression, please.' … click-click … 'Come back tomorrow, please' … and then kick them out and wait for the next? No, friend. It's more than just that. This is a strong-room of dreams. The dreamers? My people. The simple people, who you never find mentioned in the history books, who never get statues erected to them, or monuments commemorating their great deeds. People who would be forgotten, and their dreams with them, if it wasn't for Styles. That's what I do, friends. Put down, in my way, on paper the dreams and hopes of my people so that even their children's children will remember a man … 'This was our Grandfather' …

and say his name. Walk into the houses of New Brighton and on the walls you'll find hanging the story of the people the writers of the big books forget about.

(*To his display-board.*)

This one (*a photograph*) walked in here one morning. I was just passing the time. Midweek. Business is always slow then. Anyway, a knock at the door. Yes! I must explain something. I get two types of knock here. When I hear … (*knocks solemnly on the table*) … I don't even look up, man. 'Funeral parlour is next door.' But when I hear … (*energetic rap on the table … he laughs*) … that's *my* sound, and I shout 'Come in!'

In walked a chap, full of smiles, little parcel under his arm. I can still see him, man!

(STYLES *acts both roles.*)

'Mr Styles?'

I said: 'Come in!'

'Mr Styles, I've come to take a snap, Mr Styles.'

I said: 'Sit down! Sit down, my friend!'

'No, Mr Styles. I want to take the snap standing. (*Barely containing his suppressed excitement and happiness*) Mr Styles, take the card, please!'

I said: 'Certainly, friend.'

Something you mustn't do is interfere with a man's dream. If he wants to do it standing, let him stand. If he wants to sit, let him sit. Do exactly what they want! Sometimes they come in here, all smart in a suit, then off comes the jacket and shoes and socks … (*adopts a boxer's stance*) … 'Take it, Mr Styles. Take it!' And I take it. No questions! Start asking stupid questions and you destroy that dream. Anyway, this chap I'm telling you about … (*laughing warmly as he remembers*) … I've seen a lot of smiles in my business, friends, but that one gets first prize. I set up my camera, and just as I was ready to go … 'Wait, wait, Mr Styles! I want you to take the card with this.' Out of his parcel came a long piece of white paper … looked like some sort of document … he held it in front of him. (STYLES *demonstrates.*)

What might this document be?

For once I didn't have to say, 'Smile!' Just: 'Hold it!' … and, click, … finished. I asked him what the document was.

'You see, Mr Styles, I'm forty-eight years old. I work twenty-two years for the municipality and the foreman kept on saying to me if I want promotion to Boss-boy I must try to better my education. I didn't write well, Mr Styles. So I took a course with the Damelin Correspondence College. Seven years, Mr Styles! And at last I made it. Here it is. Standard Six Certificate, School Leaving, Third Class! I made it, Mr Styles. I made it. But I'm not finished. I'm going to take up for the Junior Certificate, then Matric … and you watch, Mr Styles. One day I walk out of my house, graduate, self-made! Bye-bye, Mr Styles,' … and he walked out of here happy man, self-made.

(*Back to his display-board; another photograph.*)

My best. Family Card. You know the Family Card? Good for business. Lot of people and they all want copies.

One Saturday morning. Suddenly a hell of a noise outside in the street. I thought: What's going on now? Next thing that door burst open and in they came! First the little ones, then the five- and six-year-olds. … I didn't know what was going on, man! Stupid children, coming to mess up my place. I was still trying to chase them out when the bigger boys and girls came through the door. Then it clicked. Family Card!

(*Changing his manner abruptly*)

'Come in! Come in!'

(*Ushering a crowd of people into his studio*)

… now the young men and women were coming in, then the mothers and fathers, uncles and aunties … the eldest son, a mature man, and finally …

(*Shaking his head with admiration at the memory*)

the Old Man, the Grandfather! (*The 'old man' walks slowly and with dignity into the studio and sits down in the chair.*)

I looked at him. His grey hair was a sign of wisdom. His face, weather-beaten and lined with experience. Looking at it was like paging the volume of his history, written by himself. He was a living symbol of Life, of all it means and does to a man. I adored him. He sat there – half smiling, half serious – as if he had already seen the end of his road.

The eldest son said to me: 'Mr Styles, this is my father, my mother, my brothers and sisters, their wives and husbands, our children. Twenty-seven of us, Mr Styles. We have come to take a card. My father …,' he pointed to the old man, '… my father always wanted it.'

I said: 'Certainly. Leave the rest to me.' I went to work.

(*Another graphic re-enactment of the scene as he describes it.*)

The old lady here, the eldest son there. Then the other one, with the other one. On this side I did something with the daughters, aunties, and one bachelor brother. Then in front of it all the eight-to-twelves, standing, in front of them the four-to-sevens, kneeling, and finally right on the floor everything that was left, sitting. Jesus, it was hard work, but finally I had them all sorted out and I went behind the camera.

(*Behind his camera.*)

Just starting to focus …

(*Imaginary child in front of the lens;* STYLES *chases the child back to the family group.*)

'… Sit down! Sit down!'

Back to the camera, start to focus again. … Not One Of Them Was Smiling! I tried the old trick. 'Say cheese, please.' At first they just looked at me. 'Come on! Cheese!' The children were the first to pick it up.

(*Child's voice.*) 'Cheese. Cheese. Cheese.' Then the ones a little bit bigger – 'Cheese' – then the next lot – 'Cheese' – the uncles and aunties – 'Cheese' – and finally the old man himself – 'Cheese'! I thought the roof was going off, man! People outside in the street came and looked through the window. They joined in: 'Cheese.' When I looked again the mourners from the funeral parlour were there wiping away their tears and saying 'Cheese'. Pressed my little button and there it was – New Brighton's smile, twenty-seven variations. Don't you believe those bloody fools who make out we don't know how to smile! Anyway, you should have seen me then. Moved the bachelor this side, sister-in-laws that side. Put the eldest son behind the old man. Reorganized the children. … (*Back behind his camera.*) 'Once again, please! Cheese!' Back to work … old man and old woman together, daughters behind them, sons on the side. Those that were kneeling now standing, those that were standing, now kneeling. … Ten times, friends! Each one different!

(*An exhausted* STYLES *collapses in a chair.*)

When they walked out finally I almost said Never Again! A week later the eldest son came back for the cards. I had them ready. The moment he walked through that door I could see he was in trouble. He said to me: 'Mr Styles, we almost didn't make it. My father died two days after the card. He will never see it.'

How do you think Styles will react to this?

'Come on,' I said. 'You're a man. One day or the other everyone of us must go home. Here. …' I grabbed the cards.

'Here. Look at your father and thank God for the time he was given on this earth.' We went through them together. He looked at them in silence. After the third one, the tear went slowly down his cheek.

But at the same time … I was watching him carefully … something started to happen as he saw his father there with himself, his brothers and sisters, and all the little grandchildren. He began to smile. 'That's it, brother,' I said. 'Smile! Smile at your father. Smile at the world.'

When he left, I thought of him going back to his little house somewhere in New Brighton, filled that day with the little mothers in black because a man had died. I saw my cards passing from hand to hand. I saw hands wipe away tears, and then the first timid little smiles.

You must understand one thing. We own nothing except ourselves. This world and its laws allows us nothing, except ourselves. There is nothing we can leave behind when we die, except the memory of ourselves. I know what I'm talking about, friends – I had a father, and he died.

(*To the display-board.*)

Here he is. My father. That's him. Fought in the war. Second World War. Fought at Tobruk. In Egypt. He fought in France so that this country and all the others could stay Free. When he came back they stripped him at the docks – his gun, his uniform, the dignity they'd allowed him for a few mad years because the world needed men to fight and be ready to sacrifice themselves for something called Freedom. In return they let him keep his scoff-tin and gave him a bicycle. Size twenty-eight. I remember, because it was too big for me. When he died, in a rotten old suitcase amongst some of his old rags, I found that photograph. That's all. That's all I have from him.

(*The display-board again.*)

Or this old lady, Mrs Matothlana. Used to stay in Sangocha Street. You remember! Her husband was arrested. …

(*Knock at the door.*)

Tell you about it later. Come in!

(*A man walks nervously into the studio. Dressed in an ill-fitting new double-breasted suit. He is carrying a plastic bag with a hat in it. His manner is hesitant and shy.* STYLES *takes one look at him and breaks into an enormous smile.*)

(*An aside to the audience.*) A Dream!

(*To the man.*) Come in, my friend.

First reaction

8 Look at these opinions of Styles.

a a likeable rogue
b a good, honest man doing the best he can in a difficult environment
c a cynic, interested only in money and his own happiness
d a clown
e a social commentator of great insight
f an unreliable witness

Which do you agree with? What do you think of him?

Close reading

Character

9 Look at the way Styles reacts to the news (lines 17–52). What do his comments and reactions suggest about his character? Fill in the table.

News	*Styles's comments and reactions*	*What these might suggest about his character*
Storm in Natal	1) laughs 2) ________	indifferent to the sufferings of others? amused by life
S W Africa and China		
American politics		
Car plant expansion		
Big speech about conditions of non-white workers		
Visit of Henry Ford		

10 'Six years there. Six years a bloody fool.' (line 235)

a Where is 'there'?

b Why does he think he was a fool? Pick out four or five key sentences from the next 40 lines which explain his opinion.

c What is your view? Was he a fool or not?

Staging

11 How many different parts (including short imitations of characters) does the actor play in this scene? First guess, without re-reading the scene. Then re-read the scene and list them.

12 Why is just one actor required to play all these parts? Choose the interpretation(s) that you think most likely.

a To save the expense of hiring a large cast.

b Because these are all figures in Styles's memory.

c To let the actor show off his brilliance at mimicry.

d To make the audience laugh.

e To make Styles seem superior to other people.

f This is a well-known storytelling technique.

g Some other reason (write your own).

13 In his Introduction to the play, Athol Fugard wrote that he was deeply influenced by a book by the Polish theatre director Jerzy Grotowski, *Towards A Poor Theatre* (first published in 1968). Here is an account of some of the key ideas developed by Grotowski. What connections can you see between *Sizwe Bansi Is Dead* and the ideas expressed below? Would you give a different answer to Exercise 12 after reading this passage?

Grotowski's Theatre Laboratory in Wroclaw was a place of pilgrimage for avant-garde actors, directors and playwrights in the 1960s and 1970s. The 'laboratory' of the title suggested Grotowski's 'scientific' approach to theatre. Through practical experimentation he sought to answer the questions: What is the theatre? What is unique about it? What can it do that film and television cannot?

The experiments consisted in a gradual elimination of superfluous elements from the theatrical performance in the hope of finding its essence. The list of 'superfluities' is surprisingly long: make-up, costumes, sets, lighting, sound-effects, even a stage to perform on. And what is left after these elements have been removed? 'The actor-spectator relationship' – in other words someone acting and someone watching. Grotowski described this relationship as 'perceptual, direct, live communication'. Without it, he says, theatre cannot exist.

Grotowski had the humility to admit that this was an 'ancient theoretical truth'. But its consequences for theatrical practice in the late 20th century, if rigorously applied, were revolutionary. It undermined most of what was conventionally thought of as 'theatre'. Grotowski called conventional theatre – the kind that uses lights, costumes, make-up, scenery, etc – 'the Rich Theatre', adding that it is 'rich in flaws'. He saw in it nothing but 'artistic kleptomania', 'hybrid spectacles' – with material and ideas assembled from literature, sculpture, painting, architecture, cinema and TV – presented as organic works of art but actually without 'backbone' or 'integrity'.

Rich theatre, in his view, was nonsense. Even if it tried to bring in more and more mechanical devices, it would always remain technologically inferior to films and television.

And so Poor Theatre was born. Grotowski's actors abandoned make-up, costumes, wigs, false bellies – 'everything that the actor puts on in the dressing-room before performance'. Instead they transformed themselves from character to character in front of the audience – 'in a **poor** manner, using only their own body and craft'.

The same approach was applied to setting the scene. Instead of performing in front of painted sets, the actors used nothing but gestures and movement, to transform 'the floor into a sea, a table into a confessional, a piece of iron into a living partner ...'.

By accepting poverty in the theatre, stripped of all the inessentials, Grotowski claimed to have discovered not only 'the backbone of the medium', but also 'the deep riches which lie in the very nature of the art-form'.

Symbols and ideas

14 Read the cockroach episode again (lines 315–68).

a How would you present this in the theatre? Make notes under these headings: props, lighting, sound effects, Styles's movements and voice.

b You'll notice that Styles gives the cockroaches human characteristics – he makes them speak, he calls them 'paratroopers', 'the old professor', etc. What is the point of this? Do you think this episode is meant simply to entertain the audience or does it also have a symbolic meaning? (See Chapter 5, Exercise 6, p 129 for an explanation of symbols in the theatre.)

c What does this episode suggest to you about Styles's attitude to life?

15 a Why do you think 'the writers of the big books' (lines 390–1) forget about the people of New Brighton?

b What does Styles say in the remainder of the scene (lines 393– 553) to make us realize that they are wrong to forget about these people?

16 'Smile at the world' (line 520). Does this sum up Styles's philosophy of life? What else would you add? Can you find a more suitable motto for him?

Language practice – structures

Elliptical sentences and the storytelling style

I applied for permission to use the room as a studio. After some time the first letter back: 'Your application has been received and is being considered.' A month later: 'The matter is receiving the serious consideration of the Board.' Another month: 'Your application is now on the director's table.' I nearly gave up, friends. But one day, a knock at the door – the postman – I had to sign for a registered letter. 'We are pleased to inform you ....'

17 Five of the sentences or clauses here are **elliptical** (some parts, mainly verbs, are missing) – while the others are complete.

- ***a*** Which are elliptical?
- ***b*** Why do you think some are elliptical and some complete?

18 Here are some more elliptical phrases. Convert each one into a grammatically complete sentence.

Example: But one day, a knock at the door – the postman –
But one day there was a knock at the door – it was the postman –

- ***a*** big hole in the roof, cobwebs in the corners. (line 306)
- ***b*** All over. On the floors, the walls. (lines 320–1)
- ***c*** Out of here and into the Chinaman's shop. (line 325)
- ***d*** Not them. (line 337)
- ***e*** General meeting under the floorboards. (lines 338–9)
- ***f*** Midweek. (line 394)
- ***g*** In walked a chap, full of smiles, little parcel under his arm. (line 400)
- ***h*** No questions! (line 416)
- ***i*** The old lady here, the eldest son there. (line 469)
- ***j*** Back to the camera, start to focus again .... (line 481)
- ***k*** Ten times, friends! Each one different! (lines 501–2)

19 Now look at lines 45–120, and list the elliptical phrases and sentences. Then convert each one into a grammatically complete sentence.

Language practice – vocabulary

20 'This is a strong-room of dreams. The dreamers? My people.' (lines 381–2)

a In the columns below, write down all the ideas and images that you associate with each of these key words.

STRONG-ROOM	DREAMS	MY PEOPLE

b **Group / pair work**: tell your partner(s) what you have written under each column, then listen while they tell you theirs. Ask / answer any questions about items that strike you as particularly interesting or surprising.

c **Individual or group work**: what do you think Styles means when he says, 'This is a strong-room of dreams'? Write down your interpretation.

21 Now make a similar analysis of these.

a A circus monkey (line 255)

b the volume of his history, written by himself (line 458)

c everyone of us must go home (line 511)

Extension

22 A few years after the first production of *Sizwe Bansi Is Dead*, Athol Fugard described it as 'a play which walked the tightrope between poetry and propaganda'. What do you think he meant by this? Can you identify any parts of the play that seem to be either propaganda or poetry?

23 **Debate / essay topic**: which of these two judgements do you agree with?

a 'The play is unlikely to be read in the 21st century, except by historians of apartheid.'

b 'Despite its specific historical setting, and the fast-changing political scene in South Africa, the play remains universal in its appeal.'

24 Write a short narrative or dramatic monologue based on your own experience, containing the words, 'Then I realized what a fool I'd been.'

25 **Group / pair work**: choose one of the episodes in this extract and stage it for other members of the class. (See Chapter 1, 'Staging a play', p 21.)

Beyond the text

26 Read this extract from *Shirley Valentine* by Willy Russell. It describes a crisis in the life of a housewife from Liverpool while she is on holiday in Greece. As you read, try to work out

a what happened between Shirley and Costas
b what kind of relationship Shirley has with her husband

Shirley Valentine (1988)
Willy Russell

See the Glossary section at the back of the book for vocabulary.

Later on, just lyin' there on the boat, with the sun beginnin' to dip towards the evenin', that's when the thought came to me. I tried to like, push it out of me head at first. Because it was too shocking. I kept tryin' to think of other things, to make this thought go away. But it wouldn't. It was just there in me head. An' this thought was 'If … somehow …. if … for … some … reason … I … didn't … go … back … home … who would really care? Would it cause anyone any real suffering? Would it damage anyone? Who would miss – me? Why should I go back? Why should I go back an' become that woman again when, when that woman isn't needed anymore. Her job's done. She's brought up her kids. I mean, they'd say it was awful, it was terrible to have a mother who went on holiday an' never came back. I hadn't gone round the pipe. I hadn't. I hadn't fallen in love with Costas. It had been sweet. It had been lovely. It had been a day full of kindness. But I hadn't fallen in love with him. I'd fallen in love with the idea of livin'. An' every day when I woke up, when I came down here with Jane, when we went an' had a coffee or a drink at Costas's taverna, when I was lyin' in me bed, just droppin' off to sleep, it was always there in me head – this shocking thought – 'I'm not goin' back.' 'I'm not goin' back.' (*Pause.*) An' of course – all the time I knew really. I knew I'd have to go back in the end. I knew that I was just one of millions an' millions before me who'd gone on a holiday an' had such a good time that they didn't want to go home. Because we don't do what we want to do. We do what we have to do. An' pretend it's what we want to do. An' what I wanted to do was to stay here and be Shirley Valentine. And what I had to do was to go back there, back to bein' St Joan Of The Fitted Units. An' all through the days, an' when I said goodbye to Costas, an' on the way to the airport, an' in the long queue for the check-in desk I didn't know if I'd do what I wanted to do, or what I had to do. We were standin' there, in this queue, me an' Jane an' all the others who had to go back. An' I remembered this question I was gonna ask Jane. So I said to her, 'Jane, Jane why is it that there's all this unused life?' She just said it was because of men, it was all the fault of men, an' went back to readin' her magazine. An' I thought about it an' I thought, 'That's rubbish … It's not just men who do it to women. Because I've looked at Joe, an' I know it's the same for him. He had more life in him than he could use. An' so he carries all this … waste around with him. It's the same for everyone. I know it. When I'm out when I'm in the shops, when I see people I grew up with, standin' there in the shop buyin' vegetables. An' we say how are y' we all say fine an' we pretend we are because the vegetables are fresh an' we haven't had a cold this year an' our kids grew up with their limbs intact an' never got in trouble with the police. We say we're fine. An' we carry on an' on an' on until we die. An' most of us die … long before we're dead. An' what kills us is the terrible weight of all this unused life that we carry round.' We'd got to the check-in desk. Me suitcase was on the conveyor belt with a tag on it, for England, for home. I stood there, just watchin' it as it moved away, along the conveyor belt an' through these flaps an' disappeared into this dark hole. An' I knew then. I knew I couldn't go with it … Jane just called out at first, as she saw me walkin' away. Then she realised, she knew an' she screamed at me, to come back, to come back. All the people in the queue were lookin' at me. An' I knew they all wanted me to 'come back, come back.' But I just kept walkin', across the concourse. All I had left was me handbag, the clothes I stood in, Gillian's robe, me passport an' a few drachmas. An' after I'd paid me bus fare, even the drachmas had gone. (*Pause.*) When I walked up to the taverna Costas was

talkin' to this woman, sittin' on a bar stool. As I walked in I heard him sayin' to her: 'You afraid? You afraid I want make try you ....' The poor feller, he nearly dropped his olives when he saw me. 'Don't worry Costas,' I said, 'I haven't come back for you. I've come back for the job. The job in your taverna.' Nearly three weeks I've been workin' there now. I get on well with the customers. Even the 'Dougies an' Jeanettes', we get a pair of them every week y' know. They come in, order a drink an' look all dead nervous at the menu. I always say to them, 'Would you like me to do y' chips an' egg?' An' they're made up then. Bein' a part of it here, a proper part of it – it's much better than bein' on holiday. (*She moves to the table and puts up the parasol.*) I have most of the days to meself an' just work the nights. I've got the night off tonight though. Well Joe's arrivin' tonight. The first time he phoned, y' know after Jane had got back, he screamed at me. He said I must have finally gone mad. He said I was a disgrace – to the kids, to him, to meself. It was the easiest thing in the world to just put the phone down on him. The second time he phoned he said you can't run away from life. I said I agreed with him an' now I'd found some life I had no intention of runnin' away from it. He started to scream an' shout again then; he said he knew all about me 'holiday romance', an' how I'd made a fool of meself but, but if I stopped all this arsin' round, if I got meself home, where I belonged, he said, he said he'd promise never to mention it. I said ... said ... 'The only holiday romance I've had, is with meself Joe. An' ... an' I think ... I've come to like meself, really.' I said to him, I said, 'I think I'm all right Joe. I think that if ... if I saw me, I'd say, that woman's O.K. ... She's alive. She's not remarkable, she's not gonna ... gonna be there in the history books. But she's ... she's there in the time she's livin' in. An' certainly she's got her wounds ... an' her battle scars but maybe, maybe ... a little bit of the bullshit is true an' the wounds shouldn't be hidden away – because, because even the wounds an' the scars are about bein' alive.' There was a long pause. I thought he'd gone off the phone. An' then I heard this voice, 'I knew it,' he was sayin', 'I knew it, it's the bleedin' change of life isn't it?' 'That's right Joe,' I said, 'That's right, it's a change of life. An' that's why you're wastin' your money phonin' me to try an' get me back. I'm not comin' back.'

27 Write a postcard from Shirley to a friend saying what has happened and why.

28 At line 390 in *Sizwe Bansi Is Dead*, Styles referred to 'the people the writers of the big books forget about'. Shirley makes a similar reference. What expression does she use, and how does it help her to understand her situation?

29 What similarities can you see between Shirley and Styles? Make a list and compare with a partner.

30 What do you think Shirley means by 'unused life'? Do you agree that 'it's the same for everyone ... most of us die long before we're dead'?

Authors

Athol Fugard has written this about himself:

'I was born in Middelburg, a small village in the semi-desert Karroo region of South Africa, on 11 June 1932. My mother is an Afrikaner, my father an English-speaking South African, possibly of Irish descent. I have an elder brother and a younger sister. At the time of my birth my parents owned a small general dealer's store in the village, but we sold this when I was about three years old and moved to Port Elizabeth, which has been my home ever since. Port Elizabeth is an almost featureless industrial port on the Indian Ocean. It is assaulted throughout the year by strong south-westerly and easterly winds. Close on half a million people live here – black, white, Indian, Chinese, and Coloured (mixed-race). It is also very representative of South Africa in the range of its social strata, from total affluence on the white side to the extremest poverty on the non-white. I cannot conceive of myself as separate from it.

'My life away from Port Elizabeth has included three years of studying philosophy and social anthropology at the University of Cape Town, a six-month hitch-hiking trip up Africa, two years as a seaman in the Far East, and a few trips overseas when I worked in theatre and television in England, America and Europe.

'I first became actively involved in theatre after my return from the Far East when I met my wife – Sheila Meiring – who was working as an actress in Cape Town. We formed an experimental drama group for which we wrote most of the material. In 1958, the second year of our marriage, we moved to Johannesburg, where I found a job as clerk in a Native Commissioner's Court [dealing with offences against the pass laws] ....

'My time in the Fordsburg Court in Johannesburg was traumatic for me as a white South African. We were kept very busy, averaging about one case every three minutes. During my six months in that Court Room I saw more suffering than I could cope with. I began to understand how my country functioned.

'At the same time I made my first black friends and began to visit them in the ghetto townships. Out of this life I wrote my first full-length play, *No-Good Friday*, which described the lives of black people in those townships, threatened as always by white laws and black gangsters. Through personal contacts my wife and I managed to assemble the necessary cast of ten (only a few of whom had any previous stage experience) and we began to rehearse wherever and whenever possible. *No-Good Friday* received considerable attention when first presented.' (Introduction to *Three Port Elizabeth Plays*, Oxford University Press, 1974)

His plays about South Africa are widely admired for their compassion, truth to life, and emotional power, as well as their fine craftsmanship and forceful political impact. They include *Nongogo* (1959), *The Blood Knot* (1961), *Hello and Goodbye* (1965), *People are Living There* (1968), *Boesman and Lena* (1969), *Statements after an Arrest under the Immorality Act* (1972), *The Island* (with John Kani and Winston Ntshona, 1973), *A Lesson from Aloes* (1978), *'Master Harold' and the Boys* (1982), *The Road to Mecca* (1984), *A Place with the Pigs* (1987) and *Playland* (1992).

Sizwe Bansi Is Dead is a comedy about a black worker, Sizwe Bansi, who beats the pass laws by exchanging his identity with a dead man. The play was created through improvisations with John Kani and Winston Ntshona, two actors from the Serpent Players, a drama group in New Brighton. They performed *Sizwe Bansi Is Dead* in South Africa, London and New York, where it was an immediate popular success. They have since become internationally recognised as two of South Africa's finest actors.

Willy Russell was born in 1947 and worked as a ladies' hairdresser in Liverpool for five years (1963–8) before realising that what he really wanted was a good education. So he studied to be a teacher. His experience of life in a comprehensive school in Liverpool is brought out in *Our Day Out* (shown on TV in 1977, later adapted for the stage), and his own escape from the limitations of working-class culture is dramatised in the comedy *Educating Rita* (1980, film 1983). Freedom is the major theme of his work. He has explored it, and the various means devised by modern society to confine it (respectability, apathy, competitive consumerism) in a series of eloquent comedies which have made him one of the most commercially and critically successful dramatists in contemporary Britain. They include *Breezeblock Park* (1975), *One for the Road* (1976), *Stags and Hens* (1978), *Blood Brothers* (1981) and *Shirley Valentine* (1988), which has also been made into a film. He writes:

'I believe that every play I have ever written has, ultimately, been one which celebrates the goodness of man; certainly the plays have included emptiness, despair, possibly even baseness. But it is the goodness that I hope the audience is left with. I really don't want to write plays which are resigned, menopausal, despairing, and whingeing. I don't want to use any medium as a platform for displaying the smallness and hopelessness of man. Man is man because madly, stupidly but certainly wonderfully, he kicks against the inevitability of life.'

7 Success!

Before you read

1 Look at the photograph on the previous page. Who are these men? Where are they? What are they doing? What jobs do you think they do?

2 Look at the following list of occupations and place them in order from 1 to 8 according to (a) the amount of money they earn, (b) their usefulness to society, (c) what you would like to be. Use the table below.

accountant
television personality
bank robber
children's nanny
bank clerk
housewife
gardener
show business agent

	MONEY	USEFULNESS	I'D LIKE TO BE
1 most			
2			
3			
4			
5			
6			
7			
8 least			

3 **Group / pair work**: compare your three lists. Where you disagree, listen to other people's reasons for their choices. Reach a compromise if you can. Is it possible for the whole class to agree?

Man of the Moment (1988)
Alan Ayckbourn

Man of the Moment is set at the Spanish holiday villa of Vic Parks, an ex-bank robber. During the play a television programme is being made about Vic and Douglas Beechey, who seventeen years ago became a popular hero by attacking Vic as he was robbing the bank where Douglas worked. Nerys, who later became Douglas's wife, was shot and badly disfigured in the raid. Now Douglas is forgotten, an accountant living a quiet, anonymous life in the suburbs of London, while Vic, after serving his prison sentence, has become famous as a television personality.

In the following scene, Douglas – who has been flown to Spain specially for the

TV programme – catches a glimpse of Vic's domestic life. Other characters in the scene are Sharon (employed by Vic to look after his children), Trudy (Vic's wife), Kenny (Vic's manager), and Ruy (the gardener).

See the Glossary section at the back of the book for vocabulary.

ACT 2

(SHARON *returns from the swimming pool. Walking slowly, as before, she carries an armful of the children's toys.*)

VIC: Hey, Sharon …

SHARON (*stopping*): Yes, Mr Parks?

VIC: Where're Timmy and Cindy?

SHARON: They're having their tea in the kitchen with Marta, Mr Parks.

VIC: Sit down, then.

SHARON: I've got to go and –

VIC: Sit down.

SHARON: Yes, Mr Parks.

(SHARON *sits, still holding on to the toys. She is obviously hotter than ever and slightly breathless.*)

VIC: Get your breath back.

SHARON: Thank you …

VIC: Look at her. Puffing like a grampus, aren't you?

SHARON: Yes, Mr Parks.

VIC: Sweat running off you. (*To the others.*) Look at her. Have you ever seen anyone sweating like that? It's dripping off her. I bet it's running off you underneath there, isn't it, eh? Eh?

(SHARON *doesn't reply.*)

Running down your arms? Trickling down your legs? If there's one thing I hate, it's to see a woman sweating like that. It's bad enough on a man, it's obscene on a woman, don't you agree?

(SHARON *sits unhappily.* RUY *crosses with another block of stone.*)

I'll tell you something, Sharon. Do you know why you're sitting there, sweating like that? Do you know the reason why you're sat there like a great bowl of pork dripping? Do you want to know the reason? Because you are overweight, girl. You are fat. Let's face it, Sharon, you are a fat girl, aren't you? A big, fat girl.

DOUGLAS: Oh, I don't think that's fair, she's just …

VIC: Here, let her tell you something, just a second. Sharon …

SHARON: Yes, Mr Parks …

VIC: Shall we tell them why you're so fat? Shall we? Shall we tell them your secret? It's because you are greedy, isn't it, Sharon? You eat too much. You are a guts. Aren't you? You're a glutton. Eh?

SHARON: Yes, Mr Parks.

VIC: Tell them what you ate on your last birthday, Sharon. Tell them. This girl, she told me that last year on her birthday, she sat on her own, in her flat in wherever it was – Macclesfield –

SHARON: Huddersfield …

VIC: Huddersfield. She sat there all on her own, singing happy birthday to me and she ate … What did you eat, Sharon? Tell them what you ate, go on.

SHARON (*muttering*): Twelve rum babas.

VIC: Come on, say it louder …

SHARON (*loudly*): Twelve rum babas, Mr Parks.

VIC: Twelve rum babas. Can you imagine that? Turns you over, doesn't it? Still, we're working on you, aren't we, Sharon? We're slowly melting you down, aren't we?

SHARON: Yes, Mr Parks …

VIC: Getting her fit. Giving her some exercise. Working it off her. What were you learning this morning then? What was I teaching you this morning, Sharon?

SHARON: Scuba diving, Mr Parks.

VIC: Scuba diving. She enjoyed that – didn't you?

SHARON: Yes.

VIC. You should have seen her in her big black rubber suit flailing about in the water there, first thing. Like a big shiny, beached, humpbacked whale, weren't you …

(SHARON *suddenly starts to cry very quietly.*)

DOUGLAS: Look, I'm sorry, this is very, very cruel and unnecessary and I really don't think you should go on tormenting this girl simply because –

VIC: You mind your own business –

DOUGLAS (*undaunted*): – simply because she's a shade overweight and obviously very self-conscious about it, anyway. It is cruel and it is hurtful and it is –

VIC (*suddenly yelling at him*): I said, mind your own bloody business!

(*A silence.* SHARON *gets up and runs into the house. She passes* TRUDY *who is coming out.* TRUDY *looks at the men and appears to sum up the scene.* RUY *crosses again, empty-handed.*)

(*To* DOUGLAS, *softly*) I hope I don't have to remind you again that you are a guest in this house. And the way I choose to treat my staff is entirely my concern. OK?

(DOUGLAS *is silent.* KENNY *clears his throat.*)

KENNY: They should be about set up for that interview, I should think …

TRUDY: They were nearly ready, yes.

VIC: I've been waiting here. Patiently. Plenty of things I could have been getting on with, too.

TRUDY (*brightly*): I wondered if you wanted to take up my offer and stroll down to the beach, Douglas? While they're doing their interview?

DOUGLAS: Oh, lovely, yes. Thank you very much.

VIC (*sourly*): Yes, you take him down the beach, good idea.

TRUDY (*faintly sarcastic*): Oh, dear. You haven't been disagreeing with my husband, have you? I hope not.

DOUGLAS: No, I –

TRUDY: You mustn't do that, you know. He only likes people who agree with him all the time. It's one of his little whims.

VIC: What are you talking about?

TRUDY: It comes of being surrounded by people who nod at him all day at work. He prefers us all to nod at home, too …

VIC (*innocently*): What did I do, eh? What am I meant to have done, now?

KENNY (*laughing*): Can't imagine.

TRUDY: He surrounds himself with these little nodding animals. It's like the back shelf of a car in our house. We all do it.

VIC: Bloody rubbish.

TRUDY: Yes, quite right, dear. Nod, nod.

VIC: What a load of rubbish. (*To* KENNY.) Isn't it? A load of rubbish?

KENNY (*nodding*): Oh, yes.

First reaction

4 Who is the strongest character in this scene? Who is the weakest? (Consider the possible meanings of 'strong' and 'weak' as you answer.)

5 In the next scene, two hours later, it is a moonlit evening. Ayckbourn describes it as follows.

Patches of shadow. Cicadas chirping. Very romantic. Perhaps marred slightly by some very syrupy country and western music emanating distantly from the hi-fi somewhere in the house.

What sort of scene is likely to take place in this setting?

a a dramatic confrontation between Douglas and Vic
b a love scene between two of the characters
c a murder

d a confession
e an argument between Trudy and Vic
f a scene of gentle comedy
g something else – your prediction: ____________________

Now read the scene and see which (if any) is correct. (Note: Douglas and Trudy have just returned from their walk along the beach. They begin to discuss what happened in the bank raid seventeen years ago.)

See the Glossary section at the back of the book for vocabulary.

ACT 2

TRUDY: You really don't bear any resentment for what he did? To you? To your wife? The woman you were in love with? Didn't it matter? It's like it never mattered to you at all.

DOUGLAS: Oh, it mattered. Then. Of course it did. Only – Well, it wasn't as straightforward as that. It never is. Let me try and – explain, then. It's difficult. (*Pause.*) Working with me in this bank – I was twenty-four – twenty-five at the time – working with me, alongside me – was the most beautiful woman I have ever seen in my life, anywhere. Before or since. Her name was Nerys Mills and she was a stunner. And I was – besotted. That's the only word for it. Some days I couldn't look at her at all. My hands would shake and my voice used to crack and go falsetto when I spoke and I'd feel sick in my stomach, and one day I actually started crying without any warning at all. Right in the middle of serving a customer. In the end, I had to pretend I got hay fever. And that was very inconvenient, because then I had to remember to keep having it and take nose drops and things, otherwise people would begin to wonder what was really wrong with me. Anyway, needless to say – Nerys didn't take a blind bit of notice of me. No, that's not exactly true. She was generally very nice and polite, but, so far as romance went, I think I was definitely at the bottom of the reserves as far as she was concerned. She was actually unofficially engaged to this other man – (*Darkly.*) I forget his name now. I never forget names but I've forgotten his.

TRUDY: Did he work in the bank as well?

DOUGLAS: No, no. He was a salesman. A double-glazing salesman, actually. There's an amusing story to that, I'll come back to that. Anyway, I sat there and – longed for her – day after day – month after month – fantasized about her a little – nothing unpleasant, you know …

TRUDY: No, no ...

DOUGLAS: And some mornings she'd have a chat with me between customers. And then the sun would shine all day, you know ... (*He smiles.*)

TRUDY (*smiling*): Yes ...

DOUGLAS: And other mornings, she'd come in like thunder – something obviously had gone wrong the night before with her and old double-glazing ... And then, of course, you never got a smile ...

TRUDY (*sadly*): Ah ...

DOUGLAS: And as time went by, I marked her off in my own personal ledger in the desirable but unattainable column, along with the Silver Cloud and the offer to keep wicket for Kent – and I was just resigning myself to life without her and seriously considering whether the Royal Army Pay Corps might have a vacancy somewhere – when the bank raid occurred. And that did change everything. There's no doubt about it. I don't know why I did what I did. Your husband was right, it was madness. It just seemed the only thing to do at the time, that's all. There was this stranger in a balaclava threatening the woman that I cared more than my own life for ... I couldn't help myself, you see?

TRUDY (*engrossed*): No. I see. I see.

DOUGLAS: Afterwards, I went to see her a lot in hospital. Partly through guilt. Only partly. But, you see, if I hadn't run at Vic like that, she might never have – Not that she's ever blamed me. She's never once, ever – Never. Anyway, I went to see her, as soon as they'd let us in to visit. I imagined there'd be so many blokes round the bed she'd never even see me, anyway. And there were, to start with. I was just there waving my bunch of daffodils at her from the back of the crowd. And then slowly they all drifted away. Over the weeks. Stopped coming to see her.

TRUDY: How rotten. Aren't people rotten, sometimes?

DOUGLAS: Yes, I thought that at first. Then I realized later, of course. She'd been sending them all away. Subconsciously. A beautiful woman like she'd been, she couldn't bear to be seen like – that. She couldn't stand it. I mean, she wasn't vain. Not really. But if you're used all your life to people taking pleasure in looking at you, then it must be very hurtful when they suddenly start instinctively looking away from you. You couldn't blame people, altogether. She did look a terrible mess for a time.

TRUDY: But you didn't? Look away from her?

DOUGLAS: Well, I think I probably did, yes. As I say, it was only natural early on. But, you see, if I looked away from her, it didn't matter quite so much. Because she'd never valued my opinion of her anyway. So it never worried her. And there I was, with her all to myself. Visiting every day. Jollying her up. And over the weeks we got very friendly.

TRUDY: And did she fall in love with you?

DOUGLAS: I don't know.

TRUDY: But did she never say to you … ?

DOUGLAS: No. And I didn't ask her. It didn't matter. She liked me. And more important, she needed me. That's what mattered. And I loved her. (*He smiles.*) I was going to tell you, you know, when I'd left the bank, I applied for my present job with this double-glazing company. I thought it might – you know – increase my standing with her. Since she seemed to have a liking for double-glazing men. Ridiculous. We laughed about that later. I never regretted it, though. They're a grand bunch. Anyway, she came out. And we married quietly. And we got a joint mortgage on number fifty-three and we've lived there ever since. With never a cross word, I'm happy to report. (*Pause.*) So what do I say? Yes, I do – I hate Vic because of what he did to the most beautiful woman in the world? Or, thank you very much, Vic, for being instrumental in arranging for me to marry the unattainable girl of my dreams? Difficult to know which to say, isn't it? (*Pause.*) All right. I know you might well say, what about her? What about poor old Nerys? Being forced to settle for minor league when she was naturally first division. Well, all I can say is, without prejudice, and I am not a swearing person, you appreciate – but that man she was engaged to originally – old double-glazing the first – he was a complete – pillock. He really was. He treated Nerys like – well, there were times when – not just me, you understand … We all could have done – in that bank. Including Mr Marsh. This man – he treated her as only a handsome man can treat a beautiful woman. If you know what I mean.

TRUDY: Yes. I do. I think I do.

What do you think Douglas means?

(*They listen to the music for a moment.*)

DOUGLAS (*cheerfully*): Well, that's – that's my life. Sorry if I bored you. (*Pause.*) This is very pleasant music, isn't it? Country and western? Am I right?

TRUDY (*weakly*): Yes. Vic likes it. We used to … When we were … (*Her voice tails away.*)

(DOUGLAS *waits for her to finish the sentence. She doesn't. She is evidently in some distress. She rocks about. She looks at* DOUGLAS.

Suddenly and unexpectedly, she kisses him on the mouth. Then pulls away and avoids his look. He, after taking a second to recover, avoids her in turn. They sit, pretending it hasn't happened.)

DOUGLAS (*at length*): Yes, I'm very partial to country and western music. They always manage to come up with a good tune, don't they?

TRUDY (*in a little voice*): I'm sorry. (*Then, pulling herself together.*) There's nothing we can do for you, then? Vic and I? Nothing?

DOUGLAS: Do?

TRUDY: Well, to help in any way … Money or …

DOUGLAS (*rather embarrassed*): Oh, no.

TRUDY (*equally embarrassed*): Sorry. I didn't mean to –

DOUGLAS: No, no …

TRUDY: It's just so rare to meet someone who doesn't want something from us these days … I suppose that's called being successful. Or is it because it's us who are offering? Is that why you're saying you don't want anything?

DOUGLAS: No, it's not that. I just don't think there is anything. Thank you very much. Well. I think I must away down the hill to my own hotel. They'll be serving dinner soon …

TRUDY: You're welcome to stop and have supper with us if you –

DOUGLAS: No, that's very kind of you, but you'll see quite enough of me again tomorrow.

TRUDY: Well, wait there a second, I'll fetch the keys and run you back –

DOUGLAS: No, please.

TRUDY: It's no trouble –

DOUGLAS: I'd rather walk, I really would. Really. I don't get the chance to walk around islands that much.

TRUDY (*reluctantly*): Well …

DOUGLAS: Thank you for all your hospitality today. You've been very kind. You really have. (*He starts to move back towards the gate.*) Straight down the hill, I take it?

TRUDY: Yes. Only when you get to the fork that leads to the sea – the one we took – go right instead of left.

DOUGLAS: Simple enough. Well. See you tomorrow, Trudy.

TRUDY: Goodnight, Douglas.

DOUGLAS (*turning in the gateway*): Er … (*Smiling.*) There's one thing I wouldn't have minded, I suppose. Not that you could have given it to me. But since you mentioned wanting things …

TRUDY: What's that? Anything we –

DOUGLAS: No, I was just thinking. I was a hero, I suppose, for all of a year. People wrote to me. Sent for my photograph. Asked my advice. Listened to what I had to say. I think it would have been nice to have been a hero for a bit longer …

TRUDY: You still are –

DOUGLAS: … silly. I'd probably never have missed it, only …

TRUDY: – to people like Nerys you are. And I bet there are others who still remember …

DOUGLAS: No, I think I'm best remembered now as the idiot who tackled an armed robber and nearly got someone's head blown off in the process. I think you ended up with the hero, Trudy, not poor old Nerys. You stick with him. You stick with Vic. If you're looking for heroes. See you in the morning.

(DOUGLAS *goes out through the gate.* TRUDY *stares after him.*)

TRUDY (*faintly*): Yes …

(*She gets up to go into the house. Then decides that, if she's going to cry, she'd better cry out here. She sits down again in the shadows. She hugs herself and starts to weep quietly and privately.*

In a little while, there is a faint slapping sound from the direction of the swimming pool. TRUDY *becomes aware of this and stops crying to listen.* SHARON *appears, walking along the side of the swimming pool towards the deep end. She has on her black wetsuit, rubber helmet and flippers. She carries a weighted diving belt. She is also crying. In fact, she is in a desperate, heart-broken state. She stops at the end of the swimming pool, a tragi-comic, fat, black, rubber-clad figure.*

What do you think Sharon is planning to do?

TRUDY *watches her, astonished.* SHARON, *unaware she is being watched, looks towards the house and starts to fasten the diving belt about her waist.*)

(*Cautiously*) Sharon? Sharon … What are you doing there?

SHARON (*between sobs*): Mrs Parks …

TRUDY: What are you doing, Sharon?

SHARON: I'm going to kill myself, Mrs Parks.

TRUDY (*moving to her, alarmed*): You are going to what?

SHARON: I'm sorry, Mrs Parks. I love him so much, and he doesn't care about me at all.

TRUDY: Sharon …

SHARON (*as in one breath*): He just says I'm fat and I've got to get thin and I've tried to get thin but I can't get thin whatever I do because when he says he doesn't love me I just keep eating because I'm so unhappy you see and then when I eat then I just get fatter you see and then he doesn't love me … and I love him so much, Mrs Parks, and I'm ever so sorry …

TRUDY: Yes … I'm sorry, Sharon … I know how it is, believe me I do …

SHARON: No, you don't – you can't …

TRUDY: Yes, I do. I promise, Sharon, I do …

SHARON: Nobody knows –

(*During the next, the music from the house stops as the record comes to an end.*)

TRUDY: Sharon, it's a passing thing, I promise. It's something we all go through. Most of us. God help us. It'll pass …

SHARON: No, it won't pass. I've loved Vic for years …

TRUDY: Years? What do you mean, years? You've only been with us two months …

SHARON: I seen him on the telly. I used to watch him on the telly and I used to write to him on *Ask Vic* and he used to write back to me, he did, I promise …

TRUDY: Sharon, he gets thousands of letters a week. He doesn't even read them, let alone write back …

SHARON: He did, he wrote to me and it was in his writing. And he used to tell us on the telly if we had problems how to deal with them and not to worry and then when I got this job working for him I just thought it was going to be so wonderful and he's just been horrible to me … I don't know what I've done … What have I done wrong, Mrs Parks?

(*During the next,* VIC *comes out of the house and listens, unnoticed.*)

TRUDY (*fiercely*): The only thing you did wrong, Sharon … the one and only thing you ever did wrong was to love him in the first place … Because he is not a man to love, Sharon, I promise you. Not if you can possibly avoid it. I speak as one who has tried for eight years, Sharon, to keep loving him. While that bastard has abused me and ignored me and taken me for granted – while he has been screwing his way round Television Centre and half of ITV – I have looked after his kids and his house and his bloody, bad-tempered old mother in Beckenham … And I have tried to keep loving him … I swear to God I have tried. And if you are honestly clinging on to life in the hope of getting one tiny scrap of care or consideration back from that self-centred, selfish – scum bucket – then all I can say is, you'd better jump in there now, Sharon, and cut your losses.

How would you react to this speech if you were Sharon?

(SHARON, *understandably, is a little bemused by this outburst. She stands indecisively.* VIC *steps out further on to the patio. Both women see him for the first time.*)

VIC: Well, well. You know what they say. You never hear good about yourself, do you?

TRUDY: Tell her, Vic. Talk to the girl, for God's sake.

VIC: Tell her what?

TRUDY: I just caught her trying to drown herself …

VIC (*amused*): What?

TRUDY: Vic, talk to her …

VIC: What do you want to drown yourself for, Sharon?

TRUDY: What do you think ...?

VIC: I have no idea. I have no idea why this great big girl should want to drown herself …

(SHARON *sobs and finishes fastening her belt.*)

TRUDY: Vic …

VIC: Why? Just tell me?

TRUDY: Because of what you've said to her. Done to her.

VIC: What?

TRUDY: Whatever you said – whatever you did. I don't know. I don't want to know …

VIC: I've never laid a finger on her, have I? Sharon, tell her, I've never laid a finger on you … Have I? Eh?

SHARON (*unhappily*): No, Mr Parks …

VIC: There you are. No. She confirms that …

TRUDY (*shouting*): You know bloody well what you've done to her, Vic, now do something about it …

VIC: Right, that's it, forget it. I am not being shouted at. Let her jump …

(*He turns to move into the house.* SHARON *prepares to jump into the pool.*)

TRUDY (*yelling*): Vic …

VIC (*furiously*): Let the stupid cow drown herself, what do I care? Go on. Jump, jump, jump then …

(SHARON *jumps into the pool. Weighted down by her diver's belt, she sinks rapidly under the dark water and vanishes in a trail of bubbles.*)

TRUDY (*screaming*): SHARON!

VIC (*surprised* SHARON *has done it*): Bloody hell!

Are you surprised that Sharon has jumped in? What do you think will happen now?

(VIC *moves towards the pool.*)

TRUDY: Vic, get her out. Dive in and get her out, for God's sake …

VIC: I'm not diving in there. Not in these clothes.

TRUDY: Vic, the girl is drowning.

VIC: She's not drowning. She can stay under for hours. She's built like a bathyscope …

TRUDY: Are you going in to get her, or not?

VIC: You dive in.

TRUDY: I can't get her out, she's far too big for me, she's enormous, Vic …

VIC: We could sprinkle rum babas on the surface, that'll bring her up …

TRUDY: You bastard … (*Desperately.*) Oh, dear God. (*Running to the gate and yelling.*) Douglas! Douglas! He's gone …

VIC (*peering into the pool, meanwhile*): Sharon! I can see you down there, Sharon.

TRUDY (*running to the house and calling*): Kenny! Kenny, come out here, please!

VIC: Kenny went down to the shop – we were running out of vino …

TRUDY: If she dies, Vic. If that girl dies …

VIC: Nobody would miss her except the national union of bakers …

TRUDY (*running at him in fury*): You … God, I hate you! I really so hate you! (*She attacks him with both her fists.*)

VIC (*amused and fending her off easily*): Hey, hey, hey!

TRUDY (*beating at him*): I'd so love to … hurt you … like you … hurt … other people, sometimes …

(*She lands a blow that* VIC *doesn't care for. He takes her a little more seriously.*)

VIC: Oi! Now, Trudy! That's enough. You've had your fun …

(*He starts to pinion her arms to protect himself.* TRUDY *continues to fight and* VIC *is forced to turn her away from him and grab her neck in the crook of his arm in a traditional headhold whilst pinioning her arms with his other hand.* TRUDY *is finally incapacitated. She remains there, exhausted and infuriated by her impotence against his superior strength. Barely have they finished struggling when* DOUGLAS *runs back into the garden through the gate. He is halfway to the house before he sees* VIC *and* TRUDY.)

DOUGLAS (*as he enters*): What's the problem? I – (DOUGLAS *stops and stares at them in amazement.*)

TRUDY (*weakly, choking in* VIC*'s grip*): Douglas … please!

VIC (*calmly*): Now, it's all right. Don't get excited and nobody'll get hurt, all right?

(DOUGLAS *reacts like a charger on hearing the bugle call. He gives a sudden wild yell of fury and rushes at* VIC *head down.*)

DOUGLAS: Aaaaarrrrggggghhhh!

VIC (*startled*): Jesus!

(VIC *pushes* TRUDY *to one side in order to defend himself – not for the first time in his life – from* DOUGLAS*'s sudden wild onslaught.* DOUGLAS *catches* VIC *in the midriff.* TRUDY *screams.* VIC *grunts with pain, winded. Both men lose their balance.* VIC *topples into the pool.* DOUGLAS *is left kneeling on the edge, slightly winded himself.*)

TRUDY: Douglas? Are you all right?

DOUGLAS: Yes, I … I'm … I'm sorry, I … where's Vic?

TRUDY: He's in the …

(*As she starts to speak,* VIC*'s hand grips the edge of the pool. He hauls himself up. He looks very dangerous.*)

How do you think this scene will be resolved?

VIC (*breathless*): Right. There is about to be some serious damage done, I can tell you … (*Pointing at* DOUGLAS *and* TRUDY *in turn.*) To you. And to you. All right?

(DOUGLAS *and* TRUDY *draw back, nervously.* VIC *seems about to climb out of the pool.*

Suddenly the waters part and a large black shape, barely recognizable as SHARON*, breaks surface and seizes hold of* VIC *around the neck from behind.*)

As soon as I've … Uurrgghhh!

(*He is dragged under the water by* SHARON*'s sheer weight.*)

DOUGLAS (*genuinely alarmed*): Oh, my goodness, what is it, a whale?

TRUDY: No, it's Sharon …

(*There is a great deal of frenzied threshing about under the water. Rather like an old Johnny Weissmuller film.* TRUDY *and* DOUGLAS *watch, unable to do much else.*)

TRUDY (*during this, vainly*): Sharon … Vic …

DOUGLAS (*likewise*): Vic … Sharon …

(*The waters finally still.* SHARON *comes up for air and props herself against the side of the pool, breathlessly and strangely happy.* TRUDY *and* DOUGLAS *approach her cautiously.*)

TRUDY: Sharon …?

DOUGLAS: Sharon …?

TRUDY: Are you all right?

SHARON (*gathering enough breath to speak*): Yes, thank you, Mrs Parks …

DOUGLAS (*trying to calm her desperate breathing*): Easy. Easy now …

TRUDY (*a sudden thought*): Sharon, where is Mr Parks?

SHARON (*apologetically*): I'm standing on him, Mrs Parks.

(TRUDY *and* DOUGLAS *react with alarm.*)

DOUGLAS: Sharon, for goodness sake …

TRUDY (*with* DOUGLAS): For God's sake, get off him …

(*Together, they start to haul* SHARON *out of the water.*)

SHARON (*as they do so*): I'm very sorry, Mrs Parks …

TRUDY: All right, Sharon, all right. Out you come now.

(*They land her on the poolside like a large, beached mammal.* VIC *floats to the surface. Unconscious or worse.* SHARON *lies panting while* TRUDY *and* DOUGLAS *pull* VIC *from the water.*)

(*To* DOUGLAS) Turn him over, we must get the water out of him …

DOUGLAS: Right.

(*They turn* VIC *over.*)

SHARON (*as they do so*): Can I give him the kiss of life, Mrs Parks ... ?

TRUDY: No, you can't, Sharon. Stay there, please.

(*She and* DOUGLAS *try to work on* VIC *rather ineffectually.*)

I don't know what you do. I think you have to pump his ribs somehow …

DOUGLAS: I'm afraid I don't really have much of an idea … Me and water, you know …

SHARON (*heaving herself up*): Here, let me …

TRUDY: No, Sharon, I'd rather you …

SHARON: It's all right, Mrs Parks, I've got my life-saver's medal.

TRUDY (*rather surprised*): You have?

SHARON: In the Huddersfield baths. Here, let me …

(SHARON *takes over from* TRUDY *and* DOUGLAS. *She sits astride* VIC *and pumps away vigorously.* TRUDY *and* DOUGLAS *watch her anxiously.*)

TRUDY: Anything ...?

SHARON: No, I don't think he's … He's not responding.

TRUDY: Oh, God.

SHARON: Hang on.

(*She rolls* VIC *over and tries the kiss of life a couple of times. There is no response.*)

TRUDY (*anxiously*): No?

SHARON: No. I'm sorry, Mrs Parks, I … (*Starting to cry as the realization finally hits her.*) I'm sorry. I'm ever so sorry …

(*She kneels weeping again. A silence.*)

First reaction

6 How do you feel about Vic's death? Is Sharon guilty of murder?

Close reading

The characters

7 What do the following lines suggest to you about the characters who say them?

Example: DOUGLAS: Some days I couldn't look at her at all. (line 114)
This suggests that Douglas is shy and perhaps rather afraid of women.

VIC

a Do you want to know the reason why you're sat there like a great bowl of pork dripping? Do you want to know the reason? Because you are overweight, girl. You are fat. (lines 26–9)
b I said, mind your own bloody business! (line 69)
c Let the stupid cow drown herself, what do I care? (line 372)
d I'm not diving in there. Not in these clothes. (line 380)
e We could sprinkle rum babas on the surface, that'll bring her up … (lines 388–9)
f Right. There is about to be some serious damage done … (lines 436–7)

SHARON

g Yes, Mr Parks. (line 37)
h (*Muttering*) Twelve rum babas. (line 45)
i I'm going to kill myself, Mrs Parks. (line 291)
j I don't know what I've done …. What have I done wrong, Mrs Parks? (lines 323–4)
k (*unhappily*) No, Mr Parks …. (line 363)
l (*apologetically*) I'm standing on him, Mrs Parks. (line 463)

8 Find lines in the text which could be used to illustrate the following comments on the characters.

DOUGLAS

a He is a courageous man, prepared to take action against injustice.

____

b He is a modest, reasonable man, who knows what he is capable of and what is beyond him.

____

c He is good at sympathising with other people – imagining what they are thinking and feeling.

____

d He tends to undervalue himself.

____

TRUDY

e She is sick of her husband.

____

f She seems to admire Douglas.

____

g She has become cynical about people.

____

Do you have any further comments on the characters? Cite lines that support your opinions.

9 Look at the stage direction at lines 217–21 (DOUGLAS *waits. ... it hasn't happened*), and Douglas's next speech (lines 222–4).

a Why doesn't Trudy finish her sentence?
1 Because she is in distress.
2 She has forgotten what she wants to say.
3 She feels that what she has to say is beyond words.
4 She is enjoying her romantic memories.
5 Another reason – your own interpretation: ________________

b Why does Trudy rock about?
1 She is moving to the rhythm of the music.
2 She is in distress, and this is a way of calming herself.
3 She is reverting to childhood.
4 It is an expression of frustrated emotion.
5 Another reason – your own interpretation: ________________

c Why does Trudy kiss Douglas on the mouth?
1 She is in love with him.
2 She wants to seduce him.
3 It is a way of releasing her emotion.
4 It is her way of expressing her admiration for him.
5 Another reason – your own interpretation: ________________

d What kind of look would Douglas give her after the kiss (line 219)?
1 Astonished.
2 Puzzled.
3 Romantic.
4 Frightened.
5 Your own interpretation: ________________________

e Why do they pretend it hasn't happened?
1 Because they are afraid of their emotions.
2 They realise it was a momentary aberration.
3 They know that their love is impossible.

4 They are afraid someone may be watching them.
5 Another reason – your own interpretation: ______________________

f Why does Douglas start talking about country and western music? Write your own interpretation: ______________________

10 Why does Trudy start to weep after Douglas goes (lines 275–7)? Write a set of alternative interpretations like the ones in Exercise 9, and ask another student to choose one. Compare your answers. Is there a single correct answer, do you think?

Language practice – structures

Interrupted sentences

11 Ayckbourn's dialogue (like real dialogue in everyday life) frequently contains incomplete sentences, where one character interrupts another, or one thought interrupts another. Here are some examples for you to complete as if the character had not been interrupted. (Note: to do this, you need to read each line in its context.)

a Line 9 — SHARON: I've got to go and –
b Line 31 — DOUGLAS: Oh, I don't think that's fair, she's just …
c Line 67 — DOUGLAS: It is cruel and it is hurtful and it is –
d Line 89 — DOUGLAS: No, I –
e Line 184 — TRUDY: But did she never say to you …?
f Line 205 — DOUGLAS: He treated Nerys like –
g Line 206 — DOUGLAS: Well, there were times when –
h Line 215 — TRUDY: We used to …
i Line 215 — TRUDY: When we were …
j Line 228 — TRUDY: Money or …
k Line 230 — TRUDY: Sorry. I didn't mean to –
l Line 239 — TRUDY: You're welcome to stop and have dinner with us if you –
m Line 248 — TRUDY: Well …
n Line 259 — TRUDY: Anything we –
o Line 398 — TRUDY: If that girl dies …
p Line 433 — TRUDY: He's in the …
q Line 444 — VIC: As soon as I've …
r Line 485 — SHARON: Here, let me …
s Line 486 — TRUDY: No, Sharon, I'd rather you …
t Line 500 — SHARON: I'm sorry, Mrs Parks, I …

12 A sentence in English can take three possible forms: statement, command or question. It is sometimes claimed that the most aggressive, 'macho' forms are the command and the statement, and that the mildest, most non-aggressive form is the question.

a What do you think of this idea?
b Which form would you expect Vic to use most frequently – command, statement or question?
c Look at lines 1–103 (where Vic humiliates Sharon). Write C for command, S for statement and Q for question next to each sentence spoken by Vic, then count up the three totals. Which is highest?
d Can you explain this result? How does Vic use language to bully Sharon?

Language practice – vocabulary

The language of personal criticism

13 Here are some words which might be used to describe Vic. Match each one with words of similar meaning from the box below.

cruel vain vulgar hypocritical

self-obsessed crude hard-hearted vicious proud insincere tyrannical sadistic coarse brutal loud conceited sanctimonious egocentric unfeeling

14 Imagine that Sharon is suddenly in a position of power over Vic, with the chance to humiliate him in the same way that he has humiliated her in lines 1–103. She can accuse him of whatever she chooses – cruelty, sadism, emotional inadequacy, vulgarity, hypocrisy …

Re-write the dialogue from lines 16 to 60, but with Sharon making the accusations. Use the same grammatical forms as the original, but adapt the vocabulary to the new situation. Use a dictionary to help you if necessary.

Extension

15 Write a short monologue (10 lines) expressing either Trudy's or Douglas's thoughts at the point where Trudy kisses him (line 219).

16 Design a publicity poster for a production of *Man of the Moment*, based on this extract from the play (see Chapter 1, Publicity, p 20).

17 Write a letter from Douglas to his wife describing what has happened today.

18 **Group work**: make a stage design for *Man of the Moment* based on this extract, taking into account everything that happens in it.

Beyond the Text

19 Look at lines 217–21 and 275–7, where Trudy kisses Douglas, then cries alone in the dark [Exercises 9–10 focus on these]. These are examples of 'body language' – movements, actions and gestures that are full of meaning even though no words are spoken. Here are some more examples from the play. Next to each, write down what meaning you think it might have.

ACTION	MEANING
Kenny clears his throat (line 76)	________________
Trudy stares after him (line 273)	________________
Sharon looks towards the house (line 286)	________________
Vic points at Douglas and Trudy (line 437)	________________
Sharon kneels (line 502)	________________

20 **Group / pair work**

a Make a list of some other common examples of body language from everyday life. Ask your partner to interpret their possible meanings.

b Think of some meanings and ask others to invent body language to express them.

21 Playwrights, directors and actors often use actions as dramatic **symbols**. Tennessee Williams does this in *A Streetcar Named Desire* (see Chapter 6, Exercise 6), and Alan Ayckbourn does it at line 103, where 'Kenny nods'. Notice that this is not just 'body language' (a way of saying yes) but a symbol of something much bigger – human conformity, feebleness, acceptance of bullying, etc. There are two meanings to this action – a **literal** meaning, and a **symbolic** meaning.

Now read this short play by Samuel Beckett, which communicates its meaning entirely through body language and symbolic action.

Act Without Words II (1956/1960) Samuel Beckett

See the Glossary section at the back of the book for vocabulary.

NOTE

This mime should be played on a low and narrow platform at back of stage, violently lit in its entire length, the rest of the stage being in darkness. Frieze effect.

A is slow, awkward (gags dressing and undressing), absent. B brisk, rapid, precise. The two actions therefore, though B has more to do than A, should have approximately the same duration.

ARGUMENT

Beside each other on ground, two yards from right wing, two sacks, A's and B's, A's being to right (as seen from auditorium) of B's, i.e. nearer right wing. On ground beside sack B a little pile of clothes (C) neatly folded (coat and trousers surmounted by boots and hat).

Enter goad right, strictly horizontal. The point stops a foot short of sack A. Pause. The point draws back, pauses, darts forward into sack, withdraws, recoils to a foot short of sack. Pause. The sack does not move. The point draws back again, a little further than before, pauses, darts forward again into sack, withdraws, recoils to a foot short of sack. Pause. The sack moves. Exit goad.

A, wearing shirt, crawls out of sack, halts, broods, prays, broods, gets to his feet, broods, takes a little bottle of pills from his shirt pocket, broods, swallows a pill, puts bottle back, broods, goes to clothes, broods, puts on clothes, broods, takes a large partly-eaten carrot from coat pocket, bites off a piece, chews an instant, spits it out with disgust, puts carrot back, broods, picks up two sacks, carries them bowed and staggering half-way to left wing, sets them down, broods, takes off clothes (except shirt), lets them fall in an untidy heap, broods, takes another pill, broods, kneels, prays, crawls into sack and lies still, sack A being now to left of sack B.

Pause.

Enter goad right on wheeled support (one wheel). The point stops a foot short of sack B. Pause. The point draws back, pauses, darts forward into sack, withdraws, recoils to a foot short of sack. Pause. The sack moves. Exit goad.

B, wearing shirt, crawls out of sack, gets to his feet, takes from shirt pocket and consults a large watch, puts watch back, does exercise, consults watch, takes a tooth brush from shirt pocket and brushes teeth vigorously, puts brush back, rubs scalp vigorously, takes a comb from shirt pocket and combs hair, puts comb back, consults watch, goes to clothes, puts them on, consults watch, takes a brush from coat pocket and brushes clothes vigorously, brushes hair vigorously, puts brush back, takes a little mirror from coat pocket and inspects appearance, puts mirror back, takes carrot from coat pocket, bites off a piece, chews and swallows with appetite, puts carrot back, consults watch, takes a map from coat pocket and consults it, puts map back, consults watch, takes a compass from coat pocket and consults it, puts compass back, consults watch, picks up two sacks and carries them bowed and staggering to two yards short of left wing, sets them down, consults watch, takes off clothes (except shirt), folds them in a neat pile, consults watch, does exercises, consults watch, rubs scalp, combs hair, brushes teeth, consults and winds watch, crawls into sack and lies still, sack B being now to left of sack A as originally.

Pause.

Enter goad right on wheeled support (two wheels). The point stops a foot short of sack A. Pause. The point draws back, pauses, darts forward into sack, withdraws, recoils to a foot short of sack. Pause. The sack does not move. The point draws back again, a little further than before, pauses, darts forward again into sack, withdraws, recoils to a foot short of sack. Pause. The sack moves. Exit goad.

A crawls out of sack, halts, broods, prays.

CURTAIN

POSITION I

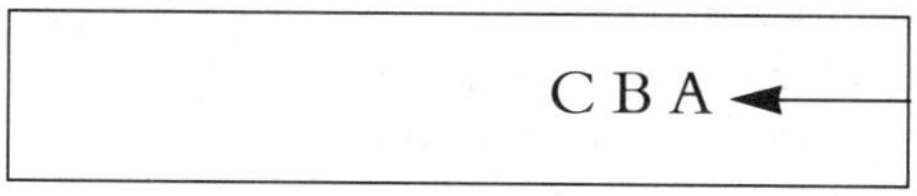

POSITION II

POSITION III

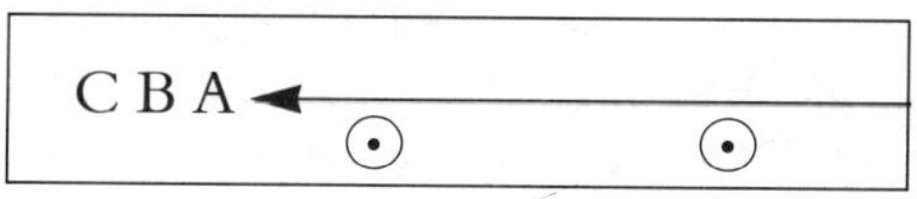

STAGE FRONT

22 What meanings would you give to the following actions?
- *a* B consults his watch
- *b* A swallows a pill
- *c* B does exercises
- *d* B consults a map
- *e* A leaves the clothes in an untidy heap
- *f* B folds the clothes in a neat pile
- *g* A and B share the clothes
- *h* A broods
- *i* A and B move each other and their sacks across the stage

Discuss your interpretations with other students. Which of your interpretations were literal and which symbolic?

23 What symbolic meaning would you give to the following actions?
- *a* the goad darting into the sacks
- *b* A needing two prods from the goad to wake up, while B needs only one

24 What does the play as a whole suggest to you about human life?

25 **Group work**: write or perform your own 'play without words' for other members of the class. Ask them to interpret its meaning. Does it have the same meaning for you as for them?

Authors

Alan Ayckbourn was born in London in 1939 and went straight into the theatre as a stage manager after leaving school. He is now a full-time theatre director, working both at the Royal National Theatre in London and at the Stephen Joseph Theatre in the Round, Scarborough. He has written over 50 comedies, many of them works of startling technical ingenuity with surprising quantities of pain and sorrow in them. He is one of the world's most commercially successful dramatists, and has demonstrated over a long and constantly evolving career that it is possible to be both a popular and a serious artist. He has been called 'wildly funny and deeply tragic', 'a left-wing writer using a right-wing form', and 'the most acute analyst of contemporary British society', although he occasionally insists that his only intention is to entertain. Other plays include *Absurd Person Singular*, *Intimate Exchanges* (a series of plays with sixteen different endings, all with the same main characters and opening scene), *Woman In Mind*, and *A Small Family Business*. His life and views are entertainingly recorded in *Conversations with Ayckbourn* by Ian Watson.

Samuel Beckett (1906–89) was born and educated in Ireland, although he spent most of his adult life in France. He wrote both novels and plays in French and English, and translated his own works from one language to the other. His best-known play is *Waiting for Godot* (1952), in which two men wait by a roadside for someone who never arrives. Although very little seems to happen in the play, it is generally regarded as one of the most important texts in 20th century world literature – expressing, among other things, the spiritual loneliness of life in a sceptical, post-religious age. Other plays include *Endgame* (1957), *Krapp's Last Tape* (1958), *Happy Days* (1961), and several works for radio. Beckett's works are abstract, puzzling, symbolic, and filled with subtle philosophical and theological references. They show characters in bleak, extreme situations, yet they often manage to be comic, popular and – as one critic put it – 'curiously exhilarating'. Beckett avoided publicity, never gave interviews to journalists, and although he accepted the Nobel Prize for Literature in 1969, would not go to Stockholm to receive it. Despite his reputation as a frightening and austere recluse (reinforced by his writings and rather severe appearance in photographs), personal reminiscences show him to have been a man of great courage, warmth and kindness. There are biographies of Beckett by Vivian Mercier (*Beckett/Beckett*) and Dierdre Bair.

8 Making History

Before you read

1 *The Plough and the Stars* is set in Dublin in 1916, at the time of a rebellion by Irish nationalists against the British government.

Imagine that you are a film director. You have been asked to make a short film (say, 20 minutes long) about the rebellion. Use the historical material given here to plan your film.

Since 1800 England had governed Ireland directly from Westminster, with growing Irish resentment. Especially after the famine years of the 1840s many Irish people felt that only the Irish could, and should, handle Ireland's problems. Attempts to win political freedom through Parliament failed because the small presence of Irish MPs could never win the support of enough sympathetic English MPs.

Then in 1910 the General Election produced a 'hung' Parliament (that is, no party had an absolute majority). The Liberals could only stay in power by the consent of the Irish Nationalist Party. And the price of Irish co-operation was a 'Home Rule' Bill, granting Ireland a measure of independence. This aroused fierce opposition in the ancient province of Ulster, where, 300 years before, large groups of Scots and Irish had planted themselves after driving out the native Irish. These Protestants were concentrated in the six north-eastern counties of Ulster and outnumbered the Catholic Irish by about three to two. In September 1912 half a million signed, some in their own blood, a solemn pledge 'never to recognise a Dublin Parliament'. In 1913, 100,000 Ulstermen joined the para-military Ulster Volunteers who trained daily for war.

Ulster's resistance to Home Rule was supported by the Conservative Party and by the army. It became clear to the British Prime Minister, Asquith, that he would not be able to force the Ulster Protestants to accept home rule, and he promised to make special arrangements for Ulster.

Southern Ireland was outraged at this. 'Irish Nationalists can never agree to the mutilation of the Irish nation,' declared their leader, John Redmond. The scholar Eoin MacNeill promptly raised the Irish Volunteers, who drew thousands to their ranks, including many secret members of the Irish Republican Brotherhood (known as Fenians), who were dedicated to overthrowing the English occupation by armed revolt. Civil war was only averted by the outbreak of war against Germany in 1914.

John Redmond urged the Irish Volunteers to fight for England in the war, and 170,000 were soon in France alongside English soldiers. The remaining 10,000, including the more militant Nationalists, broke away under MacNeill.

An old Fenian saying is 'England's difficulties are Ireland's opportunities'. In 1916 German victory seemed possible. The timing for a revolt seemed perfect. The Uprising was arranged for Easter Sunday, 23 April. Plans went wrong from the start. When a German ship carrying arms was captured by the British navy off the Irish coast, MacNeill ordered the Volunteers to stay at home on Easter Sunday. The Irish Republican Brotherhood ordered the Volunteers to come out on Easter Monday instead. So, when Patrick Pearse declared the Irish Republic from the steps of the General Post Office in Dublin, the contradictory orders resulted in only 1600 Volunteers coming out – most of them in Dublin. But the surprise was complete, because only days before, British Security in Dublin reported that the Irish were 'sound and loyal'. Irish people too were stunned and shocked. Most supported England's war effort and looked forward to Home Rule, which England promised after the war was over.

For a week the Volunteers fought professional English soldiers with courage and tenacity. Outgunned and outnumbered by over 20 to 1, Pearse surrendered. Civilians suffered over three-quarters of the 3000 casualties. As Dubliners looked at their devastated city they felt a deep resentment at the folly of the Volunteers. When the Volunteers were led off to captivity the streets were lined by sullen and angry citizens who jeered and taunted them. The prisoners would have been assaulted if the English soldiers had not been present. The Irish bishops denounced the Uprising: 'a senseless, meaningless debauch of blood ... treachery to our native land'. Pearse realised the revolutionaries must endure hatred from Irish people for a time; attitudes, he believed, would change once the Irish came to understand the reasons.

After the Uprising General Maxwell was sent to govern Ireland. To him the issue was clear: subjects of the Crown had rebelled during a national crisis when thousands of their fellow Irishmen were doing their duty in France. Gradually it dawned on Dubliners that sinister events were taking place. On 2 May a priest and relatives of Pearse, Tom Clark and Thomas MacDonagh (three of the leaders of the rebellion) were summoned by the military authorities. Next morning a terse message announced the execution of these three Volunteers.

Twelve other executions followed in the next ten days. What really horrified the Irish were the secret trials, the randomness of the executions and the clear innocence of several of the executed. After the fifteenth execution a Dublin woman wrote, 'It was like watching a stream of blood coming from under a closed door.' The Bishop of Limerick wrote to Maxwell: 'Personally, I regard your action with horror and I believe it has outraged the conscience of the country.' In the House of Commons the deputy-leader of the Irish Nationalists warned, 'You are letting loose a river of blood.'

On 12 May Asquith visited Dublin. There had been two executions that morning – and Ireland was seething with outrage. Asquith stopped further shootings, and soon after offered Home Rule to Southern Ireland (though not to Ulster) to take immediate effect.

(Adapted from Michael Hodges, *Ireland from Easter Uprising to Civil War*, Batsford 1987)

Note: some eyewitness accounts of the uprising can be found in the Extension section of this chapter, Exercise 18.

The Plough and the Stars (1926) Sean O'Casey

See the Glossary section at the back of the book for vocabulary.

ACT 3

The corner house in a street of tenements: it is the home of the Clitheroes. The house is a long, gaunt five-story tenement; its brick front is chipped and scarred with age and neglect. The wide and heavy hall door, flanked by two pillars, has a look of having been charred by a fire in the distant past. The door lurches a little to one side, disjointed by the continual and reckless banging when it is being closed by most of the residents. The diamond-paned fanlight is destitute of a single pane, the frame-work alone remaining. The windows, except the two looking into the front parlour (Clitheroe's room), are grimy, and are draped with fluttering and soiled fragments of lace curtains. The front parlour windows are hung with rich, comparatively, casement cloth. Five stone steps lead from the door to the path on the street. Branching on each side are railings to prevent people from falling into the area. At the left corner of the house runs a narrow lane, bisecting the street, and connecting it with another of the same kind. At the corner of the lane is a street lamp.

As the house is revealed, MRS GOGAN *is seen helping* MOLLSER *to a chair, which stands on the path beside the railings, at the left side of the steps. She then wraps a shawl around* MOLLSER*'s shoulders. It is some months later [than in Act 2].*

MRS GOGAN (*arranging shawl around* MOLLSER): Th' sun'll do you all th' good in th' world. A few more weeks o' this weather, an' there's no knowin' how well you'll be. … Are you comfy, now?

MOLLSER (*weakly and wearily*): Yis, ma; I'm all right.

MRS GOGAN: How are you feelin'?

MOLLSER: Betther, ma, betther. If th' horrible sinkin' feelin' ud go, I'd be all right.

MRS GOGAN: Ah, I wouldn't put much pass on that. Your stomach maybe's out of ordher. … Is th' poor breathin' any betther, d'ye think?

MOLLSER: Yis, yis, ma; a lot betther.

MRS GOGAN: Well, that's somethin' anyhow. … With th' help o' God, you'll be on th' mend from this out. … D'your legs feel any sthronger undher you, d'ye think?

MOLLSER (*irritably*): I can't tell, ma. I think so. … A little.

MRS GOGAN: Well, a little aself is somethin'. … I thought I heard you coughin' a little more than usual last night. … D'ye think you were?

MOLLSER: I wasn't, ma, I wasn't.

MRS GOGAN: I thought I heard you, for I was kep' awake all night with th' shootin'. An' thinkin' o' that madman, Fluther, runnin' about through th' night lookin' for Nora Clitheroe to bring her back when he heard she'd gone to folly her husband, an' in dhread any minute he might come staggerin' in covered with bandages, splashed all over with th' red of his own blood, an' givin' us barely time to bring th' priest to hear th' last whisper of his final confession, as his soul was passin' through th' dark doorway o' death into th' way o' th' wondherin' dead. … You don't feel cold, do you?

MOLLSER: No, ma; I'm all right.

MRS GOGAN: Keep your chest well covered, for that's th' delicate spot in you … if there's any danger, I'll whip you in again. … (*Looking up the street*) Oh, here's th' Covey an' oul' Pether hurryin' along. God Almighty, sthrange things is happenin' when them two is pullin' together.

(THE COVEY *and* PETER *come in, breathless and excited.*)

MRS GOGAN (*to the two men*): Were yous far up th' town? Did yous see any sign o' Fluther or Nora? How is things lookin'? I hear they're blazin' away out o' th' G.P.O. That th' Tommies is sthretched in heaps around Nelson's Pillar an' th' Parnell Statue, an' that th' pavin' sets in O'Connell Street is nearly covered be pools o' blood.

PETER: We seen no sign o' Nora or Fluther anywhere.

MRS GOGAN: We should ha' held her back be main force from goin' to look for her husband. … God knows what's happened to her – I'm always seein' her sthretched on her back in some hospital, moanin' with th' pain of a bullet in her vitals, an' nuns thryin' to get her to take a last look at th' crucifix!

THE COVEY: We can do nothin'. You can't stick your nose into O'Connell Street, an' Tyler's is on fire.

PETER: An' we seen th' Lancers –

THE COVEY (*interrupting*): Throttin' along, heads in th' air: spurs an' sabres jinglin', an' lances quiverin', an' lookin' as if they were assin' themselves, "Where's these blighters, till we get a prod at them?" when there was a volley from th' Post Office that stretched half o'them, an' sent th' rest gallopin' away wondherin' how far they'd have to go before they'd feel safe.

PETER (*rubbing his hands*): 'Damn it,' says I to meself, 'this looks like business!'

THE COVEY: An' then out comes General Pearse an' his staff, an', standin' in th' middle o' th' street, he reads th' Proclamation.

MRS GOGAN: What proclamation?

PETER: Declarin' an Irish Republic.

MRS GOGAN: Go to God!

PETER: The gunboat *Helga*'s shellin' Liberty Hall, an' I hear the people livin' on th' quays had to crawl on their bellies to Mass with th' bullets that were flyin' around from Boland's Mills.

MRS GOGAN: God bless us, what's goin' to be th' end of it all!

BESSIE (*looking out of the top window*): Maybe yous are satisfied now; maybe yous are satisfied now. Go on an' get guns if yous are men – Johnny get your gun, get your gun, get your gun! Yous are all nicely shanghaied now; th' boyo hasn't a sword on his thigh now! Oh, yous are all nicely shanghaied now!

MRS GOGAN (*warningly to* PETER *and* THE COVEY): S–s–sh, don't answer her. She's th' right oul' Orange bitch! She's been chantin' 'Rule, Britannia' all th' mornin'.

PETER: I hope Fluther hasn't met with any accident, he's such a wild card.

MRS GOGAN: God grant it; but last night I dreamt I seen gettin' carried into th' house a sthretcher with a figure lyin' on it, stiff an' still, dhressed in th' habit of Saint Francis. An, then, I heard th' murmurs of a crowd no one could see sayin' th' litany for th' dead; an' then it got so dark that nothin' was seen but th' white face of th' corpse, gleamin' like a white wather-lily floatin' on th' top of a dark lake. Then a tiny whisper thrickled into me ear, sayin', 'Isn't the face very like th' face o' Fluther?' an' then, with a thremblin' flutther, th' dead lips opened, an', although I couldn't hear, I knew they were sayin', 'Poor oul' Fluther, afther havin' handed in his gun at last, his shakin' soul moored in th' place where th' wicked are at rest an' th' weary cease from throublin'.'

PETER (*who has put on a pair of spectacles, and has been looking down the street*): Here they are, be God, here they are; just afther turnin' th' corner – Nora an' Fluther!

THE COVEY: She must be wounded or something – he seems to be carryin' her.

What is the mood of this opening? Do you think that things will turn out well or badly?

(FLUTHER *and* NORA *enter.* FLUTHER *has his arm around her and is half leading, half carrying her in. Her eyes are dim and hollow, her face pale and strained-looking; her hair is tossed, and her clothes are dusty.*)

MRS GOGAN (*running over to them*): God bless us, is it wounded y'are, Mrs Clitheroe, or what?

FLUTHER: Ah, she's all right, Mrs Gogan; only worn out from thravellin' an' want o' sleep. A night's rest, now, an' she'll be as fit as a fiddle. Bring her in, an' make her lie down.

MRS GOGAN (*to* NORA): Did you hear e'er a whisper o' Mr Clitheroe?

NORA (*wearily*): I could find him nowhere, Mrs Gogan. None o' them would tell me where he was. They told me I shamed my husband an' th' women of Ireland be carryin' on as I was. ... They said th' women must learn to be brave an' cease to be cowardly. ... Me who risked more for love than they would risk for hate. ... (*Raising her voice in hysterical protest*) My Jack will be killed, my Jack will be killed! ... He is to be butchered as a sacrifice to th' dead!

BESSIE (*from upper window*): Yous are all nicely shanghaied now! Sorra mend th' lasses that have been kissin' an' cuddlin' their boys into th' sheddin' of blood! ... Fillin' their minds with fairy tales that had no beginnin', but, please God, 'll have a bloody quick endin'! ... Turnin' bitther into sweet, an' sweet into bitther. ... Stabbin' in th' back th' men that are dyin' in th' threnches for them! It's a bad thing for any one that thries to jilt th' Ten Commandments, for judgements are prepared for scorners an' sthripes for th' back o' fools! (*Going away from window as she sings:*)

Rule, Britannia, Britannia rules th' waves,
Britons never, never, never shall be slaves!

FLUTHER (*with a roar up at the window*): Y'ignorant oul' throllope, you!

MRS GOGAN (*to* NORA): He'll come home safe enough to you, you'll find, Mrs Clitheroe; afther all, there's a power o' women that's handed over sons an' husbands to take a runnin' risk in th' fight they're wagin'.

NORA: I can't help thinkin' every shot fired'll be fired at Jack, an' every shot fired at Jack'll be fired at me. What do I care for th' others? I can think only of me own self. ... An' there's no woman gives a son or a husband to be killed – if they say it, they're lyin', lyin', against God, Nature, an' against themselves! ... One blasted hussy at a barricade told me to go home an' not be thryin' to dishearten th' men. ... That I wasn't worthy to bear a son to a man that was out fightin' for freedom. ... I clawed at her, an' smashed her in th' face till we were separated. ... I was pushed down th' street, an' I cursed them – cursed the rebel ruffians an' Volunteers that had dhragged me ravin' mad into th' sthreets to seek me husband!

PETER: You'll have to have patience, Nora. We all have to put up with twarthers an' tormentors in this world.

THE COVEY: If they were fightin' for anything worth while, I wouldn't mind.

FLUTHER (*to* NORA): Nothin' derogatory'll happen to Mr Clitheroe. You'll find, now, in th' finish up it'll be vice versa.

NORA: Oh, I know that wherever he is, he's thinkin' of wantin' to be with me. I know he's longin' to be passin' his hand through me hair, to be caressin' me neck, to fondle me hand an' to feel me kisses clingin' to his mouth. ... An' he stands wherever he is because he's brave? (*Vehemently*) No, but because he's a coward, a coward, a coward!

MRS GOGAN: Oh, they're not cowards anyway.

NORA (*with denunciatory anger*): I tell you they're afraid to say they're afraid! ... Oh, I saw it, I saw it, Mrs Gogan. ... At th' barricade in North King Street I saw fear glowin' in all their eyes. ... An' in th' middle o' th' sthreet was somethin' huddled up in a horrible tangled heap. ... His face was jammed again th' stones, an' his arm was twisted round his back. ... An' every twist of his body was a cry against th' terrible thing that had happened to him. ... An' I saw they were afraid to look at it. ... An' some o' them laughed at me, but th' laugh was a frightened one. ... An' some o' them shouted at me, but th' shout had in it th' shiver o' fear. ... I tell you they were afraid, afraid, afraid!

MRS GOGAN (*leading her towards the house*): Come on in, dear. If you'd been a little longer together, th' wrench asundher wouldn't have been so sharp.

NORA: Th' agony I'm in since he left me has thrust away every rough thing he done, an' every unkind word he spoke; only th' blossoms that grew out of our lives are before me now; shakin' their colours before me face, an' breathin' their sweet scent on every thought springin' up in me mind, till, sometimes, Mrs Gogan, sometimes I think I'm goin' mad!

MRS GOGAN: You'll be a lot betther when you have a little lie down.

NORA (*turning towards* FLUTHER *as she is going in*): I don't know what I'd have done, only for Fluther. I'd have been lyin' in th' streets, only for him. ... (*As she goes in*) They have dhriven away th' little happiness life had to spare for me. He has gone from me for ever, for ever. ... Oh, Jack, Jack, Jack!

How do you react to Nora's fears for her husband?

(*She is led in by* MRS GOGAN *as* BESSIE *comes out with a shawl around her shoulders. She passes by them with her head in the air. When they have gone in, she gives a mug of milk to* MOLLSER *silently.*)

FLUTHER: Which of yous has th' tossers?

THE COVEY: I have.

BESSIE (*as she is passing them to go down the street*): You an' your Leadhers an' their sham-battle soldiers has landed a body in a nice way, havin' to go an' ferret out a bit o' bread God knows where. ... Why aren't yous in th' G.P.O. if yous are men? It's paler an' paler yous are gettin'. ... A lot o' vipers, that's what th' Irish people is!

(*She goes out.*)

FLUTHER: Never mind her. ... (*To* THE COVEY) Make a start an' keep us from th' sin o' idleness. (*To* MOLLSER) Well, how are you to-day, Mollser, oul' son? What are you dhrinkin', milk?

MOLLSER: Grand, Fluther, grand, thanks. Yis, milk.

FLUTHER: You couldn't get a betther thing down you. ... This turn-up has done one good thing, anyhow; you can't get dhrink anywhere, an' if it lasts a week, I'll be so used to it that I won't think of a pint.

THE COVEY (*who has taken from his pocket two worn coins and a thin strip of wood about four inches long*): What's th' bettin'?

PETER: Heads, a juice.

FLUTHER: Harps, a tanner.

(THE COVEY *places the coins on the strip of wood, and flips them up into the air. As they jingle on the ground the distant boom of a big gun is heard. They stand for a moment listening.*)

> *What effect do you imagine this sudden 'boom of a big gun' would have on an audience in the theatre?*

FLUTHER: What th' hell's that?

THE COVEY: It's like th' boom of a big gun!

FLUTHER: Surely to God they're not goin' to use artillery on us?

THE COVEY (*scornfully*): Not goin'! (*Vehemently*) Wouldn't they use anything on us, man?

FLUTHER: Aw, holy Christ, that's not playin' th' game!

PETER (*plaintively*): What would happen if a shell landed here now?

THE COVEY (*ironically*): You'd be off to heaven in a fiery chariot.

PETER: In spite of all th' warnin's that's ringin' around us, are you going' to start your pickin' at me again?

FLUTHER: Go on, toss them again, toss them again. … Harps, a tanner.

PETER: Heads, a juice.

(THE COVEY *tosses the coins.*)

FLUTHER (*as the coins fall*): Let them roll, let them roll. Heads, be God!

(BESSIE *runs in excitedly. She has a new hat on her head, a fox fur round her neck over her shawl, three umbrellas under her right arm, and a box of biscuits under her left. She speaks rapidly and breathlessly.*)

BESSIE: They're breakin' into th' shops, they're breakin' into th' shops! Smashin' th' windows, battherin' in th' doors, an' whippin' away everything! An' th' Volunteers is firin' on them. I seen two men an' a lassie pushin' a piano down th' sthreet, an' th' sweat rollin' off them thryin' to get it up on th' pavement; an' an oul' wan that must ha' been seventy lookin' as if she'd dhrop every minute with th' dint o' heart beatin', thryin' to pull a big double bed out of a broken shop-window! I was goin' to wait till I dhressed meself from th' skin out.

MOLLSER (*to* BESSIE, *as she is going in*): Help me in, Bessie: I'm feelin' curious.

(BESSIE *leaves the looted things in the house, and, rapidly returning, helps* MOLLSER *in.*)

THE COVEY: Th' selfishness of that one – she waited till she got all she could carry before she'd come to tell anyone!

FLUTHER (*running over to the door of the house and shouting in to* BESSIE): Ay, Bessie, did you hear of e'er a pub gettin' a shake up?

BESSIE (*inside*): I didn't hear o' none.

FLUTHER (*in a burst of enthusiasm*): Well, you're goin' to hear of one soon!

What is the mood now?

THE COVEY: Come on, man, an' don't be wastin' time.

PETER (*to them as they are about to run off*): Ay, ay, are you goin' to leave me here?

FLUTHER: Are you goin' to leave yourself here?

PETER (*anxiously*): Didn't yous hear her sayin' they were firin' on them?

THE COVEY and FLUTHER (*together*): Well?

PETER: Supposin' I happened to be potted?

FLUTHER: We'd give you a Christian burial, anyhow.

THE COVEY (*ironically*): Dhressed up in your regimentals.

PETER (*to* THE COVEY, *passionately*): May th' all-lovin' God give you a hot knock one o' these days, me young Covey, tuthorin' Fluther up now to be tiltin' at me, an' crossin' me with his mockeries an' jibin'!

(*A fashionably dressed, middle-aged, stout woman comes hurriedly in, and makes for the group. She is almost fainting with fear.*)

THE WOMAN: For Gawd's sake, will one of you kind men show any safe way for me to get to Wrathmines? ... I was foolish enough to visit a friend, thinking the howl thing was a joke, and now I cawn't get a car or a tram to take me home – isn't it awful?

FLUTHER: I'm afraid, ma'am, one way is as safe as another.

WOMAN: And what am I gowing to do? Oh, isn't this awful? ... I'm so different from others. ... The mowment I hear a shot, my legs give way under me – I cawn't stir, I'm paralysed – isn't it awful?

FLUTHER (*moving away*): It's a derogatory way to be, right enough, ma'am.

WOMAN (*catching* FLUTHER*'s coat*): Creeping along the street there, with my head down and my eyes half shut, a bullet whizzed past within an inch of my nowse. ... I had to lean against the wall for a long time, gasping for breath – I nearly passed away – it was awful! ... I wonder, would you kind men come some of the way and see me safe?

FLUTHER: I have to go away, ma'am, to thry an' save a few things from th' burnin' buildin's.

THE COVEY: Come on, then, or there won't be anything left to save.

(THE COVEY *and* FLUTHER *hurry away.*)

WOMAN (*to* PETER): Wasn't it an awful thing for me to leave my friend's house? Wasn't it an idiotic thing to do? … I haven't the slightest idea where I am. … You have a kind face, sir. Could you possibly come and pilot me in the direction of Wrathmines?

PETER (*indignantly*): D'ye think I'm goin' to risk me life throttin' in front of you? An' maybe get a bullet that would gimme a game leg or something that would leave me a jibe an' a jeer to Fluther an' th' young Covey for th' rest o' me days!

(*With an indignant toss of his head he walks into the house.*)

THE WOMAN (*going out*): I know I'll fall down in a dead faint if I hear another shot go off anyway near me – isn't it awful!

What is your reaction to this woman? Is she ridiculous, pitiable, tragic – or what?

(MRS GOGAN *comes out of the house pushing a pram before her. As she enters the street,* BESSIE *rushes out, follows* MRS GOGAN, *and catches hold of the pram, stopping* MRS GOGAN*'s progress.*)

BESSIE: Here, where are you goin' with that? How quick you were, me lady, to clap your eyes on th' pram. … Maybe you don't know that Mrs Sullivan, before she went to spend Easther with her people in Dunboyne, gave me sthrict injunctions to give an accasional look to see if it was still standin' where it was left in th' corner of th' lobby.

MRS GOGAN: That remark of yours, Mrs Bessie Burgess, requires a little considheration, seein' that th' pram was left on our lobby, an' not on yours; a foot or two a little to th' left of th' jamb of me own room door; nor is it needful to mention th' name of th' person that gave a squint to see if it was there th' first thing in th' mornin', an' th' last thing in th' stillness o' th' night; never failin' to realize that her eyes couldn't be goin' wrong, be sthretchin' out her arm an' runnin' her hand over th' pram, to make sure that th' sight was no deception! Moreover, somethin's tellin' me that th' runnin' hurry of an inthrest you're takin' in it now is a sudden ambition to use th' pram for a purpose that a loyal woman of law an' ordher would stagger away from!

(*She gives the pram a sudden push that pulls* BESSIE *forward.*)

BESSIE (*still holding the pram*): There's not as much as one body in th' house that doesn't know that it wasn't Bessie Burgess that was always shakin' her voice complainin' about people leavin' bassinettes in th' way of them that, week in an' week out, had to pay their rent, an' always had to find a regular accommodation for her own furniture in her own room. … An' as for law an' ordher, puttin' aside th' harp an' shamrock, Bessie Burgess'll have as much respect as she wants for th' lion an' unicorn!

PETER (*appearing at the door*): I think I'll go with th' pair of yous an' see th' fun. A fella might as well chance it, anyhow.

MRS GOGAN (*taking no notice of* PETER, *and pushing the pram on another step*): Take your rovin' lumps o' hands from pattin' th' bassinette, if you please, ma'am; an', steppin' from th' threshold of good manners, let me tell you, Mrs Burgess, that it's a fat wondher to Jennie Gogan that a lady-like singer o' hymns like yourself would lower her thoughts from sky-thinkin' to sthretch out her arm in a sly-seekin' way to pinch anything dhriven asthray in th' confusion of th' battle our boys is makin' for th' freedom of their counthry!

PETER (*laughing and rubbing his hands together*): Hee, hee, hee, hee, hee! I'll go with th' pair o' yous an' give yous a hand.

MRS GOGAN (*with a rapid turn of her head as she shoves the pram forward*): Get up in th' prambulator an' we'll wheel you down.

BESSIE (*to* MRS GOGAN): Poverty an' hardship has sent Bessie Burgess to abide with sthrange company, but she always knew them she had to live with from backside to breakfast time; an' she can tell them, always havin' had a Christian kinch on her conscience, that a passion for thievin' an' pinchin' would find her soul a foreign place to live in, an' that her present intention is quite th' lofty-hearted one of pickin' up anything shaken up an' scatthered about in th' loose confusion of a general plundher!

(*By this time they have disappeared from view.* PETER *is following, when the boom of a big gun in the distance brings him to a quick halt.*)

PETER: God Almighty, that's th' big gun again! God forbid any harm would happen to them, but sorra mind I'd mind if they met with a dhrop in their mad endeyvours to plundher an' desthroy.

(*He looks down the street for a moment, then runs to the hall door of the house, which is open, and shuts it with a vicious pull; he then goes to the chair in which Mollser had sat, sits down, takes out his pipe, lights it and begins to smoke with his head carried at a haughty angle.* THE COVEY *comes staggering in with a ten-stone sack of flour on his back. On the top of the sack is a ham. He goes over to the door, pushes it with his head, and finds he can't open it; he turns slightly in the direction of* PETER.)

THE COVEY (*to* PETER): Who shut th' door? … (*He kicks at it*) Here, come on an' open it, will you? This isn't a mot's hand-bag

I've got on me back.

PETER: Now, me young Covey, d'ye think I'm goin' to be your lackey?

THE COVEY (*angrily*): Will you open th' door, y'oul' –

PETER (*shouting*): Don't be assin' me to open any door, don't be assin' me to open any door for you. … Makin' a shame an' a sin o' th' cause that good men are fightin' for. … Oh, God forgive th' people that, instead o' burnishin' th' work th' boys is doin' to-day with quiet honesty an' patience, is revilin' their sacrifices with a riot of lootin' an' roguery!

THE COVEY: Isn't your own eyes leppin' out o' your head with envy that you haven't th' guts to ketch a few o' th' things that God is givin' to His chosen people? … Y'oul' hypocrite, if everyone was blind you'd steal a cross off an ass's back!

PETER (*very calmly*): You're not going to make me lose me temper; you can go on with your proddin' as long as you like; goad an' goad an' goad away; hee, hee, heee! I'll not lose me temper. (*Somebody opens door and* THE COVEY *goes in.*)

THE COVEY (*inside, mockingly*): Cuckoo-oo!

PETER (*running to the door and shouting in a blaze of passion as he follows* THE COVEY *in*): You lean, long lanky lath of a lowsey bastard. … (*Following him in*) Lowsey bastard, lowsey bastard! (BESSIE *and* MRS GOGAN *enter, the pride of a great joy illuminating their faces.* BESSIE *is pushing the pram, which is filled with clothes and boots; on the top of the boots and clothes is a fancy table, which* MRS GOGAN *is holding on with her left hand, while with her right hand she holds a chair on the top of her head. They are heard talking to each other before they enter.*)

MRS GOGAN (*outside*): I don't remember ever havin' seen such lovely pairs as them, (*they appear*) with th' pointed toes an' th' cuban heels.

BESSIE: They'll go grand with th' dhresses we're afther liftin', when we've stitched a sthray bit o' silk to lift th' bodices up a little bit higher, so as to shake th' shame out o' them, an' make them fit for women that hasn't lost themselves in th' nakedness o' th' times. (*They fussily carry in the chair, the table, and some of the other goods. They return to bring in the rest.*)

How do you react to this looting?

PETER (*at door, sourly to* MRS GOGAN): Ay, you. Mollser looks as if she was goin' to faint, an' your youngster is roarin' in convulsions in her lap.

MRS GOGAN (*snappily*): She's never any other way but faintin'!
(*She goes to go in with some things in her arms, when a shot from a rifle rings out. She and* BESSIE *make a bolt for the door, which* PETER, *in a panic, tries to shut before they have got inside.*)

MRS GOGAN: Ay, ay, ay, you cowardly oul' fool, what are you thryin' to shut th' door on us for?
(*They retreat tumultuously inside. A pause; then* CAPTAIN BRENNAN *comes in supporting* LIEUTENANT LANGON, *whose arm is around* BRENNAN*'s neck.* LANGON*'s face, which is ghastly white, is momentarily convulsed with spasms of agony. He is in a state of collapse, and* BRENNAN *is almost carrying him. After a few moments* CLITHEROE, *pale, and in a state of calm nervousness, follows, looking back in the direction from which he came, a rifle, held at the ready, in his hands.*)

CAPT. BRENNAN (*savagely to* CLITHEROE): Why did you fire over their heads? Why didn't you fire to kill?

CLITHEROE: No, no, Bill; bad as they are they're Irish men an' women.

CAPT. BRENNAN (*savagely*): Irish be damned! Attackin' an' mobbin' th' men that are riskin' their lives for them. If these slum lice gather at our heels again, plug one o' them, or I'll soon shock them with a shot or two meself!

Why is Captain Brennan so angry?

LIEUT. LANGON (*moaningly*): My God, is there ne'er an ambulance knockin' around anywhere? ... Th' stomach is ripped out o' me; I feel it – o–o–oh, Christ!

CAPT. BRENNAN: Keep th' heart up, Jim; we'll soon get help, now.
(NORA *rushes wildly out of the house and flings her arms round the neck of* CLITHEROE *with a fierce and joyous insistence. Her hair is down, her face is haggard, but her eyes are agleam with the light of happy relief.*)

NORA: Jack, Jack, Jack; God be thanked ... be thanked. ... He has been kind and merciful to His poor handmaiden. ... My Jack, my own Jack, that I thought was lost is found, that I thought was dead is alive again! ... Oh, God be praised for ever, evermore! ... My poor Jack. ... Kiss me, kiss me, Jack, kiss your own Nora!

CLITHEROE (*kissing her, and speaking brokenly*): My Nora; my little, beautiful Nora, I wish to God I'd never left you.

NORA: It doesn't matter – not now, not now, Jack. It will make us dearer than ever to each other. ... Kiss me, kiss me again.

CLITHEROE: Now, for God's sake, Nora, don't make a scene.

NORA: I won't, I won't; I promise; I promise, Jack; honest to God. I'll be silent an' brave to bear th' joy of feelin' you safe in my arms again. … It's hard to force away th' tears of happiness at th' end of an awful agony.

BESSIE (*from the upper window*): Th' Minsthrel Boys aren't feelin' very comfortable now. Th' big guns has knocked all th' harps out of their hands. General Clitheroe'd rather be unlacin' his wife's bodice than standin' at a barricade. … An' th' professor of chicken-butcherin' there, finds he's up against somethin' a little tougher even than his own chickens, an' that's sayin' a lot!

CAPT. BRENNAN (*up to* BESSIE): Shut up, y'oul hag!

BESSIE (*down to* BRENNAN): Choke th' chicken, choke th' chicken, choke th' chicken!

LIEUT. LANGON: For God's sake, Bill, bring me some place where me wound'll be looked afther. … Am I to die before anything is done to save me?

CAPT. BRENNAN (*to* CLITHEROE): Come on, Jack. We've got to get help for Jim, here – have you no thought for his pain an' danger?

BESSIE: Choke th' chicken, choke th' chicken, choke th' chicken!

CLITHEROE (*to* NORA): Loosen me, darling, let me go.

NORA (*clinging to him*): No, no, no, I'll not let you go! Come on, come up to our home, Jack, my sweetheart, my lover, my husband, an' we'll forget th' last few terrible days! …

First reaction

2 From a first reading of this scene, how would you describe O'Casey's attitude to the 1916 rebellion? Is he

a sympathetic to the British?
b sympathetic to the rebels?
c indifferent?
d contemptuous of both sides?
e interested only in its effects on ordinary people?

Close reading

Stage directions

3 Which of the stage designs below corresponds to the stage directions at the start of the scene?

4 Why do you think O'Casey gives such a detailed description of the house (lines 1–15)?

5 Here are O'Casey's descriptions of the women in this scene (taken from stage directions in Act I). Can you match the descriptions with the characters?

a She is a young woman of twenty-two, alert, swift, full of nervous energy, and a little anxious to get on in the world. The firm lines of her face are considerably opposed by a soft, amorous mouth and gentle eyes. When her firmness fails her, she persuades with her feminine charm.

b She is a doleful-looking little woman of forty, insinuating manner and sallow complexion. She is fidgety and nervous, terribly talkative, has a habit of taking up things that may be near her and fiddling with them while she is speaking. Her heart is aflame with curiosity, and a fly could not come into nor go out of the house without her knowing.

c She is a woman of forty, vigorously built. Her face is a dogged one, hardened by toil, and a little coarsened by drink.

d She is about fifteen, but looks to be only about ten, for the ravages of consumption [tuberculosis] have shrivelled her up. She is pitifully worn, walks feebly, and frequently coughs.

The fighting

6 Look at Mrs Gogan's speeches and actions in lines 20–110, particularly her visions of the deaths of Fluther and Nora. Do you find these have a sinister or comic effect? Or something of both? What reasons can you give for your opinions?

7 Read through the extract again and note down all the references to the British armed forces. Next to each one, write down what impression it gives you of their strength and their ability to control the situation.

8 You will notice that the fighting in the streets of Dublin all occurs offstage – in other words it is reported rather than seen.

a In a theatrical production, what are the advantages and disadvantages of *describing* rather than *showing* military action?

b Why do you think O'Casey chose to present the rebellion in this way?

9 Look at Nora's speeches from lines 126 to 203. Below are some paraphrases of what she says. Some are accurate, some inaccurate. Decide which ones are accurate.

a Jack is braver than the other men at the barricades.
b I admit I'm being selfish, but there's nothing wrong with that.
c I got into a fight with another woman in the street.
d I think of all the times I've been unkind to Jack and I regret them.
e Jack's life is being thrown away for nothing.
f I was accused of discouraging our men.
g I saw a man lying in the street, screaming with pain.
h The terrible thing is, Jack has forgotten about me.

Structure

10 Many of O'Casey's most powerful dramatic effects are created through contrast – the mixture of comedy and tragedy, the acts of selfishness set against acts of heroism and kindness, the contradictory nature of the characters (such as Fluther glad that the pubs are closed so he can't get a drink, then excitedly running off to loot one) and so on.

One of the effects of these contrasts is emotional: the comic sight of Bessie Burgess entering with 'a new hat on her head, a fox fur round her neck over a shawl, three umbrellas under her right arm, and a box of biscuits under her left' is intensified by the atmosphere of tension and danger, and complicated by our awareness of her as a poor woman who has suddenly had the chance to own some luxuries, probably for the first time in her life.

Other effects are moral or political. (These may be simultaneous with an emotional effect.)

a Read the passage where Nora enters and describes what she has seen at the barricades (lines 126–203). Here we are presented with a clash between Nora's belief in personal happiness and the patriotic idealism of the women at the barricades. This forces the audience to choose: do they agree with Nora or the women at the barricades? What is your opinion?

b How does the choice change at lines 134–45 when Bessie interrupts and accuses them all of irresponsibility and treachery?

c Look at the end of this extract (lines 406–96). Can you pick out some contrasts from this passage? What is the effect in each case?

1 ____________________

2 ____________________

3 ____________________

4 ____________________

5 ____________________

6 ____________________

Language practice – structures

Comparisons with verbs, nouns and adverbs

11 Look at these lines from the play.

I thought I heard you coughin' **a little more than usual** last night. (lines 35–6)

Me who risked **more for love than they would risk for hate**. (lines 130–1)

If you'd been **a little longer** together th' wrench asundher **wouldn't have been so sharp**. (lines 188–90)

You **couldn't get a better thing** down you. (line 221)

One way is **as safe as another**. (line 292)

Bessie Burgess'll have **as much respect as she wants** for the lion an' unicorn. (lines 349–51)

I don't remember ever havin' seen **such lovely pairs as them**. (lines 420–1)

General Clitheroe'**d rather be unlacin' his wife's bodice than standin' at a barricade**. (lines 479–80)

Use one of each of these patterns to fill the gaps in these sentences.

a Nora ____________ at home with Jack ____________ out in the streets.
b Fluther thinks ____________ about drinking ____________ the rebellion.
c Mrs Gogan is ____________ sharp-tongued ____________ Bessie; there is no winner in their arguments.
d O'Casey makes us feel that these people have never had ____________ opportunity as this to acquire a few luxuries.
e Nora can't imagine a ____________ cause ____________ a husband and wife being left to love each other in peace.
f If the rebellion had been less violent, it ____________ dramatic.
g It is a sign of these people's tolerance that Bessie can speak as freely ____________ against the rebellion, and even against the Irish people.

12 Use one of the patterns from Exercise 11 to rewrite the following sentences so that their meaning is not changed. Your new sentences should use the words that are provided.

a One might expect O'Casey to write more positively about the rebellion than he does.
O'Casey writes more negatively ________________________
b Brennan is more committed to the rebellion than Clitheroe is.
Clitheroe is not as ________________________
c Nora believes that Jack would prefer to be at home kissing her than fighting in the streets.
rather ________________________
d This is the most anguished moment in Nora's life.
never ________________________
e Fluther is hoping to loot a pub so that he can drink all the whisky he wants.
as much ________________________
f The best thing they can think of is having a game of tossers.
nothing ________________________

13 Write five sentences of your own comparing the characters' attitudes to the rebellion.

Language practice – vocabulary

Talking about character

14 When Mrs Gogan says that Fluther has been out all night looking for Nora, this suggests something about his character: that he is concerned for her safety more than his own. We don't yet know why he has done this – is he a kind man, or does he want something from her? – but we later find out that he acted purely out of kindness.

Now look at these two statements by Fluther, and choose the interpretation that you think is most suitable.

This turn-up has done one good thing, anyhow; you can't get dhrink anywhere, an' if it lasts a week, I'll be so used to it that I won't think of a pint. (lines 221–4)

FLUTHER: Ay, Bessie, did you hear of e'er a pub gettin' a shake up?
BESSIE: I didn't hear o' none.
FLUTHER (*in a burst of enthusiasm*): Well, you're goin' to hear of one soon! (lines 270–1)

a He is a hypocrite.
b He is well intentioned but weak.
c He is foolish.
d He is unscrupulous.
e He is arrogant.

15 Here are some more of the characters' actions and words for you to interpret. Some words are given in the box below to help you.

a THE COVEY: If they were fightin' for anything worth while, I wouldn't mind. (lines 166–7)
b CAPT. BRENNAN: … If these slum lice gather at our heels again, plug one o' them, or I'll soon shock them with a shot or two meself! (lines 451–3)
c CLITHEROE: Now, for God's sake, Nora, don't make a scene. (line 472)
d PETER (*rubbing his hands*): 'Damn it,' says I to meself, 'this looks like business!' (lines 77–8)
e MRS GOGAN (*leading her towards the house*): Come on in, dear. If you'd been a little longer together, th'wrench asundher wouldn't have been so sharp. (lines 188–90)
f WOMAN: I'm so different from others. … The mowment I hear a shot, my legs give way under me – I cawn't stir, I'm paralysed – isn't it awful? (lines 293–5)

ignorant embarrassed weak excited angry detached self-pitying contemptuous experienced arrogant understanding foolish

16 Complete this table.

ADJECTIVE	NOUN	PREPOSITION AFTER
ignorant	ignorance	ignorant of / about
embarrassed		
weak		(not often used with prepositions)
excited		
angry		
detached		
self-pitying		(not often used with prepositions)
contemptuous		
experienced		
arrogant		
understanding		
foolish		

17 Write some sentences of your own about the characters, using the adjective / noun + preposition patterns in the right-hand columns above.
Example: The well-dressed woman seemed ignorant of other people's needs and feelings.

Extension

18 Here are some eye-witness accounts of the 1916 rebellion. Imagine that you were in Dublin in 1916 and witnessed some of the scenes described below or enacted in *The Plough and the Stars*. Write a letter to a friend describing your experiences.

> Thirteen Sinn Feiners walked quietly up to the lower gate of Dublin Castle. The policeman on duty put up his hand to show that there was no passage. Instantly one of the volunteers raised his rifle and shot the policeman dead. That was the first shot fired, and the first life lost, in the insurrection.
>
> (*The Times, 1st May, 1916*)

> I took a few days off in Connemara before Easter, 1916. I was returning by train from Galway when the first rumours of the insurrection were heard. Rumour upon rumour as the train went along. It was delayed at Athlone, which is about the centre of Ireland, to allow artillery from the barracks there to go ahead to

Dublin. Then I knew that there was something serious in the air. At Mullingar, fifty miles west of Dublin, the train came to a halt. It could go no further because the lines were cut. This evidently was to prevent the passage of guns to Dublin. It convinced me that the country must have risen, as it had. …

Dublin was 'up'. All the old ballads surged through my mind: 'The debt so long unpaid.' Every century had seen a rising against the oppressor and now we were in another rebellion. I felt that I was a lucky man.

There was but one car that could be hired at Mullingar. Needless to say, it was not a good one. Its owner charged enough to buy it; but what did I care? I had to get to Dublin, not to see patients on Tuesday morning but to see what was happening on Easter Monday, now.

We were going down Cabra Road when a bullet struck the windscreen and a few others whined over our heads. … At once the driver put out the headlights. Cautiously we came to the railway bridge at Cabra, which had been turned into a barricade. A boy with a rifle stood beside it. He said his name was John Fogarty. … He explained that we were mistaken for 'military' because we drove with lights undimmed. And the Republic could not afford to take chances. … He seemed full of hope for the rising. I left him so. He could not have been more than sixteen.

(Oliver St John Gogarty, *It Isn't This Time Of Year At All!*, 1954, pp 175–9)

Civilians were not molested by the rebels, and that, to my mind, shows that the rising was purely military in character, and directed against the Government. There was a little looting in the streets, and perhaps 10 or 20 shops were entered. There was, however, no violence, and it was as safe to walk about as it is in the streets of London. … You could go anywhere you liked, so long as you were not motoring or cycling, or using any kind of conveyance. … On the other hand, it was made very clear that any person in his Majesty's uniform was liable to be shot at sight.

I saw the wires in the Northumberland-road, near the Post Office, cut. They were lying across the electric tramway wires. They succeeded in cutting off the railway communication. The Sinn Feiners in the General Post Office are being fed with provisions commandeered from a well-known hotel, but I believe the food was paid for.

(*The Times, 29th April, 1916*)

From Tuesday morning onward in every suburb the soldiers kept pushing in towards the city, doing their best to clear the streets as they came along. The rebels had occupied 3 or 4 houses in every street. As one house was taken they escaped along the roof to another. The sniping was continuous, and, unfortunately, accurate. Officers told me that this was far more dangerous and trying fighting than anything they had seen in France.

The road from Trinity College, down to Westmoreland-street, over O'Connell Bridge, and through Sackville-street to Nelson's Pillar, is the broadest city thoroughfare in Europe, and in normal times the most populous thoroughfare in Dublin. Since Tuesday evening its sole occupant has been a dead volunteer, who is lying on O'Connell Bridge. …

On Wednesday night a new horror was added to the fighting in Sackville-street. Some shops had been looted at Nelson's Pillar, and a fire broke out in one of them – a toy shop. It spread quickly, and soon the whole of one of the finest blocks of buildings in Dublin was in flames. By Thursday night the fire had involved a large restaurant, the Imperial Hotel, a big drapery shop, a jeweller's shop, a picture house, and several other buildings. The flames could be seen 10 miles away. In my newspaper office, where the police had forbidden all lights, men worked by this glare. The roar of the flames and the din of the rifle fire were a truly awful combination. …

Friday evening was obviously the beginning of the end. By this time it must have been clear to even the most reckless and ignorant rebel that the game was up. On Friday night the General Post Office, the last stronghold of the insurrection, took fire, and is now a blazing ruin.

(*The Times, 1st May, 1916*)

19 **Individual /group work**: write or improvise a scene showing one of the following.

- Nora arguing with the women at the barricades
- Patrick Pearse reading the Proclamation (lines 79–82)
- the looting of a shop

20 **Group work**: choose a short section of this extract and work out how you would stage it: exits and entrances of characters, actions, movements, groupings, etc. Then rehearse and perform your scene for other groups. (See Chapter 1, 'Staging a play', p 21.)

Beyond the text

21 Read this extract from Brian Friel's play, *Translations.* It is set in a 'hedge school' organised by peasants, who study Latin, Greek, Geography and Mathematics with their teacher Hugh O'Donnell, in the village of Baile Beag (Ballybeg) in the rural west of Ireland in 1833. At that time most of the western Irish people spoke Gaelic, although the English language was already starting to take over. At the same time, the English government was engaged in two major projects: setting up national schools where English was the language of instruction, and drawing up a detailed map of Ireland (with anglicised place names) through the Ordnance Survey, the army's cartography department. Although these projects were claimed to be for the benefit of the Irish, it is clear that they also threatened the Irish culture and language.

At this point in the play, an English soldier, Lieutenant George Yolland, has disappeared. His commanding officer, Captain Lancey, now comes in to the hedge school to make an announcement. He does not speak Gaelic, and the local people do not speak English, so Lancey has been employing Owen O'Donnell, the son of the schoolmaster, as an interpreter and adviser. [Note: the whole play is written in English, although it is understood that the Irish villagers are in fact speaking Gaelic.]

As you read, note down what differences, and what similarities, you can see between this play and *The Plough and the Stars*. Make notes under these headings.

a the way the Irish people are represented
b the way the English are represented
c the way violence is represented
d how the author seems to feel about violent resistance to English rule

Translations (1980)
Brian Friel

See the Glossary section at the back of the book for vocabulary.

ACT 3

OWEN: Any news? Any word?

(LANCEY *moves into the centre of the room, looking around as he does.*)

LANCEY: I understood there was a class. Where are the others?

OWEN: There was to be a class but my father –

LANCEY: This will suffice. I will address them and it will be their responsibility to pass on what I have to say to every family in this section.

(LANCEY *indicates to* OWEN *to translate.* OWEN *hesitates, trying to assess the change in* LANCEY*'s manner and attitude.*)

I'm in a hurry, O'Donnell.

OWEN: The captain has an announcement to make.

LANCEY: Lieutenant Yolland is missing. We are searching for him. If we don't find him, or if we receive no information as to where he is to be found, I will pursue the following course of action. (*He indicates to* OWEN *to translate.*)

OWEN: They are searching for George. If they don't find him –

LANCEY: Commencing twenty-four hours from now we will shoot all livestock in Ballybeg.

(OWEN *stares at* LANCEY.)

At once.

OWEN: Beginning this time tomorrow they'll kill every animal in Baile Beag – unless they're told where George is.

LANCEY: If that doesn't bear results, commencing forty-eight hours from now we will embark on a series of evictions and levelling of every abode in the following selected areas –

OWEN: You're not – !

LANCEY: Do your job. Translate.

OWEN: If they still haven't found him in two days time they'll begin evicting and levelling every house starting with these townlands.

(LANCEY *reads from his list.*)

LANCEY: Swinefort.

OWEN: Lis na Muc.

LANCEY: Burnfoot.

OWEN: Bun na hAbhann.

LANCEY: Dromduff.

OWEN: Druim Dubh.

LANCEY: Whiteplains.

OWEN: Machaire Ban.

LANCEY: Kings Head.

OWEN: Cnoc na Ri.

LANCEY: If by then the lieutenant hasn't been found, we will proceed until a complete clearance is made of this entire section.

OWEN: If Yolland hasn't been got by then, they will ravish the whole parish.

LANCEY: I trust they know exactly what they've got to do. (*Pointing to* BRIDGET.) I know you. I know where you live. (*Pointing to* SARAH.) Who are you? Name!

(SARAH*'s mouth opens and shuts, opens and shuts. Her face becomes contorted.*)

What's your name?

(*Again* SARAH *tries frantically.*)

OWEN: Go on, Sarah. You can tell him.

(*But* SARAH *cannot. And she knows she cannot. She closes her mouth. Her head goes down.*)

OWEN: Her name is Sarah Johnny Sally.

LANCEY: Where does she live?

OWEN: Bun na hAbhann.

LANCEY: Where?

OWEN: Burnfoot.

LANCEY: I want to talk to your brother – is he here?

OWEN: Not at the moment.

LANCEY: Where is he?

OWEN: He's at a wake.

LANCEY: What wake?

(DOALTY, *who has been looking out the window all through* LANCEY*'s announcements, now speaks – calmly, almost casually.*)

DOALTY: Tell him his whole camp's on fire.

LANCEY: What's your name? (*To* OWEN.) Who's that lout?

OWEN: Doalty Dan Doalty.

LANCEY: Where does he live?

OWEN: Tulach Alainn.

LANCEY: What do we call it?

OWEN: Fair Hill. He says your whole camp is on fire.

(LANCEY *rushes to the window and looks out. Then he wheels on* DOALTY.)

LANCEY: I'll remember you, Mr Doalty. (*To* OWEN.) You carry a big responsibility in all this. (*He goes off.*)

BRIDGET: Mother of God, does he mean it, Owen?

OWEN: Yes, he does.

BRIDGET: We'll have to hide the beasts somewhere – our Seamus'll know where. Maybe at the back of Lis na nGradh – or in the

caves at the far end of the Tra Bhan. Come on, Doalty! Come on! Don't be standing about there!
(DOALTY *does not move.* BRIDGET *runs to the door and stops suddenly. She sniffs the air. Panic.*)
The sweet smell! Smell it! It's the sweet smell! Jesus, it's the potato blight!

DOALTY: It's the army tents burning, Bridget.

BRIDGET: Is it? Are you sure? Is that what it is? God, I thought we were destroyed altogether. Come on! Come on!
(*She runs off.* OWEN *goes to* SARAH *who is preparing to leave.*)

OWEN: How are you? Are you all right?
(SARAH *nods: Yes.*)

OWEN: Don't worry. It will come back to you again.
(SARAH *shakes her head.*)

OWEN: It will. You're upset now. He frightened you. That's all's wrong.
(*Again* SARAH *shakes her head, slowly, emphatically, and smiles at* OWEN. *Then she leaves.* OWEN *busies himself gathering his belongings.* DOALTY *leaves the window and goes to him.*)

DOALTY: He'll do it, too.

OWEN: Unless Yolland's found.

DOALTY: Hah!

OWEN: Then he'll certainly do it.

DOALTY: When my grandfather was a boy they did the same thing. (*Simply, altogether without irony.*) And after all the trouble you went to, mapping the place and thinking up new names for it.
(OWEN *busies himself. Pause.* DOALTY *almost dreamily.*)
I've damned little to defend but he'll not put me out without a fight. And there'll be others who think the same as me.

OWEN: That's a matter for you.

DOALTY: If we'd all stick together. If we knew how to defend ourselves.

OWEN: Against a trained army.

DOALTY: The Donnelly twins know how.

OWEN: If they could be found.

DOALTY: If they could be found. (*He goes to the door.*) Give me a shout after you've finished with Lancey. I might know something then. (*He leaves.*)
(OWEN *picks up the Name-Book. He looks at it momentarily, then puts it on top of the pile he is carrying. It falls to the floor. He stoops to pick it up – hesitates – leaves it.*)

Authors

Sean O'Casey (1880–1964) spent the first forty years of his life in the kind of poverty portrayed in *The Plough and the Stars*. He was born into a poor Protestant family, and left school at 14 to become a labourer, continuing his education through evening classes and the Trade Union movement. His first plays were rejected by Dublin's Abbey Theatre, but its founder, Lady Gregory, encouraged him to keep writing, and in 1923 the Abbey put on his play *The Shadow of a Gunman*. This was the first of three masterpieces about the slum life of Dublin in the troubled years 1916–22. The second play, *Juno and the Paycock*, was staged in 1924 and was an immediate success, enabling O'Casey to write full-time. *The Plough and the Stars* repeated the success of *Juno*, although it caused riots in the theatre for its unflattering portrayal of the Easter Rising. His fourth play, *The Silver Tassie* (an expressionist drama about a footballer injured in the 1914–18 war), was rejected by the Abbey Theatre, and O'Casey moved to England. Despite international recognition, he never again repeated the success of the three Dublin plays, although they have continued to be staged and acclaimed all over the world.

Brian Friel is one of Ireland's most admired contemporary playwrights, best known for the more recent West End and Broadway hit, *Dancing at Lughnasa*. *Translations* (1980) was his fifteenth play. It was first produced by the Field Day Theatre Company which Friel founded in 1980 with the poet Seamus Heaney and the actor Stephen Rea with the aim of re-appraising the political and cultural situation in Northern Ireland. 'They aim,' as one critic wrote, 'to examine and analyse the established opinions, slogans, myths and war-cries which have gone to the creation of the present troubles in Ireland.' Another writer, the dramatist Thomas Kilroy, has described Field Day as providing 'a platform for the life of the mind, of whatever persuasion, at a time when mindlessness threatens to engulf us all.'

Glossary

1 Anatomy of a Play

Our Country's Good

Note: the play that is being rehearsed, *The Recruiting Officer*, has a number of archaic 18th century expressions. The convicts rehearsing the play also use a number of archaic slang expressions.

27 toss pot: *drunkard*
34–5 Screw jaws Salt bitch: *insults*
47 arse: (vulgar) *bottom*
49 bow: (pronounced / baʊ /) *bending forward from the waist, as actors do when the audience applauds*
58 cast: (verb) *to assign a part to an actor*
78 scuttle off: *run away*
82 arms-a-cross: *arms crossed, a traditional sign of melancholy (see line 105)*
90 buzzed: (archaic slang) *stolen*
wiper, wipe: (archaic slang) *handkerchief*
91 drawer: (archaic slang) *thief*
crew: *company, group of people*
94 the pot calling the kettle black: (proverb) *when someone accuses another person of a fault he is guilty of himself (Sideway is a pickpocket)*
95 stalks: *walks angrily*
96 prigged: (archaic slang) *stole*
99 mittens: *hands* (literally, *gloves*)
100 rum diver: (archaic slang) *pickpocket*
104 Methinks: (archaic) *I think*
105 melancholy: *sad*
110 Garrick: *David Garrick (1717–79), the most famous actor of the time*
113 'Oh that this …': *the opening line of Hamlet's first soliloquy (Hamlet, I.ii)*
119 establish: *make clear to the audience*
melancholy: *sadness*
134 safe and sound returned: *you have come back safe and healthy*
142 euh: *sound made when a speaker hesitates*
174 chic: (French, pronounced / ʃiːk /) *elegant, fashionable*
187 *Liz rushes through her lines without thinking about the meaning, which requires a pause (a full stop) after 'cousin Sylvia'; she also does this at lines 238–40 (pause needed after 'year')*
189 heads of shires: *capital towns of counties*
192 give the spleen: *make people melancholy and irritable*
222 masticate: *chew*
238 nice: *delicate*
239 constitution: *health*
241 prithee: (archaic) *please*
put on such an air: *behave in such a superior way (this is a pun on the previous use of 'air' (lines 233 and 239) meaning the air we breathe)*
279 spleen, colic, vapours: *irritable feelings, stomach pains, depression*
281 slink away: *move away in a stealthy, guilty way*
287 Tssaach: *sound indicating disapproval*
297 thespists: (jocular / contemptuous) *actors*
299 renegade: *rebellious*
303 calamity: *disaster*
306 worms its way: *enters cunningly, aiming to deceive or destroy*
324 lingers: *stays, waits*
325 Ouusstta, Arara, tss: *exclamations (of surprise, approval, disapproval)*
327 shambles: *ruin, mess*

2 Language, Class and Power

Pygmalion

1 Wimpole Street: *a street of expensive houses in central London*

4 file cabinets: *(now known as 'filing cabinets') drawers with numbered compartments for storing papers*

6 phonograph: *instrument for recording and reproducing sounds using wax cylinders (early version of a record player or gramophone) (see line 10)*

laryngoscope: *medical instrument for inspecting the throat*

7 bellows: *instrument for blowing air*

lamp chimney: *glass cylinder placed over the flame of an oil lamp*

singing flames: *apparatus for measuring sound according to its effect on a flame*

8 indiarubber: *rubber*

tuning-fork: *fork-shaped instrument that makes a perfect musical note when struck; used for tuning musical instruments, giving singers their first note, etc*

14 coal-scuttle: *bucket for coal*

23 stray: *with no fixed place of its own*

24 Piranesi: *Italian engraver (1720–78), known for his views of ancient Rome*

25 mezzotint: *a type of engraving*

30 frock-coat: *long jacket*

38 petulance: *bad temper, anger*

41 the whole show: *everything*

47 done up: *finished, exhausted*

51 fancied myself: *thought I was clever*

64 common: *low-class*

79–80 Bell's Visible Speech, Romic: *phonetic notations*

84 the flower girl: *Higgins and Pickering met her selling flowers in Act I.*

in state: *acting in a grand manner*

91 feather-weight cross: *small problem*

95 jotted down: *he made phonetic notes on her accent*

96 Lisson Grove: *a poor district of London, just north of Wimpole Street*

lingo: (colloquial) *language*

97 Be off with you: *Go away*

99 saucy: *impudent, rude*

aint: (Cockney or working-class London dialect) *haven't or isn't*

104 above giving lessons: *too proud to give lessons*

109–10 yə-oo, tə-oo: *phonetic versions of 'you' and 'too' as she pronounces them*

112 stupent: (archaic) *amazed*

117 baggage: (offensive) *woman*

120 whimper: *make a pitiful sound, like a frightened dog*

125 stead of sellin: (Cockney) *instead of selling*

127 genteel: *like the people of the upper classes*

129 zif: *as if*

137 what you chucked at me: *Higgins threw some coins to her*

138 Youd a drop in: *You were drunk*

139 peremptorily: *brusquely, suddenly*

147 hearthrug: *small carpet in front of the fireplace*

153 Eliza, Betsy and Bess: *different forms of 'Elizabeth'*

166 face: *impudence*

168 shilling: *monetary unit, no longer used (20 shillings = £1)*

172 guinea: *monetary unit, no longer used, equivalent to 105 pence today*

175 Figure it out: *Calculate it*

176 half-a-crown: *2 shillings and sixpence (8 half-crowns = £1)*
180 By George: *exclamation showing surprise*
184 Hold your tongue: *Keep quiet*
189 snivelling: *crying pitifully*
203 gev: *phonetic version of 'gave' in Liza's accent*
207 Serve you right: *You deserve the punishment (for talking to her that way)*
209 garden party: *an elegant social occasion that Higgins and Pickering have been invited to; Pickering wants to see if Higgins can teach Eliza to speak so well that everyone at the garden party will think she is upper-class*
216 afore: *before*
217 turn her head: *make her feel proud and conceited*
226 draggletailed guttersnipe: *badly-dressed street child*
229–30 pass her off: *disguise her*
231 Monkey Brand: *strong kitchen soap for cleaning pans*
235 Whiteley: *a big shop in London*
239 prudery: *excessive modesty or sense of shame (it was commonly regarded by uneducated people as wicked to be naked, even when washing)*
241 wallop: *hit very hard*
250 zephyr: *a mild and pleasant breeze; Higgins's moods are compared to winds*
252 modulation: *control of pitch, volume and expression in the voice*
256 station in life: *social position, status*
269 Garn: *exclamation of ridicule*
272 drudge of fifty: *slave fifty years old*
273 whood: *who would (who'd)*
276 strewn: *covered*
277 done with: *finished with*
280 off his chump: *off his head, mad*
balmies: *madmen*
292 take you out of the gutter: *rescue you from a life of poverty in the streets*
300–1 sixth stepmother: *her father's sixth wife*
done without them: *lived without their help*
311 housekeeping book: *book of household expenses*
317 remonstrance: *telling someone that they have done wrong*
339 takes the floor: (stage action) *moves to the centre of the stage*
345 the like of you: *people like you*
346 whips out his penknife: *quickly takes out a pocket-knife*
347 bolts it: *eats it very fast, without chewing*
348 pledge: *sign or promise*
371 the Guards: *the most prestigious regiment in the army*
372 marquis: *lord, one of several ranks in the English aristocracy*
400 Buckingham Palace: *the London home of the King or Queen*
402 Tower of London: *an ancient fortress used for centuries as a prison*
403 presumptuous: *too bold*
415 Bundle her off: *Take her quickly*
426 letting myself in for: *becoming involved in*
430 plaints: *complaints, protests*

Roots

1 ramshackle: *messy, badly built*
Norfolk: *county in East Anglia (eastern part of England)*
laid on: *provided*
2 rambles: *is in disorder*
4 amenities: *machines to help the housewife (washing machine, etc)*
5 clobber: *objects of all kinds*

6–7 Tilley lamps and Primus stoves: *lights and cookers fuelled with paraffin (kerosene)*
17–18 wan', wi', mornin': *phonetic spellings indicating Jenny's Norfolk accent*
grumpy: *bad-tempered*
19 chubby: *quite fat*
20 dungarees: *working clothes*
24 Waas: *What's*
25 guts: *stomach*
a'tween: *between*
27 git: get
28 Blust: (Norfolk accent) *Blast! (an expletive)*
yit: *yet*
38 daft: *stupid*
40 I hed it: (phonetic spelling) *I had it (indigestion)*
47 driv: *drove*
ole: *old*
Armstrong: *type of car*
48 Well … rum thing: *that's very strange (ent* (dialect) *= isn't)*
51 whist drive: *meeting where people play the card game whist*
54 Ole crows: *The women, compared to crows which live on dead animals*
57 Yoo-hoo: *sound calling for attention*
61 gal: *girl*
69 harvest festival: *traditional religious celebration of the harvest*
70 Watcha: (slang) *Hello*
bor: *form of address used in Norfolk dialect (short for 'neighbour')*
74 wanna: *want to*
80 Ent: *Aren't*
101 Watcha got?: *What have you got?*
102 Watcha see: *What you see*
103 hev: *have*
107 Yearp: *Yes*
111 Soon ever: *As soon as*
115–16 ent never bin: *hasn't ever been*
118 riled: *angry*
124 Manchester Guardian: *a serious newspaper, mildly left-wing*
126 Blimey Joe: (slang) *exclamation showing surprise*
133 bor: *person (see line 70)*
141 sneak … away: *take (the comic) away secretly*
142 his-self: *himself*
158 barmy: *mad*
159 gaiters: *leather or cloth covering for the lower part of the legs*
allotment: *rented vegetable garden*
160 row: (verb, pronounced / raʊ /) *quarrel, fight*
164 stamps: *insurance payment for unemployment or sickness*
193 chores: *household jobs (washing, cleaning, etc)*
198 go on wi' you: *you're joking!*
199 blushin': *red-faced with embarrassment*

3 Family Life

Long Day's Journey Into Night

5 consumption: *tuberculosis (TB), a disease, often fatal*
12 hick burg: (US slang) *provincial, undistinguished town*
13 quack: (US / GB slang) *bad doctor*
14 Run him down: *Speak badly about him*
24 mortgaged: *(property) bought with borrowed money*
26 lousy: *usually this means 'bad'; here it simply expresses Jamie's anger*
26–7 the sky … limit: *you would pay any price*
28 sneers: *mocking insults*
29 put on frills: *dress and behave elaborately*
34 You can't change the leopard's spots: (proverb) *A person's*

habits and character never change

39 season: *theatrical season, period when plays are performed*

40 whores: *prostitutes*

44 stinks so: *is so bad*

46 turned over a new leaf: *decided to change your habits*

51 loaf: *live lazily, doing nothing*

52 lunk: (US slang) *fool, stupid person*

sponge on me: *live on my money*

54 fired: *expelled, forced to leave*

65 wryly: *in a bitter, slightly mocking way*

68 vilest: *worst, most horrible*

71 bum: (US slang) *tramp, worthless character*

74 make your mark: *become successful*

84 knee-high: *a child*

85 constitution: *physical condition, health*

86 make out: *imply*

90 prep school: (US) *private secondary school*

dissipating … Broadway sport: *leading a life of pleasure and vice instead of working; being a playboy (cf lines 39–40); Broadway is the entertainment district of New York*

92 hulk: *strong man*

94 bundle of nerves: *extremely nervous*

104 hovel: *poor, filthy house*

bog: *wet ground (often found in Ireland)*

105 gabbing: *talking stupidly and at length*

110 stung: *annoyed*

115 pumping him full of: *giving him a lot of*

118 knave: *bad character*

121 put Edmund wise to things: *teach him about life*

122 raise hell: *live wildly*

123 pal: *friend*

135 rot: *lies, nonsense*

140 stunts he's pulled: *dangerous, foolish things he has done*

144 dives: *cheap bars*

rotgut: *cheap alcoholic drinks (which rot the 'gut' or digestive system)*

145 Broadway: *see line 91*

146 bonded Bourbon: *good quality whisky*

148 guts: (slang) *courage*

149 whining: *complaining, looking for pity*

150 broke: (slang) *without money*

155 paper: *newspaper*

157 hick town rag: (slang) *low-quality newspaper in a small town*

bull they hand you: (slang) *lies they tell you*

158 bum: (slang) *useless*

160 gets him by: *allows him to continue*

162 on the big time: *in the serious professional world, at the highest level*

167 lay off me: *stop attacking me*

168 damnable: *very bad or unfortunate*

170 furtive: *secret, hidden*

186 sanatorium: *hospital*

191 Outside of nerves: *Apart from her nervous state*

197 jumping down my throat: (slang) *shouting at me, criticising me aggressively*

213 foghorn: *alarm to warn ships during fog that they are near land*

223–4 is beyond me: *I can't understand it*

225 Don't pull that: (slang, aggressive) *Don't talk nonsense*

227 mollifyingly: *in an effort to make peace, gently*

231 she first – : *ie began to take drugs*

241 driving at: *trying to say or imply*

252 spell: *short period of time*

255 Wonders will never cease: (proverb) *Life is full of surprises (she is being ironic)*

257 iron man: (US slang) *dollar*
258 carouse on: *get drunk on*
274 flurriedly: *nervously and quickly*
277 repulsion: *feeling of disgust*
286–7 sweat … middle: *make you sweat and lose weight*
287 booze fat: *fat that comes from drinking too much*
295 flounders on: *continues clumsily*
301 rebuffed: *feeling rejected*
305 roving: *wandering, moving without a purpose*
315 rotten: *ill*
318 teasing: *making a joke, making fun*
332 evading: *avoiding, not looking at*
forcing a laugh: *trying to laugh*

My Mother Said I Never Should

Act 1 Scene 6

1 council flat: *cheap apartment owned by the city council*
Mosside: *poor area of Manchester, a city in the north of England*
3 mugs: *large coffee cups*
strewn: *scattered untidily about*
transistor: *radio*
4 blares: *plays loudly*
5 Moses basket: *basket for carrying a baby*
7 holdall: *large soft travelling bag*
8 DJ: *disc jockey (radio presenter on a pop music programme)*
9 wrap up warm: *wear warm clothes*
10 Pennines: *range of mountains in northern England*
11 forecast: *expected weather*
13 black ice: *invisible ice on roads*
14 Honky Tonk Woman: *famous song by the Rolling Stones*
24 haphazard: *improvised*
25 coos: *makes a soothing, gentle sound*
30 dangles: *hangs*
37 Oh shit: (offensive) *an expression of anger or frustration*
44 tower blocks: *tall blocks of apartments*
76 Mothercare: *shop selling baby clothes and equipment*
78 carrier: *bag*
86 VD: *venereal disease*
87 Stuck for word: *Not knowing what word to use*
99 degree: *university course (literally, the qualification at the end of the course)*
102 snuffling: *noisy breathing*
105 high chair: *chair on long legs for small children*
107 precious: *word expressing affection – like 'dear' or 'darling'*
160 billows out: *throws open suddenly*

Act 3 Scene 5

1 semi: *semi-detached house, typical of English suburbs*
Raynes Park: *a suburb in south-west London*
3 tranny: (colloquial) *transistor radio*
5 grubby: *dirty*
lacquered: *varnished (the briefcase is expensive)*
6 up all night: *they have not slept*
7 LBC: *a radio station in London*
congestion: *traffic*
North Circular: *a 'ring road' going around central London to the north*
8 Blackwall Tunnel: *a road tunnel under the River Thames in east London*
11 Mini: *a popular small car*
All You Need Is Love: *a famous song by the Beatles*
14 cope with it: *react successfully to it; she finds Rosie's silence upsetting*

18 opening: *first day of an art exhibition*
19 brill: (colloquial) *brilliant, excellent*
24 she: *Jackie's mother, Margaret*
26 secondaries: *secondary cancers, in other parts of the body*
39 split up: *separated, divorced*
40 family stuff: *family documents*
54 Gran ... Grandad: *grandmother and grandfather (affectionate terms)*
72 joints: *hashish or marijuana cigarettes*
81 Lyme Park: *a park near Manchester*
84 the Guardian: *a newspaper*
86 power cuts: *periods without electricity*
88 open fire: *a fireplace in the house, burning logs or coal* trendy: *fashionable* Didsbury: *wealthy area of Manchester*
90 Punjabi: *from the Punjab (north-west India / Pakistan)*
104 Oldham: *a town near Manchester*

4 'We're Right and You're Wrong'

The Crucible

Note: Miller uses a number of archaisms – words or grammatical forms either no longer used in English, or now used with a different meaning. These are marked with an asterisk (*).

8 tracking down: *finding*
9 the Old Boy: *the Devil, Satan*
20 ails*: *is unwell*
24 Thinks on it*: *Thinks about it*
25 afflicted: *sick*
28 spoke on*: *spoke about*
30 queer: *strange, unusual*
38 she'd* fly: *she wanted to fly*
41 afloat*: *started, going on*
46 bruise of hell: *mark of the Devil's work*
58 conjurin': *(conjuring) magic, supernatural practices*
59 Goody*: (short for Goodwife) *old term of address to a married woman: Mrs*
62 she should learn*: *in order to learn*
63 conjure up the dead: *bring the dead back to life using supernatural practices*
67 work*: *event, occurrence*
71 Aye: *Yes*
78 stripped ... disguises: *unmasked, without disguise* brute: *bestial*
79 familiar spirits: *demons, evil spirits* incubi, succubi: *male and female demons believed to enter people's dreams and have sex with them in their sleep*
81 him: *the Devil*
88 open up: *(i) cut open, (ii) cure, (iii) understand*
89 boil: *infection of the skin, forming a red lump filled with pus (used by Parris as a metaphor for evil)*
105 mark this*: *listen carefully*
111 admire*: *be filled with wonder (here it means 'be very curious')*
123 stir: *move*
125 licentious: *immoral, wicked*
129 minister: *parish priest (Parris is the minister of Salem)*
132 afflict: *harm*
135 bids: *commands*
137–8 In nomine ... infernos: (Latin) *In the name of the Lord God and His Son, go to hell (this is addressed to the evil spirits possessing Betty)*
141 common dancing is all: *ordinary dancing is the only thing we were doing*
142 kettle*: *cooking pot (often associated with witchcraft)*
158 blanched: *white with fear*
163 Barbados: *the language of*

Barbados, her home in the Caribbean
168 evade: *avoid, escape*
169 brew: *soup, drink*
175 Lucifer: *name for the Devil*
184 I give she: *I gave her*
185 enlisted: *recruited, like soldiers*
186 truck: *deal, trade*
188 me: *my*
195 charm: *spells, magical words and actions*
197 corruptions: *wicked things*
200 not a stitch: *no clothes*
207 compact: (verb) *make a treaty or contract*
227 would be*: *want to be*
269 utterly*: *fully*
295 shrivelled: *became dry and lifeless, withered*
300 the Devil is out: *the Devil is active*
305 enraptured: *overcome with great emotion or joy*
320 glee: *excited happiness*
325 irons*: *chains, handcuffs, etc to restrain the accused women*
329 ecstatic: *wildly excited*

The Birthday Party

2 Don't mess me about: *Stop trying to annoy me!*
5 We're booked out: *All the rooms are full (the play is set in a small hotel)*
9 a good game: (slang) *profitable*
22 crabby: *itchy*
23 boghouse: (slang) *toilet*
24 clogged up: *blocked*
32 These are unlicensed premises: *We have no licence to sell alcohol*
44 your cup of tea: (colloquial) *suitable for you*
45 angle: *point of view*
52 get on my breasts: (vulgar) *get on my nerves, annoy me*
84 kick the shite out of him: (vulgar) *beat him up*
95 'The Mountains of Mourne': *a popular Irish song (the Mourne Mountains are in north-east Ireland)*
107 a washout: *useless, a failure*
108 get on everybody's wick: *annoy everybody (cf line 52)*
driving … off her conk: (slang) *making her become mad*
123 Black and Tan: *McCann's version of a 'black and white' or indisputable fact (the Black and Tans were British soldiers sent to suppress the Irish independence movement after World War I. They were notorious for their ruthless methods)*
126 on the wrong horse: *making a mistake*
139 Enos or Andrews: *brand names of 'fruit salts', a remedy for stomach disorders*
141 fizz: (verb) *bubble (fruit salts do this when they are mixed with water)*
160 Lyons Corner House: *a café, one of a 'chain' owned by the Lyons company; one branch was near Marble Arch, in London*
174 arsenic: *a poison*
180 porch: *entrance to a church*
181 skeddadled: (slang) *ran away*
182 left her in the lurch: *abandoned her*
183 in the pudding club: (slang) *pregnant*
217 all along the line: *totally, in every instance*
219 lechery: *excessive sexuality*
224 Mother defiler: *person who makes love to his mother*
225 pick your nose: *take the mucus out of your nose with your finger*
233 building society: *a bank that lends money for buying houses*
235 the cloth: *the church*
238 verminate: *infect with parasites – a similar idea to line 224*
239 Albigensenist heresy: *an anti-*

clerical movement in 12th–13th century southern France, brutally eradicated by Pope Innocent III

240 Who watered the wicket in Melbourne?: *an obscure question about the history of cricket*

241 Oliver Plunkett: *(Saint Oliver Plunkett) Irish archbishop (1629–1681), the last Roman Catholic to be martyred for his faith in England*

242 Why did the chicken cross the road?: *a well-known riddle (the answer is usually 'Because it wanted to get to the other side')*

258 overthrow: *a cricketing term suggesting something accidental and irritating*

261 Drogheda: *town in Ireland, site of a massacre by English soldiers under Cromwell in 1649*

262 pong: (slang) *bad smell*

278 Judas: *the disciple that betrayed Jesus (McCann continues the accusations of treachery)*

285 sweatpig: *a sweating pig*

5 Lost in New Orleans

A Streetcar Named Desire

2 Elysian Fields: *Paradise in ancient Greek mythology*
the L & N: *the Louisiana and Nashville Railroad*

3 river: *the Mississippi*

4 raffish: *slightly disreputable*

5 frame: *built of wood*
rickety: *old and starting to fall to pieces*
galleries: *balconies*

6 gables: *triangular structures shaped like the letter A*

9 lyricism: *poetic beauty*
attenuates: *softens*

11 redolences: *smells*

14 tinny: *cheap and not very well tuned*

15 infatuated: *this usually means 'foolishly or madly in love'; the meaning here is that the pianist loves playing*

17 taking the air: *outside the house enjoying the fresh air*

24 St Barnabas: *the reference is not clear; presumably, a figure in the woman's dream*

29 the Four Deuces: *a bar or night-club with gambling and music*

30 Red hot: *the vendor is selling spicy 'hot dogs' (frankfurter sausages in a bread roll, a traditional US food)*

31 clip joint: *low quality night club with high prices*

41–2 even money / odds: (gambling terms) *the return on a bet – either the same amount as the bet or a multiple*

44 bellowing: *shouting very loudly*

48 holler: (US) *shout*

52 heaves: *throws*

59 Be over: *I'll come*

61 poor boy's sandwich: local sandwich made of French bread and meat

67 Catch what: *a play on the double meaning of 'catch' – you catch a ball or catch a disease (here a sexual disease)*

69 valise: *suitcase*

71 incongruous: *very different, contrasting strongly*

72 fluffy: *soft and feathery* bodice: *top part of a dress*

74 garden district: *fashionable, rich part of the city*

80 streetcar: (US) *tram or trolleybus*

80–1 Desire, Cemeteries: *destination-signs of streetcars in the city*
block: (US) *an approximate measure of distance, the length of a block of buildings*

93 party: *person*
116 primarily: *mainly*
124 Por nada: (Spanish) *It's nothing*
133 Belle Reve: *the name of their family home; it means 'beautiful dream' in French*
137 drop: *collapse from fatigue*
138 set down: (US) *sit down*
140 make myself scarce: *go away*
142 drop by: *go to*
hustle her up: *tell her to come quickly*
146 purse: (US) *handbag*
150 tumbler: *glass*
159 Stella for Star: *'stella' means 'star' in Latin*
161 spasmodic: *repeated at irregular intervals*
175 liquor: *alcoholic drink*
177 I spy: *a children's game where one player chooses something he can see ('spy') and other players guess what it is; Blanche is trying to sound playful*
182 mix: *dilute the whisky*
183 coke: *Coca Cola*
188 to chase it: *in a separate glass, to follow the whisky*
195 Edgar Allan Poe: *American writer (1809–49) famous for his macabre stories and poems*
196–7 ghoul-haunted woodland of Weir: *a phrase from the poem 'Ulalume' by Poe*
203 Why, that you ... : *'Why' is an exclamation, sometimes used to suggest impatience or surprise; cf lines 213, 446*
220 volunteer: *offer*
222 fired: *dismissed from her job*
225 tamping: *tapping the end of it against a hard surface*
228 wire: *telegram*
235 God love you for a liar: *I know you're lying but thank you*
237 plump as a partridge: *a good, healthy, rounded shape; a partridge is a bird*
it's so becoming to you: *it makes you look beautiful, it suits you*
242 in a feather bob: *quite short, with the ends fluffed or curled*
252 a cherub in choir: *a boy in a choir (a symbol of innocence)*
256 nip: *a small drink*
to put the stopper on: *to put the top or cork back in the bottle; here it also means to stop (drinking)*
265 slipping: *losing their youthful freshness*
267 one particle: *one little bit, at all*
279 dubiously: *doubtfully*
280 gives much: *is very soft*
281 decent: *morally correct*
285 highbrow: *intellectual, sophisticated*
291 Polacks: (US) *derogatory term for Poles*
293 heterogeneous: *varied*
293–4 types: *characters (293); unusual characters (294)*
296 I guess: (US) *I suppose (GB)*
put up: *stay*
301 overwrought: *emotionally tired*
303 in-law: *relative of a wife or husband*
314 decorations: *medals awarded for bravery and good service*
316 brass: *medals*
324 on the road: *travelling*
342 reproach: *blame, express disapproval of*
342 looked out for: *thought only of*
346 hold it together: *keep it going*
361 linoleum: *a cheap, tough waterproof material*
372 big with it: *she had a disfiguring disease*
373 coffin: *wooden box for burying the dead*
376 hoarse: *rough-sounding*
384 the place: *ie their family home, Belle Reve*
let go: *(1) did not maintain it properly ; (2) sold it*
387 the Grim Reaper: *death (which 'reaps' or harvests the living)*
389 it slipped through my fingers: *I lost it*
390 cent: *smallest US coin*
404 And the old lady ... : *Steve is*

telling joke about an old lady and a policeman; the joke is crudely suggestive (it depends on pronouncing 'Mass' as 'my ass' – ie 'my bottom')

409 poker: *a card game with betting*

414 Break it up: *Stop that*

417 Jax beer: *beer from Jacksonville*

422 You want it in the papers?: (ironic) *Do you want me to announce it in the newspapers? (ie that I'm not coming home for lunch)*

431 heartiness: *virile or 'macho' behaviour*

434 gaudy: *brightly coloured (like a cockerel)*

seed-bearer: *male animal, carrying seed*

sizes up: *judges*

441 the little woman: (affectionate) *my wife*

446 Laurel: *city 160 km north-east of New Orleans*

450 Have a shot?: (US slang) *Would you like some whisky?*

469 shack up: (US slang) *stay in someone's house*

479–80 I'll strike you as the unrefined type: *you will think I am rough and crude*

Guess the Author

1 drop-leaf table: *a table that folds*

2 utensils: *knife, fork, etc*

4 scrim: *a thin transparent cloth hung in front of the actors*

8 say grace: *say a prayer before eating*

15 mastication: *chewing*

26 secretion: *production of fluids by the body*

27 Metropolitan: *famous opera house in New York*

28 excused from the table: *Amanda treats her adult son and daughter as if they were children; adults are not usually expected to ask to leave the table*

32 blancmange: *a dessert made with milk*

33 portières: *cloth hangings, curtains*

36 darkey: *black servant (the term would be offensive today)*

39 callers: *visitors*

52 nigger: *same meaning as 'darkey' (line 36) (now even more offensive)*

63 slighted: *neglected (she means she was pretty and had a good figure)*

64 nimble: *quick*

70 the book: *the script of the play – he should look as if he is not fully involved in the scene*

72 planters: *farmers*

76 OÙ SONT LES NEIGES: (Where are the snows?) *a proverbial phrase suggesting nostalgia for past glories (the reference is to a poem by the French poet Villon); this phrase, like the image of Amanda at line 60, is projected onto a screen*

80 bonds: *certificates of money deposited, on which interest is paid*

82 beaux: *fashionable young men (from French 'beau', good-looking)*

86 came into: *inherited*

acres: *measure of land area (1 acre = 4046.9 square metres)*

87 on the rebound: *after a disappointment with another lover*

89–90 had set her cap for: *wanted to marry*

94 turned up their toes to the daisies: *died*

97 Wall Street: *heart of New York's business district*

Midas: *mythical Greek king – everything he touched turned to gold; 'the Midas touch' is proverbial for success in business*

102–3 typewriter chart … shorthand:

Laura is studying to be a secretary

105 flounces: *moves in an elaborately graceful way*

111–12 in a fugitive manner: *as if trying to escape*

122 an old maid: *old and unmarried*

6 Freedom and Laughter

Sizwe Bansi Is Dead

1 African township: *separate part of an urban area reserved for black Africans under the segregation laws of apartheid*

2 Port Elizabeth: *large city (population 560,000) in the Eastern Cape, a big industrial centre (see 'Authors' for Fugard's description of the city)*

3 Reference Books: *(also known as 'pass-books') identity documents which black South Africans had to carry, showing where they were permitted to live, travel and look for work; the pass-book laws were repealed in 1991*

6 Prop.: *proprietor, owner*

9 tripod: *three-legged stand for a camera*

11 'props': *normally, objects used in a stage performance; here they are used by customers posing for photographs*

14 dapper: *neat, well-dressed*

15 dustcoat: *protective cotton coat (as worn by doctors, pharmacists, etc)*

17 headlines: *summaries in large bold print at the top of each column of news; these headlines are from the year 1972 and were taken from a real newspaper by John Kani, the actor who first played Styles; different headlines were used in later performances*

buffets: *hits*

22 South West Africa: *now Namibia; in 1972 it was still a disputed territory*

23 China gets in there … : *if China gets in there …*

25 eavesdropping on: *secretly listening to*

29 Nixon: *Richard Nixon, US President 1969–74*

30 buggerall: (vulgar) *nothing*

32 plant: *factory* rand: *South African currency*

Ja: (Afrikaans) *Yes (see note on line 56)*

39 bloody: *an expletive, expressing anger (cf line 49)*

44 ruefully: *with sadness and regret*

50 made my head go around: *made me dizzy*

51 notice-board: *place where written announcements (notices) are put up*

54 Baas: (Afrikaans) *boss*

56 Afrikaans: *South African language based on Dutch*

57 line: *work in factories is usually done along 'production lines' or 'assembly lines'; workers like Styles stand in one place on a line and repeat the same specialised action hundreds of times each day*

60 Yessus: *Jesus*

61 mop: *sponge on a long handle for washing floors*

68 canteen: *restaurant for the factory staff*

74 spot-checked: *the work was inspected*

80 *Styles continues to mimic Mr Bradley*

84 tow motor: *a motor for towing or pulling*

93 engine blocks: *the central parts of an engine*

94 Iscor: *the Iron and Steel Corporation of South Africa*

105 Gqokra … Ndawo: *these words are in the Xhosa language, which Bradley does not speak;*

although Bradley suspects that Styles is playing a trick on him, the words are quite innocent and mean 'Put On Safety Glasses Here'

112 foreman … manager: *senior grades in the factory's hierarchy; Styles is at a lower grade*

129 big-shot: (slang) *important man*

cunt: (offensive slang) *stupid or unpleasant person*

135 overall: *protective clothing worn in factories*

139 thirty-eight, forty-two: *the sizes of the overalls*

141 spanners … wrench: *examples of tools for working on machines*

142 hot test section: *where parts of the engines are tested while hot*

143 asbestos: *fire-proof material*

145 spot: *the place on the line where he worked*

Armstrong: *Neil Armstrong, US astronaut, the first man to step on the moon (21 July 1969)*

163 bastard: (offensive) *unpleasant person*

168, 169 blustering, groping for words: *unsure what to say*

169 Makulu: *'Grandmother' in the Xhosa language (cf lines 172, 179)*

185 niggers: (offensive) *black people*

Harlem: *area of New York where mainly black people live*

strike: *when workers refuse to work because of a disagreement with the management*

193 talking shit: (offensive slang) *talking nonsense*

200 Tshotsholoza … : *a work-song*

202 tighten the cylinder-head nut: *this is Styles's job on the assembly line*

212 spark-plug walk out: *the Guard suspects the workers of stealing spark-plugs – either to sell or use in their own cars*

214 Galaxies: *luxury cars made by Ford*

215 zoom up: *arrive at high speed*

220 fawning: *making a grotesque show of respect*

223 hefty: *big and strong*

231 main switchboard: *where electrical power for the machines is switched on or off*

240 fleas, bedbugs, etc: *annoying insects*

251 gold wrist-watch: *present given to a worker when he retires*

252 sign you off: *stop employing you*

276 cards: *formal photographs, printed on card*

285 circumcised: *part of the Xhosa ceremonial of manhood*

286 generation gap: *differences of opinion and misunderstandings between parents and children*

287 To hell with them: (mildly offensive) *Never mind them*

288 shutdown: *holiday (the factory is closed or 'shut down')*

292 in my line: *in my business (funerals)*

297 Board: *a group of officials, a committee*

303 Red Location: *area of the town where the studio is; a 'location' is a 'township' (see line 1)*

305 sobered me up: *made me more realistic* (literally, *took away my feeling of drunkenness)*

307 put me off: *discourage me*

316 cockroach: *a large, strong beetle* (*Blatta orientalis*)

319 paratroopers: *soldiers who enter a war zone by parachute – usually very tough characters*

325 Chinaman: *ie a Chinese shop-keeper*

329–30 Two-tin Charlie: *the mime that follows is a fantasy 'western', in which Styles uses tins of Doom as pistols*

338 meeting: *ie of the cockroaches*
342 a general inoculation: *injections to protect health*
349 peter out: *run out (no more Doom left in the tins)*
354 feelers: *antennae (protruding from an insect's head)*
364 Kitsy Kitsy Kitsy: *he is calling to the cat*
377 Reference Book: *see line 3*
381 strong-room: *locked room in a bank where valuables are kept*
407 snap: *photograph*
428 Boss-boy: *'boy' is a patronising term for blacks*
430 Correspondence College: *where students study at home and receive educational materials by post*
431 Standard Six Certificate: *normally achieved at age 12*
433–4 Junior Certificate, Matric: *normally taken at ages 15 and 17*
511 go home: (euphemism) *die*
539 scoff-tin: *tin box provided by the army for one's food*

Shirley Valentine

Note: As in *Pygmalion*, *Roots*, and *The Plough and the Stars*, there are some phonetic spellings here: mainly final letters dropped from *you*, *and*, and words ending *-ing*.

3 like: *no specific meaning: 'like' is a form of hesitation as Shirley struggles to find the right word*
6 me: *my*
14–15 gone round the pipe: (slang) *become mad*
19 Jane: *Shirley's friend, who came to Greece on holiday with her*
20 taverna: *Greek restaurant*
20, 21 me: *my*
21 droppin' off to sleep: *falling asleep*
30 St Joan Of the Fitted Units: *a joke on saints' names and the fate of the suburban housewife; St Joan of France was renowned for her patience in an unhappy marriage; 'fitted units' are kitchen cupboards; the idea is that of the saintly wife and mother, who is miserable but uncomplaining*
40 rubbish: *nonsense*
41 Joe: *Shirley's husband*
48 limbs: *arms and legs*
53 conveyor belt: *moving belt that carries suitcases*
tag: *card, label*
61 concourse: *hall or open space inside an airport*
63 drachmas: *Greek money*
67 feller: *fellow, man*
he nearly dropped his olives: *he was astonished; here 'olives' suggests testicles*
71 the 'Dougies an' Jeanettes': *earlier in the play Shirley describes a couple with these names; they complain about everything in Greece, especially the food*
73 dead nervous: (slang) *very nervous*
74 do: *cook*
chips an' egg: *a traditional English dish*
made up: (dialect) *happy*
77 parasol: *large umbrella for protection against the sun; here it is placed above a restaurant table outside the taverna*
meself: *myself*
82 put the phone down on him: *put down the phone while he was still talking*
88 arsin' round: (vulgar) *doing foolish things, playing around*
got meself home: *went home*
97 bullshit: (vulgar) *pretentious or sentimental talk*
101 bleedin': *an expletive, expressing anger*

102 change of life: *euphemism for menopause*

102–4 *Shirley takes the words 'change of life' literally, understanding Joe's meaning but ignoring it*

7 Success!

Man of the Moment

16 grampus: *someone who breathes loudly* (literally, *a kind of whale)*

28 dripping: *fat that drips from roasting meat*

36 guts: (slang, usually 'greedyguts') *person who over-eats*

glutton: *same meaning as 'guts', but not slang; gluttony is one of the Seven Deadly Sins*

40, 41 Macclesfield, Huddersfield: *towns in the north of England*

45 rum babas: *sweet cakes flavoured with rum and soaked in sticky syrup*

48 turns you over: *(it) makes you feel sick*

58 flailing about: *waving her arms and legs about awkwardly*

65 mind your own business: *don't interfere in my life*

66 a shade: *a little*

77 about set up: *almost ready*

91 whims: *irrational desires*

93 It comes of: *It is a result of*

99 back shelf of a car: *sometimes ornamented with plastic animals which nod as the car moves along*

113 a stunner: (colloquial) *an exceptionally beautiful woman*

besotted: *madly in love*

115 falsetto: *a male voice singing or speaking unnaturally high*

119 hay fever: *running nose, sore eyes, etc, caused by pollen or dust in the air during summer*

122–3 didn't take a blind bit of notice of: *completely ignored*

125 bottom of the reserves: *the last person she would choose (a sporting term – the 'reserves' are the second or B team)*

130 double-glazing: *adding a second layer of glass to the windows in a house in order to insulate it from the cold*

142 old double-glazing: *her fiancé, the double-glazing salesman*

145 marked off: *wrote*

146 ledger: *book of financial accounts, printed in columns; Douglas imagines his life as being recorded in an account book – a traditional Christian image, and very apt for him as a bank-clerk*

147 Silver Cloud: *a Rolls Royce 'Silver Cloud', a very expensive car*

keep wicket for Kent: *a fantasy of being a great sportsman ('keeping wicket' is part of the game of cricket); Kent is a county in southern England*

149 Royal Army Pay Corps: *the accountancy section of the British Army*

152 what I did: *Douglas ran at Vic while he was holding Nerys hostage; the result was that Vic shot Nerys in the head*

154 balaclava: *woollen hat shaped like a helmet which hides much of the face and with holes for the eyes (used by the bank robbers to avoid recognition)*

156 engrossed: *deeply interested*

161 blokes: (slang) *men*

164 drifted away: *gradually left*

180 Jollying her up: *Cheering her up, encouraging her*

190 standing: *importance*

192 a grand bunch: *pleasant people (his colleagues at work)*

193–4 mortgage on number fifty-three: *bank loan to buy their house*

194–5 With never a cross word: *Never arguing or quarrelling*

201, 202 minor league, first division: *low level / high level professional football – Nerys is compared to a star footballer who is forced to accept playing in a minor team*

205 pillock: (vulgar slang) *idiot*

222 partial to: *keen on, fond of*

223 come up with: *invent*

225 pulling herself together: *taking control of herself*

242 run you back: *take you back to your hotel in the car*

252 fork: *place where a road divides into two roads going in different directions*

271 stick with him: *stay with him*

281–2 wetsuit, rubber helmet, flippers: *scuba diving equipment*

284 rubber-clad: *dressed in a rubber suit*

314 telly: (colloquial) *television*

315 *Ask Vic*: *the name of Vic's TV programme*

331 bastard: (offensive) *unpleasant, vicious person*

332 screwing his way round Television Centre: *having sex with large numbers of women at the headquarters of BBC Television*

333 ITV: *Independent Television (a commercial TV channel)*

334 bloody: *an expletive, showing how much she dislikes Vic's mother*

Beckenham: *a suburb of London*

337 scrap: *small piece*

338 scum bucket: (slang) *vile, worthless person*

361 laid a finger on her: *touched her (here in a sexual way)*

367 I am not being shouted at: *I will not accept being shouted at*

383 bathyscope: *strongly-built submarine used for deep sea exploration*

397 vino: (Spanish) *wine*

406 lands a blow that Vic doesn't care for: *hits him hard, arousing his anger*

409 pinion: *hold (her arms) to her sides so that they cannot move*

422 charger: *cavalry horse used in battle*

427 onslaught: *attack*

428 midriff: *centre of the body*

429 winded: *unable to breathe for a few moments*

449 Johnny Weissmuller: *actor and Olympic swimmer famous for his role as Tarzan in films of the 1930s and 1940s*

477 kiss of life: (technically, 'mouth-to-mouth resuscitation') *method of reviving someone who has stopped breathing by blowing into the mouth*

487 life-saver's medal: *Sharon has learned how to save people from drowning; the medal is like a certificate showing that she has passed her exams in the subject*

489 baths: *public swimming pool*

491 pumps away: *she swings his arms or presses on his chest to revive him*

Act Without Words II

4 Frieze effect: *ie the action should look like a frieze – a painted or sculpted band of decoration along the top of a wall*

5 gags: *makes comic mistakes*

absent: *thinking of other things*

9 argument: *subject-matter, what happens; the word also means 'dispute'*

10 wing: *area at the side of the stage, unseen by the audience*

13–14 surmounted by boots and hat: *with boots and hat on top*

15 goad: *a pointed stick*

(originally used for driving cattle)
16 darts: *moves quickly and suddenly*
17 recoils: *moves back quickly*
22 broods: *thinks*
39 consults: *looks at*
41 scalp: *skin on the top and back of the head*
50 compass: *instrument for finding one's position; a magnetic needle points to the north on a dial*

8 Making History

The Plough and the Stars

Note on spellings: O'Casey often uses phonetic spellings to indicate his characters' Dublin accent. There are three typical tricks of spelling that he uses: (1) inserting 'h' after the letters 't' and 'd', to suggest the slightly aspirated, soft pronunciation of these consonants (*betther* for *better*, line 25), (2) omitting the final 'g' from '-ing' endings (*knowin'* line 22), (3) writing *o' th'* for *of the*. He also uses other phonetic spellings from time to time.

Title: the flag of the Irish Citizen Army, the trade union militia of which O'Casey was at one time secretary. The plough symbolises labour, the stars the aspirations of the Labour Movement.

1 tenements: *houses with rented rooms, usually low quality*
2 gaunt: *bare and forbidding*
3 flanked by two pillars: *it has a pillar on each side*
5 lurches: *leans*
6 reckless: *thoughtless, without consideration*
7 the diamond-paned … single pane: *the fan-shaped window above the door has no glass in it*
9 parlour: *sitting room*
grimy: *very dirty*
11 casement cloth: *cotton curtains*
13 area: *a small courtyard leading to the basement of the house*
14 bisecting: *cutting in half*
18 shawl: *woollen cloth used to cover the head and shoulders, part of traditional Irish women's costume*
22 there's no knowin' how well you'll be: *you'll be much better*
comfy: *comfortable*
23 Yis: *Yes*
27 put much pass on: *pay much attention to*
28 out of ordher: *unwell*
32 from this out: *from now on*
35 aself: *itself*
42 folly: *follow*
43 dhread: *dread, intense fear*
staggerin': *walking unsteadily*
46–7 as his soul … dead: *Mrs Gogan's elaborate way of saying 'as he was dying'*
51 whip you in: *bring you quickly in*
52 Covey: *the name suggests a 'know-all', a man who thinks he knows everything*
oul': *old*
53–4 sthrange … together: *Covey and Peter are constantly quarrelling, so it is strange to see them walking together*
56 yous: *you*
58 blazin' away out o' th' G.P.O.: *shooting from the General Post Office (the rebels' headquarters)*
Tommies: (slang) *English soldiers*
59–60 Nelson's Pillar, the Parnell Statue, O'Connell Street: *famous landmarks of central Dublin*
60 pavin' sets: *paving stones*
be: *by*
63 be main force: *by force*
66 vitals: *vital organs, internal parts of the body*
67 crucifix: *image of Christ crucified*

69 Tyler's: *a shoe-shop in O'Connell Street*

70 Lancers: *cavalry soldiers, originally armed with lances (long spears)*

71 Throttin': *Trotting (a horse moving at a fast walk)*
spurs: *metal spikes on a rider's boots, used to make the horse go faster*

72 sabres: *swords* jinglin': *making a metallic sound*
quiverin': *shaking*

73 assin': *asking*
blighters: (slang) *people*
get a prod at them: *hit them with our lances*

74 volley: *several shots fired simultaneously*

75 stretched: *knocked down*
gallopin': *galloping – the horse's fastest run*

84 Liberty Hall: *the headquarters of the Transport and General Workers Union, a rebel stronghold in 1916*

85 on th' quays: *in houses built along the banks of the River Liffey*
Mass: *Catholic church service*

86 Boland's Mills: *another rebel stronghold*

91 shanghaied: *in trouble (to 'shanghai' literally means to drug a man and force him to go to sea)*
boyo: *clever, confident person; she uses the word mockingly*

94 Orange: *Protestant, sympathizing with the English*
bitch: (literally, female dog) *insulting term for a woman*

95 Rule Britannia: *a patriotic English song (quoted at line 144)*

97 wild card: *unpredictable character*

99 sthretcher: (stretcher) *portable bed for carrying the sick or wounded*

100 habit of Saint Francis: *clothes of a monk*

101 litany: *prayers in church*

103 wather lily: *water lily*

104 thrickled: (trickled) *flowed like a thin stream of water*

108 moored: *tied up like a ship at a dock – the whole sentence is another of Mrs Gogan's poetic expressions for death*

112–13 after turnin': (Irish colloquial) *turned*

122 thravellin': *travelling; here it means walking around looking for her husband*

122–3 as fit as a fiddle: *in perfect health*

124 e'er a whisper o': *any news of*

128 be carryin' on: *by behaving*

132 butchered: *killed like an animal*

135 Sorra mend th' lasses: *she wishes a punishment on the girls*

140 threnches: *in France, where many thousand Irishmen were fighting in the war against Germany; much of the war was fought in inhuman conditions from defensive trenches dug into the ground*

140–1 thries … Commandments: *tries to ignore the laws of God*

141–2 judgements … fools: *a Biblical quotation (the meaning is that the rebels will be punished)*

146 throllope: (trollop) *insulting term for a woman*

149 a power o': *many*

150 take a runnin' risk: *Mrs Gogan mixes two idioms in this odd but vivid phrase; one normally 'takes' or 'runs' a risk; perhaps 'running' refers to the street-fighting*

157 hussy: (derogatory) *woman; ('blasted ' is an expletive)*
barricade: *improvised defences put up in the streets*

158 dishearten: *discourage*

160 clawed: *scratched, attacked with her hands*

162 ruffians: *criminals, violent people*
165 twarthers: *thwarters (people who thwart or obstruct you)*
166–7 If they ... wouldn't mind: *Covey is a socialist, who has said earlier that he will not join the rebellion because it will not bring freedom to the poor*
168 derogatory: *bad*
169 finish up: *end*
vice versa: *the opposite*
177 denunciatory: *denouncing, condemning*
188 If you'd ... : *ie you and your husband*
189 wrench asundher: *sudden separation*
200 only for: *without the help of*
208 tossers: *pieces of wood for tossing coins in the air; the game is explained at lines 229–30*
211 sham: *false*
landed a body in a nice way: *made life difficult for everyone*
212 ferret out: *search for*
214 vipers: *poisonous snakes (a symbol of treachery)*
217 Make a start: *Start the coin-tossing game*
219 oul' son: *friendly form of address, like 'my dear'*
222 turn-up: *sudden occurrence (the rebellion)*
224 a pint: *beer*
227–8 Heads ... Harps: *the two sides of an Irish coin; the head represents the King of England, the harp Ireland*
a juice: *a deuce (2 pence)*
a tanner: *6 pence*
237 not playin' th' game: *not fair, against the rules*
241 your pickin' at me: *your finding fault with me*
254 whippin' away: *stealing*
255 lassie: *girl*
257 oul' wan: *old one*
258 th ' dint o' heart beatin': *the strain on her heart*
262 curious: *odd, strange*
268 gettin' a shake up: *being looted*
279 potted: (slang) *shot*
281 regimentals: *ceremonial uniform of Peter's Volunteer regiment*
283 give you a hot knock: *strike angrily at you*
tuthorin' ... up: (tutoring) *teaching*
284–5 tiltin' at: *attacking, mocking*
crossin' ... jibin': *making me angry with mockery and insults*
288 Gawd: *God (phonetic spelling to indicate a middle-class accent)*
289 Wrathmines: *Rathmines, a middle-class suburb of Dublin*
290–1 howl, cawn't: *whole, can't*
301 passed away: *died*
312 pilot: *guide*
314 throttin': *running (see line 71)*
315–16 gimme a game leg: *make me lame*
321 pram: *carriage for a baby*
325 clap your eyes on: *see*
327 Dunboyne: *a village near Dublin*
sthrict injunctions: *strict orders (not to be disobeyed)*
328 accasional: *occasional*
330–41 *another of Mrs Gogan's elaborate and colourful speeches; she accuses Bessie of wanting the pram for carrying looted goods*
331 seein' that: *since*
332 jamb: *doorpost (upright part of door frame)*
334 squint: *sideways look*
336 be: *by*
346 bassinette: *pram*
week in an' week out: *every week*
347–8 a regular accommodation: *space*
349 harp, shamrock: *symbols of Ireland*
350–1 lion and unicorn: *symbols of England*
353 fella: *fellow, man*

355 Take … pattin': *Take your hands off*

356–7 steppin … manners: *forgetting good manners for a moment*

357 fat: *great*

358 singer o' hymns: *ie she makes a show of being a Christian*

359 sky-thinkin': *thinking of God*

360 sly-seekin': *trying to be cunning*
pinch: (slang) *steal*

360–1 dhriven asthray: (driven astray) *lost*

366 prambulator: (perambulator) *pram*

367–75 *Bessie says that she is not intending to steal anything, only to pick up anything left by others stealing*

369 from backside to breakfast time: *a crude expression, meaning 'thoroughly'*

370 kinch: *control*

373 lofty-hearted: *noble, unselfish*

379 sorra mind I'd mind: *I would not mind*

380 met with a dhrop: *were struck down*

391 mot: (slang) *woman*

394 lackey: *servant*

396 assin': *asking*

399 burnishin': *contributing to* (literally, *polish, give a shine to)*

400 revilin': *debasing, spoiling* (literally, *speaking badly of)*

401 roguery: *criminal actions*

402 leppin: *dialect form of 'leaping'*

403 guts: (slang) *courage*
ketch: *catch, pick up*

404 chosen people: *a phrase normally used of the Israelites in the Old Testament of the Bible; here he means the poor*

405 you'd steal … back: *a proverbial expression for a thief (donkeys have a cross-shaped marking on their backs)*

407 proddin': *teasing*
goad … away: *annoy me as much as you like*

412–13 *an elaborately-phrased insult: 'lanky' means tall and thin, a 'lath' is a narrow stick, 'lowsey' (= lousy) means infested with lice (parasitical insects), or poor in quality, and 'bastard' (the key word here) is an offensive way of telling someone he has behaved badly*

416 fancy: *expensive*

420–3 *she is talking about shoes with square heels, fashionable at that time*

423–6 *Bessie says the shoes will look good with the dresses they have taken, which they will alter to make them more modest*

423 afther: *see line 112*
liftin': (slang) *stealing*

424 sthray bit: *an odd piece, used for patching and altering*
bodice: *top part of a dress*

427 fussily: *very carefully*

430 youngster: *child*

431 convulsions: *violent, uncontrolled movements of the body*

434 make a bolt for: *run towards*

438 tumultuously: *very noisily*

441 spasms: *sudden pains*

450 mobbin': *crowding around*

451 slum lice: *Brennan is referring contemptuously to the poor of Dublin; 'slum' is poor, unhealthy housing; 'lice' (plural of 'louse') are parasitical insects that live on animals and humans, especially in unhygienic conditions*

452 plug: (slang) *shoot*

455 knockin' around: *available*

457 Keep th' heart up: *Be brave, don't despair*

460 haggard: *worn and ugly after extreme emotion*
agleam: *shining*

463 handmaiden: *a Biblical term, meaning a female servant*

464–5 lost … found … dead … alive:

an echo of the parable of the Prodigal Son from the Bible

472 don't make a scene: *don't be so emotional in public, control yourself*

477 Minsthrel Boys: *a reference to 'The Minstrel Boy', a patriotic poem by Thomas Moore (1779–1852) in which a boy goes to war carrying his sword and harp*

479–80 unlacin' … bodice: *undressing his wife*

480–1 professor of chicken-butcherin': *Captain Brennan is a chicken butcher by trade*

481 up against: *confronted with, facing (she means he now has to face the British army)*

483 y'oul hag: *you old hag (abusive term for a woman)*

484 Choke: *Kill (she is mocking him)*

Translations

5 suffice: *be sufficient, enough*

18 livestock: *farm animals*

23 bear: *produce*

24 embark on: *begin*
evictions: *forcing people to leave their homes*
levelling: *destruction*

25 abode: *house*

33–40 Swinefort, Burnfoot … Kings Head: *place-names anglicized by Lancey and his men*

45 ravish: *destroy*

51 contorted: *twisted (Sarah has a speech handicap)*

65 wake: *(Irish) funeral*

70 lout: *crude, stupid man*

76–7 wheels on Doalty: *turns angrily to face him*

89 potato blight: *a disease that destroys potatoes*

111 put me out: *force me away from my home*

Key

1 Anatomy of a Play

1 1 spotlights; 2 auditorium; 3 costume; 4 make-up; 5 director; 6 rehearsal; 7 stage manager; 8 scenery; 9 props; 10 backstage; 11 wings

2 ***a – 4; b – 13; c – 2; d – 1; e – 3; f – 10; g – 11; h – 12; i – 7; j – 8; k – 9; l – 6; m – 5***

A Rehearsal

1

Our Country's Good	*The Recruiting Officer*
Mary Brenham	Silvia
Liz Morden	Melinda
Duckling Smith	Lucy (Melinda's maid)
Dabby Bryant	Rose, a country girl
Henry Kable	Captain Plume
John Arscott	Sergeant Kite
Robert Sideway	Mr Worthy
James Freeman	Justice Balance
John Wisehammer	Captain Brazen

The play is directed by Ralph Clark.

2

0 NATURAL	50	100% ARTIFICIAL
Liz, Dabby, Duckling	Mary	Sideway

2 Language, Class and Power

3 Orwell – money; Wells – accent

4 Shaw writes 'thats' instead of 'that's', and 'havnt' instead of 'haven't'. On the other hand 'It's' (= it is) is spelt in the normal way, perhaps to distinguish it from the possessive 'its'.

6 ***c***

7

HIGGINS	PICKERING	MRS PEARCE	LIZA
impulsive	down-to-earth	down-to-earth	impulsive
noisy	practical	practical	noisy
insensitive	discreet	discreet	blunt
blunt	considerate	considerate	brusque
brusque	well-mannered	well-mannered	
	sensible	sensible	
	friendly		

8 open response, though ***c*** or ***e*** seem most probable

9 These are all rich in suggestions. Here are some possibilities:

a He is fascinated by her as an object of scientific study, though unmoved by her poverty.
b He is impulsive. He rejects conventional wisdom and prudence. He may be romantic.
c He thinks of her as an object, not a person.
d He is either very diplomatic, or cunning, or unconscious of the effects of what he says and does.
e He is patronizing to Mrs Pearce. He seems to think that human relationships are only a question of 'amusement'. He cares nothing for Liza's feelings.
f He is impractical. He is unsympathetic. (He may possibly be joking?)
g He is trying to tempt her, and one has to ask why. Perhaps because he is tempted by her himself? There is also something cynical about this – the rich man tempting the poor girl with things she has never had.
h See ***b***. Higgins is also something of a wit.

10 ***b*** and ***h*** are similar; ***f*** and ***g*** are contradictory. This suggests that he is impulsive and perhaps rather confused. His moods and opinions can change quite abruptly.

11 ***a***, ***c***, ***g*** and ***h*** are all probable.
b The way she speaks in lines 71–2 show that she is not shy.
d Lines 67–8 tell us that she knows Higgins well.
e Lines 65–8 suggest that she understands Higgins's work.
f There is nothing to suggest this in the text.

12 ***a*** lines 200–1, 248–9, 264–5, 278, 328–31
b lines 248–9, 264–5, 278, 294–6, 328–31, 361–2
c lines 200–1, 244, 267–8, 295–8, 308–9, 328–31, 361–2, 409–14
d lines 219–22, 278, 294–6

13 lines 200–1, or possibly 219–22

14 Open response, although ***c***, and ***e***, and the first part of ***d*** ('She is a narrow-minded figure') are less likely.

15 ***a*** and ***b***

16 ***a*** Probably because she is offended by the way Higgins and Mrs Pearce speak to her.
b Pickering uses a question, Higgins and Mrs Pearce use the imperative.
c There are differences in the characters' manner and intonation: Higgins speaks 'peremptorily' and 'thundering at her', Mrs Pearce speaks 'severely', and Pickering is 'very courteous'.

17

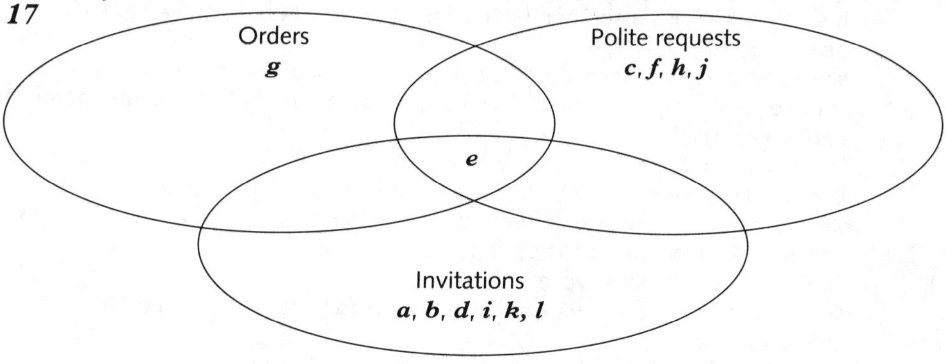

18 ***a*** Would you mind shewing her up (please), Mrs Pearce?
Could / Would you shew her up please, Mrs Pearce?
b Would you mind giving me that handkerchief (,please)?

Could / Can I have that handkerchief, please?
Would / Could you give me that handkerchief, please?
c Would you mind taking her away and cleaning her, Mrs Pearce?
Could / Would you take her away and clean her please, Mrs Pearce?

20 *a* I came in a taxi. *[present tense instead of past simple]*
b If you were a gentleman, you might ask me to sit down. *['was' for 'were' in 2nd person singular]*
c Didn't I tell you / Haven't I told you I'm bringing you business? *[present tense instead of past simple or present perfect]*
d They won't take me unless I can talk in a more genteel way / more genteelly. *[adjective instead of adverbial phrase or adverb]*
e I haven't (got) any parents. *Or* I don't have any parents. *['ain't' for 'haven't'; double negative]*
f The one that turned me out was my sixth stepmother. *[incorrect use of pronoun]*
g I did without them. *[use of past participle instead of past simple]*
h I've got (*or* I have) my feelings the same as anyone else (*or* just like anyone else) *[omission of 'have' with 'got' in present tense; omission of 'the' with 'same']*
i You care for nothing (*or* you don't care for anything) but yourself. *[double negative]*
j I wouldn't have eaten it. *[past simple instead of past participle]*
k I don't want gold or diamonds. *[double negative – twice]*
l I've always been a good girl. *[omission of 'have' in present perfect]*

25 *a* The characters on stage are all working class (judging by their accent, conversation, and habits), although Beatie is clearly in transition towards the middle-class, which is where her boyfriend Ronnie seems to belong.
b The differences stressed here are in reading habits (the *Manchester Guardian* as opposed to comics, lines 117–25), the use of leisure (playing and listening to music, painting, reading books, lines 128–31), knowing how to argue and discuss (lines 172–88), and making love in the afternoon (a sign of free-thinking, regarded as highly suspicious by Jimmy and Jenny, lines 188–202).

26 He seems to mean 'use the language *better*'. This would mean using her mind and her talents better too. Reasons given in this extract are: 1) it will enable her to defend her rights (lines 161–70); 2) it will widen her cultural horizons (lines 175–7); 3) it will enable her to settle disagreements by reasoned argument rather than quarrels (lines 178–81). 4) Looking at lines 111–13, one might add that talking in her native dialect is associated with being 'lazy', so 'using the language' would mean being more energetic too.

27 line 12 *Shut you up / get you to sleep* (*you* is omitted in standard English)
lines 15–16 *Father come home and find you awake* (for 'if Father comes home and finds you awake')
line 17 *gal* (for 'girl')
lines 17–18 *don't wan' / wi' me / mornin'* (omission of 'l' from 'don't want'; dropping of final consonants from *want, with, morning*, etc; also in lines 24, 25, 27)
line 24 *Waas matter* (for 'What's the matter')
line 25 *a'tween* (for 'between')
line 28 *Blust* (for 'Blast'); *yit* (for 'yet'. Also *git* for 'get', lines 27 and 39)
line 32 *'tis* (for 'it is')
lines 36 *she say / it go* (for 'she says / it goes'); *so bad* ('so badly')
lines 40–1 *hed / hevn't* ('had / hadn't')

3 Family Life

8 open response, though some possible answers are:
a James Tyrone is disappointed in his sons and his wife, and possibly blames himself for some of their problems.
b Mary is addicted to morphine and feels guilty about it.
c Jamie is a failure and hates being reminded of it by his father; he is also worried by his mother's behaviour.
d Edmund is seriously ill.
e They are dishonest with each other, they accuse each other constantly, they blame each other for their own unhappiness.

9 This is not very useful. It tells us 'who' and 'when' but not 'where', or what the characters do.

10 ***a – 7; b – 11; c – 4; d – 12; e – 3; f – 6; g – 9; h – 1; i – 10; j – 5; k – 8; l – 2***

11 *kind*: They're glad to have him. Some of the poems and parodies he's written are damned good. He's certainly made a damned good start.
unkind: A hick town rag! Whatever bull they hand you, they tell me he's a pretty bum reporter ... Not that they'd ever get him anywhere on the big time.

12 *a* He is bitter, cynical, weary.
b He is caring, but also defensive; the comment about 'the usual brothers' is cynical.
c He is trying to be optimistic and caring.
d He is proud.
e He is defensive, aggressive, bitter.
f He is trying to be optimistic and caring.
g She often blames others; she is bitter.
h She is self-obsessed.
i She is trying to be optimistic; she is defensive.
j Jamie is being defensive here. His words suggest that Edmund is adventurous.
k He is talented, but in an unusual way.
l He is weary.

13 *a* I sneer at myself in private.
b You're unhealthy now.
c ... but you were wrong, and I still blame you.
d You're proud, but you have nothing to be proud of.
e You're fat and out of shape from the drunken life you've led.
f We were proud of you when you gave up morphine. Now we're terrified that you've started taking it again.
g Let's talk about something else.

14 *a* This implies that he feels guilty for what he has just said.
b This suggests that he is deeply moved.
c This implies that he is being as gentle as he can, although there is still something hard and unforgiving about him.
d This suggests that he finds the words hard to say. He knows they are likely to have a bad effect on his father.
e 'Forced' implies that he does not really feel it. In other words he suspects Jamie is right but is not prepared to admit it.
f This suggests that he is keen to believe that her behaviour is innocent.
g This suggests that she is extremely nervous and tense.
h The implication is that they both know the truth but are trying to avoid showing that they know.

15 This is probably because the characters tend to be dishonest with each other, and constantly suspect one another of meaning more than they say.

16 ***a*** accuse, suspect; ***b*** blame; ***c*** blame; ***d*** suspect, pretend, claim; ***e*** defend

17 ***a*** Tyrone accuses Jamie of never having saved a dollar in his life.
b Tyrone accuses Jamie of throwing (*or* having thrown) away his salary every week on whores and whiskey.
c Jamie defends himself by saying that he earns his board and lodging working on the grounds.
d Tyrone claims that he couldn't have sent Edmund to a better doctor.
e Tyrone blames Jamie more than anyone.
f Jamie suspects that it's the special stuff that gets Edmund by.
g Jamie blames the doctor.

18 (sample answers):
a Jamie accuses his father of hiring cheap doctors to save money and of giving up hope for Edmund's health.
b Tyrone defends himself by saying that the doctors he chose were good ones, and by attacking Jamie.
c Tyrone accuses Jamie of being evil-minded, lazy and a failure.
d Jamie defends himself by claiming that his father forced him into a job he never wanted.
e Jamie suspects his mother of taking drugs again.

20 TYRONE: ***b, e, g, k, l, o, r, w***
MARY: ***a, d, f, i, n, q***
JAMIE: ***b, p, s, t, x***
EDMUND: ***c, h, j, m, u, v***
Note that these answers are based on O'Neill's stage directions (see Exercise 22). Other answers are possible.

24 ***c***

27 ***a*** open response
b There are similarities in theme (parents and children, betrayal, deception, forgiveness), and in the characters (the way the parents claim to do things for their children's sakes, but in fact do them for their own).
c The treatment of time is noticeably different. O'Neill's play shows a single day, Keatley's has separate scenes 16 years apart. In O'Neill the past is brought into the present through dialogue (the characters' memories and accusations); in Keatley, past and present are separately dramatised. The representation of Rosie in the first scene is interesting too. Whereas O'Neill is naturalistic (the characters look as they would in real life), Keatley is not – for the baby Rosie she uses a 'Moses basket of blankets' with an adult actress who 'can be seen making the sounds of the baby crying'. In a similar way, at the end of this scene, a sheet representing Rosie is suddenly shaken out, and becomes an ordinary sheet again. (This approach to theatrical illusion – in which the mechanism of the illusion is openly displayed to the audience – shows the influence of the German playwright Bertolt Brecht, who called this technique the 'alienation effect'.)

4 'We're Right And You're Wrong'

2 true: ***e, f, g, h, i, l, m, n, o***
false: ***a, b, c, d, j, k***

3 open response but ***d*** is most likely

5 ***d***

6 ***a*** lines 5–6, 8–9, 42–6, 76–83; ***b*** 8–9, 81–3

7 ***b***

8 This is personal. In ***a*** she may well mean what she says. In ***b*** Parris interprets her words in his way, which may or not be how she intends them. In ***c*** she seems to mean 'I suspect you do go to Satan'.

9 *Abigail claims* that Tituba makes her drink blood, sends her spirit on her in church, makes her laugh when she should be praying, and brings her obscene dreams at night.
Tituba claims that Abigail comes to her and asks for conjuring and charms.
a Abigail; ***b*** personal response – perhaps because Tituba is a slave and he thinks her less reliable, or because Parris seems to support Abigail; ***c*** personal response; ***d*** the testimony of an independent witness would be helpful, as would separate questioning of the witnesses.

10 ***a*** the threat of hanging; ***b*** It suggests that it may be false, since she has no choice: she must either 'confess' or die.

11 The interrogation is carried out in a grossly improper way, with the threat of violence if the 'right' answers are not given (lines 209–14), the names of possible 'guilty' people suggested to Tituba (lines 247–8), physical and emotional pressure on the witnesses (lines 259, 277) and the interrogators in a highly excited state of mind. It seems most unlikely that the confessions are true.

12 ***a*** Someone take these, please!
b Is your child sick too?
c He doesn't believe in witches.
d I never said anything about witches one way or the other.
e ... waving her arms as though she wanted to fly.
f Now, sir, what was your first warning of this strangeness?
g Don't be afraid now.
h Sit down here.
i What does it mean when (*or* if) someone reads strange books?
j I have often woken up at night and found her in a corner reading a book.
k It makes me uncomfortable (*or* uneasy)!
l I don't know. She spoke in a Barbados dialect.

13 He say Mr Parris must be kill! Mr Parris no goodly man, Mr Parris mean man and no gentle man, and he bid me rise out of my bed and cut your throat! ... But I tell him 'No! I don't hate that man. I don't want kill that man.' But he say, 'You work for me, Tituba, and I make you free! I give you pretty dress to wear, and put you way high up in the air, and you gone fly back to Barbados!' And I say, 'You lie, Devil, you *lie*!' And then he come one stormy night to me, and he say, 'Look, I have *white* people belong to me.' And I look – and there was Goody Good.

14 Note: the main tense of Tituba's narration can be either past simple or what is known as 'dramatic present' (a present tense used to make the story more exciting). He says (*or* said) Mr Parris must be killed. Mr Parris is not a good man. Mr Parris is a mean man, and not a gentle man. And he bids (*or* bade) me rise out of my bed and cut your throat! ... But I tell (*or* told) him 'No! I don't hate that man. I don't want to kill that man.' But he says (*or* said), 'You work for me, Tituba, and I will make you free! I will give you a pretty dress to wear, and put you way high up in the air, and you will fly back to Barbados!' And I say (*or* said) 'You lie, Devil, you lie!' (*or* You're lying, Devil, you're lying!) And then he comes (*or* came) one stormy night to me, and he says (*or* said), 'Look, I have *white* people belonging to me.' And I look (*or* looked) – and there was Goody Good.

15 ***a*** Tituba almost always uses the present tense, even when talking about the past or the future.
b She does not inflect verbs (*he say, must be kill,* etc); she often omits verbs and articles (*Mr Parris mean man*); she omits 'to' in the phrase *I don't want kill that man*.

16 open response; ungrammatical language often gives an impression of ignorance, so this may be one reason why they choose not to believe her when she denies Abigail's accusations.

18

a mystery	***e*** heathens	***i*** persecuted	***m*** believed
b parishioners	***f*** Christians	***j*** parishioners	***n*** light
c heathens	***g*** believed	***k*** sect	***o*** belief
d convert	***h*** homage	***l*** defiled	***p*** discipline

19 open response

23 open response

24 ***a*** Pinter deliberately leaves the situation unexplained. At times it seems that McCann and Goldberg represent a secret political or terrorist organization, at others they sound like salesmen, school-teachers, parents, businessmen, doctors, psychiatrists, priests, philosophers or police. By the end of the play the most likely explanation seems to be that they are hired killers. This form of theatre, part comedy, part thriller, part existential mystery, is sometimes called 'comedy of menace'.
b open response

5 Lost In New Orleans

2 In fact her stay turns out to be a disaster. Stanley never feels comfortable with Blanche, or she with him. He mistrusts her from the start, and later in the play he cruelly exposes her as a liar.

3 ***a*** a different social class; perhaps also a different psychological type
b She knows that Blanche will judge him to be 'inferior' (in fact this happens later in the play, where Blanche describes Stanley as 'sub-human').

4 Stanley's syntax is less correct, and both his vocabulary and topics of conversation are far more limited, more basic. He is clearly less educated than they are.

5 ***a*** She is vain, and rather bossy towards her sister.
b She is used to more elegant surroundings, and is snobbish. This remark also shows that she is insensitive to her sister's feelings.
c She lies about the amount she drinks (often a sign of alcoholism).
d She blames Stella for leaving, although she pretends not to. This adds to the feeling that she is a deceitful person, who possibly deceives herself too.
e This suggests that Stella is trying not hurt her sister's feelings, that she is a considerate person, but also that she plays along with the pretences that Blanche imposes on her, suggesting that she is a weaker character.
f This implies that she knows Blanche and her snobbery well, but has decided to be different from Blanche and live by her own standards.
g She is clearly very attached to Stanley, and perhaps rather insecure.
h This suggests that she is capable of standing up to Blanche, and is perhaps a stronger character than she seems.
i The suggestion here is that Stanley is crude, vigorous and playful. (The meat is also a symbol of his 'red-blooded' nature. See Exercise 6.)

j This shows that he is quite shrewd: he is not deceived by her pretence of not drinking. But he is also prepared to make a joke of it, not to take the matter too seriously.

k This suggests that his physical sensations are more important to him than good manners. And even though he shows some delicacy by asking if Blanche minds, he starts to remove his shirt before she has a chance to reply. This suggests that he doesn't care whether she minds or not.

6 (some possible answers):

a hot-blooded people, a lot of raw emotion in the air

b Moths are traditional symbols of fragility and self-destruction (they fly into candle-flames) or for the transience of earthly possessions (they eat clothes and furs). Blanche's alcoholism, and her loss of the family plantation, fit this quite neatly. Moths are also nocturnal insects, active at a time when most humans are asleep, and so rather strange. There is certainly something strange about Blanche.

c Blanche is on a streetcar ride through life, driven by desire towards death and an after-life. The suggestion is that she will complete this journey (or something like it) in the play.

d The house is now just a beautiful dream – a fantasy.

e Animals often stand for the instinctive (as opposed to the intellectual or spiritual) side of human life: 'nature' as against 'civilisation'. Blanche pretends to be very 'civilised', and the cat's screech shocks her with its reminder of the world of instinct.

f, g On both occasions this is clearly meant to suggest a special intensity of emotion.

7 ***a*** Unlike Stella's home, Belle Reve is large and elegant.
Unlike Stella, Stanley comes from a poor background.
Unlike Stella, Blanche stayed at Belle Reve.
Unlike the men they once went out with, Stanley is crude and unsophisticated.
Unlike Stella, Blanche lacks self-control.
Unlike Stella, Blanche is nervous and energetic.

b Belle Reve differs from (*or* is unlike) Stella's home in that it is large and elegant.
Stanley differs from (*or* is unlike) Stella in that he comes from a poor background.
Blanche differs from (*or* is unlike) Stella in that she stayed at Belle Reve.
Stanley differs from (*or* is unlike) the men they once went out with in that he is crude and unsophisticated.
Blanche differs from (*or* is unlike) Stella in that she lacks self-control.
Blanche differs from (*or* is unlike) Stella in that she is nervous and energetic.

9

a get	***h*** make	***o*** get	***v*** put
b take	***i*** doing	***p*** let	***w*** putting
c take	***j*** Put or Take	***q*** do	***x*** taking
d make	***k*** goes	***r*** going	***y*** made
e been (gone)	***l*** do	***s*** do	***z*** get
f let	***m*** go, make, get	***t*** get	
g take	***n*** take	***u*** let	

10 ***a*** They are used very frequently.

b This shows that his style is very similar to everyday conversation (at least in vocabulary). One could describe the style as *colloquial* or *conversational.*

15 The play is *The Glass Menagerie,* written by Tennessee Williams in 1944. The character of Amanda and her fixation on her lost past in Southern high society is very reminiscent of Blanche. Both the Southern setting and the use of music also suggest *A Streetcar Named Desire.*

6 Freedom and Laughter

1 *a*
2 *c*
3 *d*
4 *d*
5 *e*
6 *d* only
7 *e*
9 open response to *What these might suggest about his character.* It is of course too early in the play to judge Styles. Here we are looking at first impressions. Some suggested answers:

News	*Styles's comments and reactions*	*What these might his suggest about character*
Storm in Natal	1. laughs 2. 'I'm watching it'	indifferent to the sufferings of others? amused by life
S W Africa and China	1. 'be careful' 2. laughs 3. 'No comment'	concerned, amused, but cautious (or pretends to be)
American politics	'means buggerall to us'	interested only in what affects him or black South Africans directly
Car plant expansion	that means expanded factories, no expansion to pay packets; fed-up	cynical, shrewd, judges events by their effect on black workers; politically aware
Big speech about conditions of non-white workers	'talk ended in the bloody newspaper, never in the pay-packet'	angry, embittered; practical, hard-headed
Visit of Henry Ford	a few more cents in the pay-packet	pragmatic; impressed more by money than pride in the company

10 *a* the Ford factory
b He explains why in lines 249–269. Key sentences are 'Run up and down the whole bloody day! Your life doesn't belong to you. You've sold it. For what, Styles? Gold wrist-watch in twenty-five years time … A bloody circus monkey! Selling most of his time on this earth to another man. Out of every twenty-four hours I could

only properly call mine the six when I was sleeping. What the hell is the use of that? ... You call that living?'

c open response

11
1. Styles
2. 'Baas' Bradley (lines 56ff)
3. the factory bosses (line 66)
4. the big factory boss (line 71)
5. the man in the General Store (line 136)
6. the 'fawning men' (line 220)
7. Henry Ford (lines 225–6)
8. the white staff at the switchboard (line 232)
9. the children (lines 265–6)
10. Styles's father (lines 280–5)
11. the cockroaches (lines 321–3)
12. Two-tin Charlie (lines 331–6, 348–52)
13. the old professor cockroach (lines 340–4)
14. Dhlamini (lines 356–61)
15. the client full of smiles (lines 403–36)
16. the client in the boxer's stance (lines 415)
17. the Grandfather (lines 454–5)
18. the eldest son (lines 462–6)
19. the family photograph (children, uncles and aunts, the old man, people in the street, Styles behind the camera – lines 469–502)

12 All are possible, although ***e*** seems unlikely.

13 Noticeable similarities are: no sound effects, almost everything onstage coming from the actor, the idea of the actor transforming himself while the audience watches, and transforming the space and objects around him through mime and gesture. Generally, the play seems to be an excellent example of 'Poor Theatre'.

14 ***a*** open response (one could present this in either a 'Poor' or a 'Rich' style)

b, ***c*** open response, although a symbolic interpretation is certainly possible. Styles seems at first to have some sympathy with the cockroaches – they could be symbols of oppressed humanity, like his fellow workers in the Ford factory – but in the end it's a fight for survival between them and him, suggesting that his philosophy is after all the Darwinian principle of 'survival of the fittest'. This neatly expresses two contrasting aspects of Styles's character – he is a mixture of concern for others and determination to survive.

15 ***a*** This is probably because they think of them as unexceptional.

b Styles reminds us that the people of New Brighton are **people**, with dreams, hopes, feelings, and memories, and that every human life is unique and valuable.

16 This sums up a lot of Styles (the joker, the optimist, the showman), but not all. One might add that he is a 'fighter', who is determined to survive, and very serious about his people.

17 ***a***
1. After some time the first letter back;
2. A month later;
3. Another month;
4. But one day, a knock at the door – the postman;
5. 'We are pleased to inform you ...'

b The elliptical clauses show Styles telling his story in his quick, concise, racy style, leaving out all unnecessary details. The grammatically complete clauses and sentences are either quotations from official letters written in a formal style, or describe formal procedures. The exception is 'I nearly gave up, friends' – which would be hard to reduce any further!

18 ***a*** There was a big hole in the roof, and (there were) cobwebs in the corners.
b They were all over – on the floors, the walls.
c I went (*or* walked, or ran) out of here and into the Chinaman's shop.
d They did not sleep.
e There was a general meeting under the floorboards.
f It was midweek.
g In walked a chap, full of smiles, with a little parcel under his arm.
h I ask no questions!
i I put the old lady here, the eldest son there.
j I went back to the camera, and started to focus again …
k I did it ten times, friends! Each one was different!

19

	lines	*complete sentences*
45	Big news for us, man!	That was big news for us, man!
48	Ja, a Thursday morning.	Ja, it was a Thursday morning.
49	Those big bloody machines that used to make so much noise made my head go around…? Silent!	Those big bloody machines that used to make so much noise (that) they made my head go round were silent!
51	Went to the notice-board and read: Mr Ford's visit today!	I went to the notice-board and read: Mr Ford's visit is today!
53	The one in charge of us… hey! I remember him. General Foreman Mr 'Baas' Bradley. Good man, that one …	The one in charge of us – hey! I remember him. He was General Foreman Mr 'Baas' Bradley – a good man, that one …
59	Nothing specific, you know, little bit here, little bit there.	It was nothing specific, you know, a little bit here, a little bit there.
66	Big day for the plant!	It's a (or This is a) big day for the plant!
69	that day? Sleeves rolled up, running around us	That day he had his sleeves rolled up, and he was running around us
71	Spotless, my boys! Over there, John …	The factory must be spotless, my boys! Look over there, John …
74	spot-checked after fifteen minutes!	it was spot-checked after fifteen minutes!
76	First stage of General Cleaning finished.	The first stage of General Cleaning was finished.
79	W-h-i-t-e l-i-n-e	He painted a W-h-i-t-e l-i-n-e.
81	Been here five years and I never seen a white line before. Then:	I've been here five years and I've never seen a white line before. Then Mr Bradley painted:
86	Safety-precautions after six years. Then another gallon of paint.	We had (or They were introducing) safety-precautions after six years. Then he brought another gallon of paint.
88	Y-e-l-l-o-w l-i-n-e-	He painted a Y-e-l-l-o-w l-i-n-e.
90	Then another gallon: G-r-e-e-n l-i-n-e-	Then he brought another gallon and painted a G-r-e-e-n l-i-n-e.

	lines	*complete sentences*
94	Dangerous world, that. Big machines! One mistake there and you're in trouble.	It was a dangerous world, that. They were (or There were) big machines! Make one mistake there and you're in trouble.
99	Then my big moment.	Then came (or it was) my big moment.
111	Kneeling there on the floor … foreman, general foreman, plant supervisor, plant manager … and Styles? Standing!	Kneeling there on the floor were the foreman, the general foreman, the plant supervisor, the plant manger … and Styles? I was standing!
120	Plant was looking nice, man! Colourful!	The plant was looking nice, man! It looked (or It was) colourful!

20 ***a, b*** open response
c many possible meanings – suggested interpretation: the studio is a place where people's dreams are protected – from time, death, misfortune, injustice. Their dreams may be many things: their fantasies, their hopes, their vision of themselves as they would like to be, even their existence on earth (preserved after they die in the photograph). 'My people' in the cultural context of the play clearly means 'fellow black South Africans', but it also means the simple people, who are never mentioned in the history books.

21 ***a*** A circus monkey lives an unnatural, restricted life, performing tricks for the entertainment of others instead of living its natural life in the wild. Styles feels he was like a monkey in not living his own life.
b The man's face is like a history book which he has written himself. The phrase is a reminder of 'the writers of the big books' (line 391), who would certainly ignore this man. Again Styles implies that such people must not be ignored, since they have stories, lives, 'histories' of their own.
c When Styles says 'go home' he means 'die'. Since most people think of 'home' as a place of comfort, shelter and rest, this suggests that Styles thinks of death as not a frightening or terrible thing, but something peaceful and consoling. It may also suggest that he is religious, (or using conventional religious language to comfort his customer).

22 open response

26 ***a*** They had a day out together on a boat and made love.
b open response; note that he seems to regard her just as a housewife with no real feelings, and that he thinks entirely in conventional terms and clichés (he said I was a disgrace … he said you can't run away from life … he said he knew all about me 'holiday romance' … he was sayin', 'I knew it, it's the bleedin' change of life isn't it?'). Shirley has begun to think for herself now, and to see life (including words and their meanings) in a new way.

28 'She's not remarkable, she's not gonna be there in the history books. But she's there in the time she's livin' in.' The distinction between 'being there in the history books' and 'being there in the time she's livin' in' seems to help Shirley understand the purpose of her life. This is not to be 'remarkable' but to be fully alive in her time (the contemporary world, the present).

29 There are similarities both of character and circumstances. Both have led ordinary lives and felt imprisoned by them. Both are lively, observant, and independent-minded. Both are 'fighters' who have decided to change their lives whatever this may cost.

30 open response, though the meaning seems to be that we have desires, dreams and possibilities which we never realise – 'because we don't do what we want to do. We do what we have to do. An' pretend it's what we want to do.'

7 Success!

1 open response

2 open response

4 'Strong' may mean several things: *physically strong* (Ruy perhaps, or Vic), *morally strong* (Douglas, Trudy), or *dominating* (Vic). The weakest is either Sharon or Kenny.

5 open response

7 possible answers:

VIC

a This suggests that he is cruel and inconsiderate.

b This suggests that he has a violent temper, and is dictatorial.

c This suggests that he is completely indifferent to Sharon's suffering.

d This suggests that he is extremely vain and selfish (he values his clothes more than enother person's life).

e This suggests that he is witty, but in a heartless, cruel way.

f This suggests that he is violent.

SHARON

g This suggests that Sharon is a weak character, incapable of standing up for herself, even when Vic is being offensive and cruel to her.

h This suggests that she realises she is greedy (as Vic says), and probably feels ashamed about it, since she mutters rather than speaking aloud.

i This shows that she is desperately unhappy, but it also suggests that she has some determination.

j This suggests that she is a humble and maybe rather insecure person, who seems to be in the habit of blaming herself, even when the fault is clearly someone else's.

k This suggests that she is still in love with Vic, even though he has been cruel to her.

l This suggests that she is a stronger character than we suspected: she has at last found the determination to solve her problem (albeit in a rather strange and savage way); at the same time her apologetic tone shows that she is quite aware of what she has done. Her politeness ('Mrs Parks') is remarkable too, suggesting that Sharon's awareness of her place in society – her insecurity too, perhaps – remain at the front of her mind even in extreme moments such as this.

8 DOUGLAS

a lines 62–4, 66–8, 422–4; ***b*** 123–6, 145–50; ***c*** 167–74; ***d*** 178–9, 212–13, 268–70

TRUDY

e There is plenty of evidence of this: lines 87–101, 309–10, 326–39, 365–6, 390, 401–2, 404–5

f lines 264–7

g (possibly line 166), lines 232–4

9 Of the interpretations given, the following are possible: ***a – 1*** or ***3***; ***b – 2*** or ***4***; ***c – 3*** or ***4***; ***d – 1***, ***2***, ***4***, or perhaps all three; ***e – 1*** or ***2***

f He probably does this because he is embarrassed and feels he must say something to change the subject; the music is merely a convenient topic of conversation.

10 open response; the text does not explain Trudy's tears, although it suggests that she admires and envies Douglas's quiet devotion to his wife, and recognizes in his marriage a quality of love which is absent from her own. Perhaps she fully realises now for the first time that she has married the wrong kind of man, as she later reveals to Sharon (lines 326–39).

11 There are several possibilities for each one. Some are given here.

a look after them / put these toys away / get them ready for bed
b a little overweight / a big girl / well-built / like anybody else
c unnecessary / spiteful / humiliating / not going to help her
d haven't / was only trying to say that he was hurting Sharon
e that she loved you / felt something for you
f an animal / a slave / a dog
g I could have hit him
h go to concerts / sing together / listen a lot
i younger / in love / going out together / courting
j anything / something
k embarrass you / suggest that you were poor or in need / imply that that was why you came
l like / prefer / you'd rather / don't want to eat at the hotel
m if you're quite sure / are you sure? / it's up to you / it's all the same to me / I'm happy either way
n can do
o I'll hold you responsible / I'll never forgive you
p pool / swimming pool / water
q got out of the pool / got out of here
r help / try to revive him / do something
s didn't / left it to us / went in
t think he's dead / think I've killed him / I'm afraid it's too late / didn't know what I was doing / didn't mean to kill him

12 ***a*** open response

b open response, though it might be reasonable to expect commands or statements to predominate.

c The highest is questions, followed by statements, then commands.

d various possibilities here; Vic's questions are frequently rhetorical (he is not looking for an answer, they are statements disguised as questions: 'Running down your arms? Trickling down your legs?' [line 22]) or question tags ('you are a fat girl, aren't you?' [line 30] 'Turns you over, doesn't it?' [lines 48–9]). These have the effect of making Sharon participate in her own humiliation. In other words, they are not real questions. One might also comment, perhaps a little cynically, that Vic is a television interviewer and has learned the art of using questions to manipulate people, and even as a form of bullying.

13 cruel: hard-hearted, vicious, tyrannical, sadistic, brutal, unfeeling
vain: self-obsessed, proud, conceited, egocentric
vulgar: crude, coarse, loud
hypocritical: insincere, sanctimonious

19

ACTION	MEANING
Kenny clears his throat	he is embarrassed
Trudy stares after him	she is moved by what he has said
Sharon looks towards the house	she doesn't want anyone to see her (or perhaps she secretly does?)
Vic points at Douglas and Trudy	he is threatening them
Sharon kneels	she is penitent

22 some possible interpretations:
a B wants to know the time, or likes to know how long things take, or is waiting for someone
b A is ill, or thinks he is
c B likes to keep fit
d B wants to know where he is, or is planning a journey, or is curious about a place he has heard of
e A is a lazy, untidy person
f B is a neat, methodical person
g A and B are too poor to buy their own clothes
h A is worried about something
i A and B are trying to get somewhere and have arranged to help each other

23 open response; some possible interpretations:
a time, work, duty, or conscience
b some people have a more active conscience or sense of duty than others

24 open response; a possible interpretation is that A and B together represent all of humanity, or two contradictory tendencies in human nature (energy and laziness, for example, or method and chaos); Beckett also makes the intriguing suggestion that these two characters or tendencies depend on each other in some mysterious way.

8 Making History

2 open response, but ***e*** seems most probable

3 ***a***

4 There are various possibilities: 1) he wants the stage designer to create exactly the right impression with the set; 2) the house is symbolic of Ireland (or England's relationship with Ireland); 3) the house is an important detail in understanding the lives of the characters.

5 ***a*** Nora; ***b*** Mrs Gogan; ***c*** Bessie; ***d*** Mollser

6 You could make a case for all three (comic, sinister or both). What she says is obviously sinister, and the impression is strengthened by the presence of the 'shrivelled, pitifully worn' Mollser. But there is also something comic in the exaggerated and melodramatic way she describes her visions, as well as her apparent relish of them.

7 Th' Tommies is sthretched in heaps around Nelson's pillar (lines 58–9); th' Lancers (lines 70–6); the gunboat *Helga* (lines 84–6); the distant boom of a big gun (lines 230–4, 376–8); a shot from a rifle rings out (lines 433–4); the wounded Lieutenant Langon (lines 438–42); th' big guns has knocked all the harps out of their hands (lines 478–9). In the first two references, the impression given is one of an army taken by surprise and suffering serious losses. But the later references make it clear that the British have enormous military strength.

8 ***a*** *advantages*: it is hard (and expensive) to show military action in a convincing way on stage;
disadvantages: violence can have a very powerful shock-effect in the theatre, which is likely to be lost if the violence is merely reported.
b O'Casey was clearly more interested in the effects of the fighting on the ordinary people of Dublin than in the fighting itself. He may also have deliberately avoided the emotional effect of showing the violence so that the audience would consider the whole subject in an objective way.

9 ***b***, ***c***, ***e***, ***f*** are accurate; in ***g*** the 'cry' is metaphorical (the man is dead)

10 *a* open response
b Bessie brings in a third point of view. She thinks the men should be helping Britain in the war against Germany, so she disagrees with the women at the barricades and with Nora.
c 1) Peter is calm then suddenly angry (lines 406–13); comic effect
2) Mrs Gogan and Bessie are friendly and co-operative after clashing earlier on. Also their sudden 'wealth' contrasts with their long-term poverty, and Bessie's moralising about the 'nakedness o' th' times' contrasts with her readiness to take advantage of the situation by looting (lines 414–28); comic / pathetic effect; morally and politically suggestive too (they're friendly when they have something to gain by it, or when they have enough, or when they are excited)
3) Mrs Gogan is suddenly unconcerned by Mollser's health (line 432). Strong emotional and moral effect, suggesting her extreme excitement at suddenly owning luxuries.
4) The rifle-shot, followed by the entrance of Langon, Brennan and Clitheroe, creates a sudden change of mood. Emotional effect.
5) Brennan's aggression towards the 'slum lice' contrasts with Clitheroe's more compassionate view ('they're Irish men and women') and with his own concern for Langon. The effect is emotional, moral and political.
6) The visual contrast between the two 'couples' on the stage: Nora and Clitheroe kissing, set against Brennan supporting the dying Langon. This has a powerful emotional effect, with political implications, reinforced by Bessie's comment at lines 479–80: 'General Clitheroe'd rather be unlacin' his wife's bodice than standin' at a barricade.' Clitheroe has to make a choice between his wife and his country – between love and possible death.

11 *a* Nora would rather be at home with Jack than out in the streets.
b Fluther thinks more about drinking than (he does) about the rebellion (*or* … as much about drinking as he does about rebellion).
c Mrs Gogan is as sharp-tongued as Bessie; there is no winner in their arguments.
d O'Casey makes us feel that these people have never had such a good opportunity as this to acquire a few luxuries (*or* … have never had a better opportunity to acquire …).
e Nora can't imagine a better cause than a husband and wife being left to love each other in peace.
f If the rebellion had been less violent, it would (*or* might) not have been so dramatic.
g It is a sign of these people's tolerance that Bessie can speak as freely as she wants against the rebellion, and even against the Irish people.

12 *a* O'Casey writes more negatively about the rebellion than one might expect.
b Clitheroe is not as committed to the rebellion as Brennan is.
c Nora believes Jack would rather be at home kissing her than fighting in the streets.
d Nora has never felt such anguish (*or* so much anguish, *or* so anguished) as she does now.
e Fluther is hoping to loot a pub so that he can drink as much whisky as he wants.
f They can think of nothing better (to do) than having a game of tossers.

14 *b*, possibly *c*

15 *a* detached, contemptuous; *b* arrogant, contemptuous, angry; *c* embarrassed, weak; *d* excited; *e* understanding, experienced, detached; *f* ignorant, weak, self-pitying, foolish

16

ADJECTIVE	NOUN	PREPOSITION AFTER
ignorant	ignorance	ignorant of / about
embarrassed	embarrassment	embarrassed about
weak	weakness	(not often used with prepositions)
excited	excitement	excited about / over
angry	anger	angry about
detached	detachment	detached from
self-pitying	self-pity	(not often used with prepositions)
contemptuous	contempt	contemptuous about / towards
experienced	experience	experienced in / at
arrogant	arrogance	arrogant about / towards
understanding	understanding	understanding about / towards
foolish	foolishness	foolish about / over

21 ***a*** Friel's Irish are presented as more dignified than O'Casey's (although the play has quite a few drunkards in it).

b The English in both plays appear as powerful, determined and ruthless – primarily a military presence.

c In both plays the violence is reported rather than seen. However Friel stresses the brutality of the English more.

d Friel seems more sympathetic than O'Casey to the idea of violent resistance by the Irish.